# INTERNATIONAL INTEGRATION, MARKET STRUCTURE AND PRICES

# International Integration, Market Structure and Prices

YVES BOURDET

**ROUTLEDGE**
London and New York

First published in 1988 by
Routledge
11 New Fetter Lane, London EC4P 4EE
29 West 35th Street, New York, NY 10001

Printed and bound in Great Britain by
Mackays of Chatham PLC, Chatham, Kent

British Library Cataloguing in Publication Data

Bourdet, Yves
    International integration, market structure
    and prices.
    1. International economic integration
    I. Title
    337.1
ISBN 0-415-00393-8

**Library of Congress Cataloging-in-Publication Data**


ISBN 0-415-00393-8

# Contents

# List of Figures

# List of Tables

*For my parents*

# Acknowledgements

The present study has its origins in my interest, on the one hand, in the interplay between international trade and different forms of market imperfections, and on the other, in West European problems. The analysis of international economic integration in relation to the West European passenger car industry and markets can be regarded as an appropriate way for satisfying this two-fold interest.

During my work I have benefited from the help of many people. My first debt of gratitude goes to my supervisor Bo Södersten. His use of the right arguments (most often in French) at critical moments of my work has been a great source of support. I am also very indebted to Göte Hansson and Mats Lundahl. Their highly varied and continuous encouragements have been an invaluable help. Furthermore, their sincere engagement and constructive criticisms have led to substantial improvement in the work and have permitted its completion. I also owe a special thanks to Lars Lundberg and Lennart Hjalmarsson, who went through the book and suggested improvements.

Many colleagues at the Department of Economics at the University of Lund have been generous and stimulating. Among those who have given penetrating advice and friendly help, I would wish to particularly mention Lena Ekelund, Anne-Marie Pålsson, Åsa Weibull, Krister Andersson, Bengt Assarsson, Hans Carlsson, Stefan Hedlund and Erik Norrman. Special thanks are due to Erling Peterson, who offered constructive suggestions on particular areas, and to Björn Thalberg and David Edgerton, who provided valuable criticisms on the final draft.

A special word of gratitude to Alan Harkess and Jaya Reddy who converted my Franglais into English.

The financial assistance received from the Scandinavian Chamber of Commerce and the Institute of Economic Research at the University of Lund for the publication of the book is also gratefully acknowledged.

Needless to say, the author is solely responsible for the remaining errors and all the opinions expressed.

Depuis combien de millénaires peinent-elles ainsi, et combien de millénaires lui faudra-t-il peiner encore, à cette race ridicule, tragique et inlassable? Combien de nouvelles cathédrales vont-elles bâtir pour adorer le Dieu qui leur donna des reins aussi frêles et une charge aussi lourde?

Romain Gary, Education européenne, p. 282

Je crois que l'automobile est aujourd'hui l'équivalent assez exact des grandes cathédrales gothiques: je veux dire une grande création d'époque, conçue passionnément par des artistes inconnus, consommée dans son image, sinon dans son usage, par un peuple entier qui s'approprie en elle un objet parfaitement magique.

Roland Barthes, Mythologies, p. 150

# 1

# Introduction

## THE SCOPE OF THE STUDY

International integration of industrial markets is the subject of this book. More precisely, the study focuses on international economic integration in relation to the passenger car industry and market in the West European car-making countries, West Germany, France, Italy, Sweden and the United Kingdom, over the past two and a half decades.

International integration is usually defined as both a process and a state of affairs:[1] a process because it covers all the trade policy measures introduced over time to remove trade obstacles and to bring markets insulated by history closer to each other; a state of affairs because its full completion results in the creation of a new and larger market from several originally different national markets.

The revival of protectionism has been the key feature of the international trading system over the past decade.[2] The introduction of new trade barriers between markets, which are either unified with regard to tariffs or are moving towards such a unification, implies that the scope of the above definition of integration should be extended in order to comprise disintegrating trade measures and trends. In other words, contemporary studies of international integration should place greater emphasis on disintegrating forces, their origin and their extent, in order to understand the scope and limits of integration.

Previous studies of international integration have concentrated more particularly on the trade effects of the removal of obstacles to trade — mostly tariffs — at a rather high level of aggregation.[3] The main reason behind this orientation is to be found in the incorporation of integration theory within trade theory. A far-reaching consequence of this incorporation has been the neglect of two aspects of international economic integration, market structure and firm conduct, and institutional factors. The influence of these factors has grown and has become increasingly apparent. However, they have not received the attention they deserve in this context since their analysis falls within two other fields of economics, industrial economics and political economy. The neglect of these factors has been all the more prejudicial to the understanding of economic integration since both have contributed a great deal to the emergence of disintegrating measures and of corporate and institutional obstacles to resource reallocation between countries.

It is interesting to note that pioneer studies of international economic integration, like Scitovsky's study at the end of the 1950s or Balassa's first study at the very beginning of the 1960s, to a much lesser extent focused exclusively on the trade effects of integration.[4] They dealt with other aspects of international integration as well — such as competition and economies of scale — which were regarded as important for the dynamics and outcome of the integration process.

The neglect of political factors in the process of integration is another characteristic of current integration studies in economics. This undoubtedly constitutes a shortcoming if political factors are found to affect the growth of international trade and welfare following integration. Two examples, suggested by Albert Hirschman, illustrate the way political factors can influence economic integration.[5] First, the removal of tariffs among union members and the need to reallocate resources are very likely to increase the demand for non-tariff forms of protective measures — or for a more active industrial policy — from highly concentrated and highly organised producers whose existence is threatened by increased competition from abroad. Second, the formation of an economic union creates incentives for union producers to organise at the union level in order to obtain protective measures directed against non-member countries and, hence, to capture business from non-member producers. Both kinds of demands can favour the emergence of trade-impeding non-tariff barriers which modify the predictions of economists about the growth of international trade following integration. It should be emphasised that the success of corporate attempts depends on political considerations.

2

It will be argued during the course of the present analysis that the incorporation of industrial and political aspects in empirical work can contribute a great deal to the understanding of the process of international integration in Western Europe and its limits. This 'innovation' comes largely as a result of the inability of traditional integration theory to explain what has been observed in the real world, namely disintegrating measures and obstacles to the reallocation of resources between countries. This new approach entails a certain number of methodological difficulties.

The first difficulty ensues from the American origin of the dominant paradigm created for the purpose of analysing industrial competition. As a result, until recent years, the analysis of industrial markets and firm conduct has been mainly concerned with a closed economy and ignored the role of the international environment.[6]

The high degree of openness of West European countries suggests that the dominant approach cannot be applied to their economies without substantial modifications. Another limitation of the traditional approach when applied to West European economies is the emphasis put on structural market conditions. This is probably a consequence of the large size of the American industrial markets. The relatively smaller size of the European markets and the resulting lower number of firms imply that cooperation among them should be easier and that firm conduct is less likely to be constrained by structural conditions in Western Europe. Hence, a larger and more autonomous place for firm conduct seems necessary in European studies.

The dissatisfaction of West European economists with the dominant paradigm in industrial economics gave rise to a certain number of studies — mostly cross-sectional studies — the purpose of which was to highlight the interaction between international trade and industrial economics.[7] Most of them have been made during the last ten years and have concentrated on the way international linkages affect diverse elements of market structure (such as concentration) and performance (such as profitability and efficiency).[8] Their main conclusion is that market performance is not determined solely by the forces of international trade but rather by the interplay of these forces with diverse elements of market structure and firm behaviour.

The second difficulty arises from the very fragmentary state of knowledge about the interplay between firm conduct and the

3

political sphere — at the national as well as the supranational level — in affecting the process of international market integration. For example, how does firm conduct affect the decisions taken by the national governments concerning integration-impeding non-tariff barriers? How does firm conduct influence the decisions concerning the process of integration taken by the Commission, which is the body of the European Economic Community (EEC) charged to implement the Treaty of Rome? Does the fact that — unlike national governments — the Commission is not *directly* responsible to voters and thus consumers for its decisions make it more devoted to interest groups and industrial lobbies? And so on.

The neglect of the interaction between the political sphere and the economy in traditional trade theory has given rise to a new field of research inspired by the public choice approach and concerned with the political economy approach to protection.[9] This approach relates the level of protection across industries to a certain number of industry characteristics — such as the degree of concentration, the number of employees, the rate of growth of output and the average skill level and age of employees — which are expected to influence the ability of an industry to obtain some form of protection against foreign competition. Most empirical work on the subject has concentrated on tariff protection and on the *national* market for protection probably because of the US origin of the theory. It may be suggested that this approach might prove well suited to the analysis of the emergence of non-tariff barriers to trade. Further, the recent extension of this approach to international economic relations might be helpful to the understanding of certain aspects of international integration such as, for example, the market for protection in the EEC.[10]

In summary, the purpose of this book is to use the West European passenger car industry and markets to illustrate the interaction between international integration, market structure and firm conduct and the political sphere at the national as well as at the supranational level.

## THE NEED FOR CASE AND COMPARATIVE STUDIES

One of the main differences between the present analysis and previous analyses of international integration is that we will concentrate on only one industry over a rather long period. This is unique since, to our knowledge, there is no systematic industry study of integration in the literature.

The case study approach has two main advantages and one limitation. First, by putting flesh on the interplay between international trade, industrial economics and the political sphere, the case study approach with its implicit time-series dimension seems to us the most appropriate method for capturing the complex way in which these different factors interact with each other in the process of integration and disintegration of West European markets. More precisely, it may be suggested that the way in which firms and industry pressure groups influence national and supranational choices, and thus international integration, can hardly be understood without a detailed analysis of the decision-making process at the industry or market level.

Second, research in industrial economics has focused its attention on the existence of a large number of 'market imperfections' such as product differentiation, consumer brand loyalty, high barriers to entry and market or extra-market power. These market imperfections are likely to affect international economic integration through imports and exports. This impact should be easier to assess in case studies than in cross-sectional studies, since imperfections vary widely from industry to industry and product to product, and no proxy variable can capture their trade effects in cross-sectional studies.

The less systematic conclusions that can be drawn from detailed studies of individual industries and markets undoubtedly constitute their main limitation. Several case studies are in fact necessary in order to reach more general conclusions.

Unlike the majority of trade studies, which in most cases contain an implicit comparative dimension, industrial studies have very rarely adopted a comparative orientation.[11] This is mainly due to the paucity of industrial data in West European countries until the very end of the 1960s and to the fact that the classification of industries varies between countries. The comparative perspective used here provides a supplement to the case study approach. Such a transnational perspective has three main virtues.[12]

First, the interaction between international trade, industrial aspects of markets and the public sphere should be easier to analyse when several countries are included in the analysis. This is because the nature and form of interaction are often peculiar to a country and thus vary from country to country as the result of several factors: different trade-off relationships between government and industry, the presence in some countries of state-owned firms, different political systems and different divisions of responsibility between government and bureaucrats for trade policy.

Second, cross-country comparisons allow for a powerful test of the random-effect hypothesis in industrial economics.[13] This tells us that it is chance rather than the extent of economies of scale or barriers to entry which explains several characteristics of market structure (such as degree of concentration and degree of organisation of the industry) that may have a great impact on the allocative outcome of international integration.

Third, the impact of technological determinants (such as the extent of economies of scale) upon changes in market structure should be more easily separated from the impact of institutional determinants (such as public merger policy and all sorts of institutional barriers to entry or exit) in a transnational perspective.

## WHY THE PASSENGER CAR INDUSTRY?

Three main reasons motivate the choice of the passenger car industry as the subject of this case study. First, disaggregated data and accurate information on several aspects of industrial structure, firm behaviour and market performance are available for this industry for a fairly long period. Second, the passenger car industry plays an important role in the economies of the five countries examined, West Germany, France, Italy, Sweden and the United Kingdom. Third, the oligopolistic structure of the industry makes it a suitable research subject for economists who want to shed some light on the role of imperfectly competitive market structure and firm conduct in the process of international integration.

Table 1.1 illustrates the importance of the passenger car industry in terms of employment, export and import in the five countries examined. The figures cover employment in the whole motor vehicle industry and thus are somewhat larger than the employment figures for just the passenger car industry. It is clear, nevertheless, that the passenger car industry employs a significant share of the industrial labour force and, consequently, is of great importance for these countries.

**Table 1.1**: Passenger car industry employment,[a] export and import[b]

|  | W. Germany | France | Italy | Sweden | Britain |
|---|---|---|---|---|---|
| Employment ('000) | 661.9 | 429.4 | 198.1 | 60.7 | 296 |
| (in % of industrial employment) | 6.5 | 6.2 | 2.8 | 4.8 | 3.8 |
| Exports (1982) (in millions US$) | 15,791 | 4,952 | 1,537 | 1,442 | 1,677 |
| (in % of total exp.) | 8.8 | 5.5 | 2.1 | 6.3 | 1.9 |
| Imports (1982) (in millions US$) | 3,367 | 3,940 | 3,840 | 728 | 5,044 |
| (in % of total imp.) | 2.1 | 3.5 | 4.5 | 3.1 | 5.5 |

*Sources: Eurostat* (1985), Statistical Office of the European Communities, Luxembourg; *Swedish Statistical Yearbook* (1984), Statistiska centralbyrån, Stockholm; UN, *Yearbook of International Trade Statistics* (1982), New York.
[a]The employment figures correspond to NACE 35 (motor vehicle employment) and to NACE 1-5 for all industrial employment. The figures pertain to 1984 for West Germany and Britain, to 1983 for France and Italy and to 1981 for Sweden.
[b]The trade figures correspond to SITC 781 (passenger vehicles).

Another way to illustrate the importance of an industry over time is to see which phase of the product life cycle the industry has reached.[14] Most industrial products go through the normal product cycle and reach a decline phase after the introduction, growth and maturity phases. In the decline phase, countries that were original producers and net exporters generally become net importers. Unlike the majority of products, as illustrated by Figure 1.1, passenger cars benefit from an extended maturity phase of several decades. Recent research on the future of the passenger car industry suggests that industrial car-making countries still have a comparative advantage in the production of passenger cars and that the motor vehicle industry is very likely to remain located in these countries for many years yet.[15] Thus, the extended maturity phase illustrated in Figure 1.1 is likely to last, and the passenger car industry should remain an important industry in Western Europe in the foreseeable future. In this respect, it should be added that significant differences exist among the West European car-making countries, and that a country like England has been engaged in the decline phase of the product life cycle since the 1960s.

As mentioned above, an additional reason for selecting the West European passenger car industry for the present work has

**Figure 1.1:** Product life cycle for passenger cars

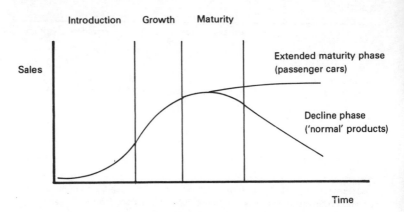

*Source:* Based on van Duijn (1983), pp. 22–26.

been its oligopolistic structure. This appears clearly in Table 1.2 which gives the main car manufacturers by country and their production in thousands of units in 1960, 1975 and 1984. Total production figures confirm that West European passenger car firms have been faced with slowly growing — nearly saturated — markets since the mid-1970s. The production figures of Table 1.2 are not corrected for the various takeovers and mergers that took place in most countries over the past two and a half decades.[16]

## PLAN OF THE STUDY

The plan of the book is influenced by the definition of international economic integration in terms of process and state of affairs. Chapters 2 to 6 concentrate on the process of integration, while Chapters 7 and 8 deal with integration regarded as a state of affairs.

Chapter 2 focuses on the relation between trade policy and international economic integration. It surveys the different trade policy steps taken since the end of the 1950s and examines in detail the measures designed to remove obstacles to trade between countries. Emphasis is put on the form of integration — customs union versus free trade area. Chapter 2 also scrutinises the non-tariff measures which have been erected mostly

**Table 1.2:** Passenger car firms and subsidiaries

| Firms | Production ('000) | | |
|---|---|---|---|
| | 1960 | 1975 | 1984 |
| West Germany | | | |
| Volkswagen | 787.4 | 1,050.3 | 1,203.3 |
| Opel (General Motors) | 351 | 655.9 | 776.5 |
| Ford | 192.7 | 413.1 | 539.8 |
| Daimler-Benz | 122.7 | 350.1 | 469.4 |
| BMW | 44 | 217.5 | 412.5 |
| NSU | 30 | 205.2 | 344.7 |
| France | | | |
| Renault | 464.1 | 1,042.3 | 1,428.5 |
| Peugeot | 173.6 | 563.8 | 736.6 |
| Citroën | 231.7 | 546.8 | 473.8 |
| Simca–Chrysler–Talbot | 204.2 | 383.2 | 73.6 |
| Italy | | | |
| Fiat | 510.5 | 1,006.7 | 1,014.3 |
| Alfa-Romeo | 47.9 | 189.7 | 200.1 |
| Lancia | 21 | 45.7 | 102.7 |
| Autobianchi | 14.8 | 71.4 | 88.3 |
| Sweden | | | |
| Volvo | 96.5 | 225.5 | 250.5 |
| Saab | 28 | 91 | 102 |
| United Kingdom | | | |
| Ford | 405 | 329.6 | 273.8 |
| Austin | 240 ⎫ | British Leyland | |
| Morris | 155 ⎪ | | |
| Standard Triumph | 110 ⎬ | 605.1 | 383.3 |
| Rover | 18 ⎪ | | |
| Jaguar | 23 ⎭ | | |
| Vauxhall (General Motors) | 145 | 98.6 | 117.1 |
| Rootes–Chrysler–Talbot | 135 | 226.6 | 95.1 |
| Total | 4,551.1 | 8,318.1 | 9,119.2 |
| Total production in the five countries | 5,005.5 | 8,384.9 | 9,204.2 |

*Sources: L'Argus de l'automobile et des locomotions,* yearly statistical issues 1961, 1976 and 1985.

since the mid-1970s and which, undeniably, have hampered a higher degree of integration of West European passenger car markets. On this occasion, much consideration is given to the interplay between firm behaviour and the political sphere in raising non-tariff barriers. Furthermore, it is shown that the emergence of non-tariff barriers has affected the form of integration in Western Europe and transformed the European Economic Community into a de facto free-trade area.

Chapter 3 is devoted to the estimation of the impact of trade policy on passenger car trade flows. First, it illustrates the changes in openness in the passenger car sector of the countries examined over the last two and a half decades. Second, it attempts to estimate with the help of regression analysis the trade effects of trade policy defined in its broadest sense, that is including traditional trade policy measures as well as new non-tariff measures.

The main purpose of Chapter 4 is to highlight the interacting factors behind changes in market structure over time. Three factors, economies of scale, foreign competition (and international integration) and public policy, are examined. A detailed analysis is devoted to the extent of economies of scale in the passenger car industry and to their changing impact on the firm's ability to survive. A related question explored in the first part is the manner in which firms relax their scale constraint. A second part of this chapter analyses the way in which increasing competition from abroad has influenced market structures. Two effects are considered. First, we concentrate on the fresh entry effect of foreign firms into domestic markets in the wake of tariff abolition. Second, we take up the effect of foreign competition on the exit of small and medium-sized firms suffering from small-scale disadvantages. Finally, in the third part of the chapter, an analysis is made of the impact of public policy on market structure and competitive conditions through merger policy and barriers to exit. Merger policies in the countries considered are compared in a first stage. In a second stage, we see how public policy has affected mergers in the West European passenger car industry. The role of economies of scale in these mergers, the impact of foreign competition and the actual logic of public policy are also investigated during the course of the analysis.

In Chapter 5 the changes in market structure that occurred during the integration process are measured with the help of two market structure indexes providing complementary information on competitive conditions. In a second stage, an attempt is made to see to what extent these changes can be ascribed to the three main factors presented in Chapter 4. The time-series dimension of the study implies further that some light is shed on

10

firm behaviour which is embodied in changes in market structure over time.

Chapter 6 attempts to see how the interplay between international integration, market structure and firm conduct and the national political sphere affects the formation of prices in the unified economic area. First the expected price effects of different forms of integration — customs unions versus free trade areas — are presented with the help of a partial equilibrium model. Then, a certain number of market imperfections are introduced and it is shown how these can favour the emergence of price disparities in a tariff-integrated area. It is pointed out that the permanence of price disparities within an integrated area depends on political considerations.

In Chapter 7 the interaction between international integration and certain market imperfections, and their effect on the formation of prices is illustrated. The role of market structure and firm conduct for the emergence and permanence of passenger car price disparities among the countries considered is examined in a second part, which confronts with reality the predictions derived from the theory. The possible role of other factors, such as exchange rate volatility and price control policies, is also investigated. In order to provide an understanding of the permanence of price disparities, the study then focuses on the interaction between, on the one hand, car manufacturers and their trade associations and, on the other hand, public policy at the national and supranational (i.e. EEC) levels.

Chapter 8 summarises the results of the study and presents a number of conclusions on the nature and future of economic integration in Western Europe, on the nature, social costs and policy implications of market power, on the role of market conduct and public policy in integration and on the limits of the process of integration.

## NOTES

1. 'We propose to define economic integration as a process and as a state of affairs. Regarded as a process, it encompasses measures designed to abolish discrimination between economic units belonging to different national states; viewed as a state of affairs, it can be represented by the absence of various forms of discrimination between national economies' (Balassa 1961, p. 1).

2. See for example Salvatore (1985), Balassa (1978) and Page (1981).

3. See for example Robson (1980), Chapter 11, and Balassa (1975), pp. 79–117.

4. Scitovsky (1958) and Balassa (1961).

5. Hirschman (1981), pp. 266–84.

6. See for example Bain (1968), Shepherd (1979) and Scherer (1980).

7. See for example the special issue of the *Journal of Industrial Economics* on International Trade and Industrial Organisation, Caves (1980a), Jacquemin and de Jong (1976) and OECD (1984a).

8. For a review of these studies, see Caves (1980a), pp. 113–17, and Caves and Khalilzadeh-Shirazi (1977), pp. 111–27.

9. See Baldwin (1982), pp. 263–86, and Anderson and Baldwin (1981).

10. See Frey (1984), Chapter 1, and Verreydt and Waelbroeck (1982), pp. 369–93.

11. Notable and pioneer exceptions are Bain (1966), Stigler (1966) and Phlips (1971).

12. On cross-country studies in industrial economics, see Adams (1976) and Caves (1976).

13. On the random-effect hypothesis, see Shepherd (1979), p. 226.

14. See Vernon (1970) and Wells (1972).

15. See the Report of the International Automobile Program of MIT, Altschuler *et al.* (1984), pp. 181–97.

16. An exception is British Leyland, which did not provide separate figures for some of its subsidiaries during the last decade. The separate figures for Jaguar in 1984 reflect its privatisation in August 1984.

# 2

# Trade Policy and International Integration

During the post-Second World War period, European trade policy evolved through a number of stages, the purpose of which was to promote trade and, in the long run, to create a totally integrated economic area. The formation of the European Economic Community (EEC) in 1959 and of the European Free Trade Association (EFTA) in 1960, the adhesion of the United Kingdom and other countries to the EEC in 1973, and the signing the same year of free-trade agreements for industrial products between the EEC and the remaining members of EFTA can be regarded as the *main* chronological stepping stones in the establishment of a free trade area for manufactures in Western Europe. Apart from a number of 'sensitive' products — such as certain paper, steel, aluminium or zinc products — which were subject to a slower rate of tariff dismantlement, the enlarged European free-trade area (including the EEC and EFTA countries) was first achieved in July 1977 when the remaining import duties on intra-European trade in manufactures were abolished after a four-year transitional period.

As regards trade relations with non-European countries, trade policy has been chiefly shaped by the different 'rounds' of tariff negotiations that took place under the auspices of the General Agreement on Tariffs and Trade (GATT). Their main result has been to bring trade nearer to free trade and to further the process of world integration. Negotiations within the GATT and the Organisation for European Economic Cooperation (OEEC) contributed to the removal of quantitative restrictions during the second half of the 1950s, while the Dillon, Kennedy and Tokyo rounds succeeded in lowering the level of tariff

13

protection for manufactured products over the last three decades. It should be noted that the two first 'rounds' also affected intra-European trade during the 1960s and the first half of the 1970s when Western Europe was still divided into two trading blocs, the EEC and EFTA.

The relation between trade policy and international economic integration is the subject of this chapter. The first purpose is to explore the role of the above-mentioned trade policy steps in the process of integration of West European passenger car markets. As suggested in Chapter 1, contemporary studies of integration should also take up disintegrating measures and trends. The second purpose of the present chapter is thus to examine the scope and origin of non-tariff barriers in passenger car trade and to discuss their disintegrating effects.

The chapter is divided into three sections. The first two deal mainly with the traditional trade policy instruments of tariffs and quotas. The first one is devoted to trade policies in the 1960s. It illustrates the rapid liberalisation of trade during this period and presents in detail the measures designed to bring national passenger car markets closer to each other. Emphasis is laid on the form of the integration chosen by those countries that are members of the EEC and EFTA, namely customs union and free-trade area.

The second section is concerned with trade policies in the 1970s and the early 1980s. It concentrates on the minor changes in tariff policy that ensued from the entry of Britain into the EEC and the free-trade agreement between the EEC and Sweden. It also takes up the implications of these changes for the form of the integration process in Western Europe. The impact of the negotiations for trade liberalisation that took place under the sponsorship of the GATT and which influenced the different steps of West European trade policy is also scrutinised in the two first sections.

The third section deals exclusively with the scope and origin of measures impeding integration. Such measures take non-tariff forms because national governments and the EEC have lost control over tariff policy as a result of the different rounds of multilateral trade negotiations and membership in the EEC or EFTA. The focus will be on the four kinds of barriers considered to be most distorting in passenger car trade, namely quantitative import restrictions, discriminatory purchase taxes, technical and administrative hindrances and public subsidies to private firms. The detailed analysis of the emergence of these non-tariff barriers illustrates the role of some industrial and political factors in the process of integration. It can be regarded as a case-study test of the political economy approach to protection.

According to this theory, an industry is likely to receive protection from abroad if it possesses a certain number of characteristics that affect either the demand or the supply of protection.[1] We may expect the passenger car industry to obtain protection from abroad because it possesses the main required characteristics. First, the industry consists of a small number of firms (see Table 1.2). It is thus easier to organise lobbying for protection among members of the industry and avoid the deterrent effect on collective action of the 'free rider' problem. Second, the passenger car industry is large in terms of employment (see Table 1.1). Protection from abroad is thus likely because labour has the votes, and the political benefits of providing protection for the industry are substantial. Third, the passenger car industry has experienced a low rate of growth of output over the past ten years (see Table 1.2). This should increase the demand for protection because declining industries have a greater incentive to seek protection. Finally, a large proportion of the total passenger car industry workforce is unskilled. Workers are thus very likely to add to the management's demand for protection because of the greater difficulties for unskilled workers in finding new jobs.

The emergence of non-tariff barriers in the wake of integration may be the result of two different processes.[2] On the one hand, the removal of tariffs and the need to reallocate production among member countries should increase the demand for non-tariff protection from threatened industries that possess the characteristics required by the political economy of protection. In this case, non-tariff barriers are very likely to be directed against union members and to be substituted for tariff barriers. On the other hand, the formation of an economic union creates an incentive for union industries to organise at the union level to capture business from non-member producers. In this second case, non-tariff barriers are likely to be directed against non-member countries and can be introduced fairly independently of tariff reductions. Another aim of the third section will be to illustrate these two different

15

processes of formation of non-tariff barriers in the West European passenger car industry.

Finally, a worthwile related question that will be answered is whether the introduction of non-tariff barriers has changed the nature of the integration process in Western Europe. More particularly, we will show that the emergence of non-tariff barriers during the last decade has transformed the European customs union (EEC) into a de facto free-trade area.

## TRADE LIBERALISATION IN THE 1960s

Among the countries under study and for most industrial products, large tariff disparities existed prior to the inception of the integration process. West Germany and Sweden had generally low tariffs whereas Britain, France and Italy had generally high tariffs.[3] Table 2.1 illustrates this in the case of passenger car customs duties by showing that the latter countries were protected by high tariff rates (30 per cent or more) while the former were protected by relatively low tariff rates (around 15 per cent).

In Britain and West Germany, the tariff rates imposed on passenger car imports were changed during the second half of the 1950s. In the former country, the old McKenna duty of 33.3

**Table 2.1:** Nominal tariffs for passenger cars in 1952 and 1959 (as a percentage of the price)

|      | France | W. Germany | Italy | Sweden | Britain |
|------|--------|------------|-------|--------|---------|
| 1952 | 30     | 32         | 45[a] | 15     | 33.3    |
|      |        |            | 40    |        |         |
|      |        |            | 35    |        |         |
| 1959 | 30     | 14[b]      | 45    | 15     | 30      |
|      |        | 17         | 40    |        |         |
|      |        |            | 35    |        |         |

Sources: The data for 1952 are based on a study made by the GATT secretariat, available in United Nations (1957), Chapter 4, p. 15. The data for 1959 were supplied by the different trade associations and as regards Sweden collected in Tulltaxa 1959, Norstedt, Stockholm.

[a] 45, 40 and 35 for passenger cars with an engine capacity of less than 15,000 cubic centimetres (cc), larger than 1,500 cc but less than 4,000 cc and larger than 4,000 cc, respectively.

[b] 14 and 17 for passenger cars of less and more than 2,000 cc respectively.

16

per cent levied on imported passenger cars since 1915 was reduced to 30 per cent at the end of 1956.[4] In West Germany, as a result of *konjunkturpolitische Zollsenkungen,* the tariff rate was more than halved within a very short period, 1956–1957.[5] First, in 1956, import duties imposed on passenger cars were reduced to 17 per cent for cars with an engine capacity of less than 2,000 cubic centimetres (cc) and 21 per cent for cars of more than 2,000 cc. Then, in August 1957, a new tariff cut brought down these two tariff rates to 14 per cent and 17 per cent respectively.

Two events, the Rome Treaty and the Stockholm Convention, greatly modified this tariff picture and contributed most to shaping West European trade policy during the 1960s. Both events have significantly reduced obstacles between national markets and thus sped up economic integration in Western Europe. The same tendency towards the liberalisation of trade could be noticed in trade relations with non-European countries, principally as a result of the Kennedy Round of trade negotiations.

### The European Economic Community

The Treaty of Rome, which established the European Economic Community, was signed in Rome by Belgium, France, West Germany, Italy, Luxembourg and the Netherlands (the Six) on 25 March 1957 and came into force on 1 January 1958. Its main purpose was the creation of a common market free from all tariff barriers and other obstacles to trade between member countries. A customs union was considered the most suitable way to achieve this common market. Therefore, the Six decided to abolish by stages tariffs among them, to remove the remaining quantitative restrictions and to unify their customs system *vis-à-vis* third countries.

The gradual dismantling of internal tariffs began on 1 January 1959 and was completed on 1 July 1968 (see Figure 2.1). The actual schedule for the tariff-cutting process was two years shorter than the one laid down in the Treaty of Rome. Further, the internal tariff elimination began earlier but was terminated later within the EEC than within EFTA.

Figure 2.2 conveys an overall picture of the progressive elimination of customs duties for passenger cars within the Common

17

**Figure 2.1:** Tariff elimination within the EEC and EFTA, 1959–1968

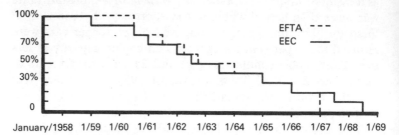

January/1958  1/59  1/60  1/61  1/62  1/63  1/64  1/65  1/66  1/67  1/68  1/69

*Sources:* Curzon (1974), p. 67; Nême and Nême (1970), p. 50.

Market (for West Germany and Italy only one of the existing tariff rates is presented in the figure). Two reasons explain the absence of perfect synchronisation in the dismantling of internal tariffs. Firstly, West Germany, which had applied considerable tariff reductions in 1956 and 1957, was exempted from the first tariff cuts in 1959 and 1960. Secondly, unilateral tariff reductions were applied by some governments. For example, on 1 April 1961, the French government decided on a unilateral reduction by 10 per cent of the tariff on intra-EEC trade.

In order to harmonise their customs systems with third countries, the EEC members agreed on a common external tariff equal to the unweighted arithmetic average of the pre-union tariffs applied in each of the six member countries on 1 January 1957. This basic rule for setting the common external tariff was not followed for passenger cars, and it was only after a process of negotiations that the Six agreed on a 22 per cent tariff rate.[6] However, this planned common external tariff was never applied but was reduced by one-fifth as a result of the negotiations within the framework of the Dillon Round in 1960 and 1961.[7] The gradual alignment of the individual tariffs up or down towards the downward adjusted common external tariff (17.6 per cent) took place in several stages (see Figure 2.2). It resulted in a lowering of tariff protection towards third countries in France and Italy and a slight increase in West Germany.

In the late 1960s and early 1970s, the Kennedy Round resulted in further concessions in the common external rate. The concessions amounted to 35–40 per cent for industrial

18

**Figure 2.2:** Tariff disarmament for passenger cars within the EEC

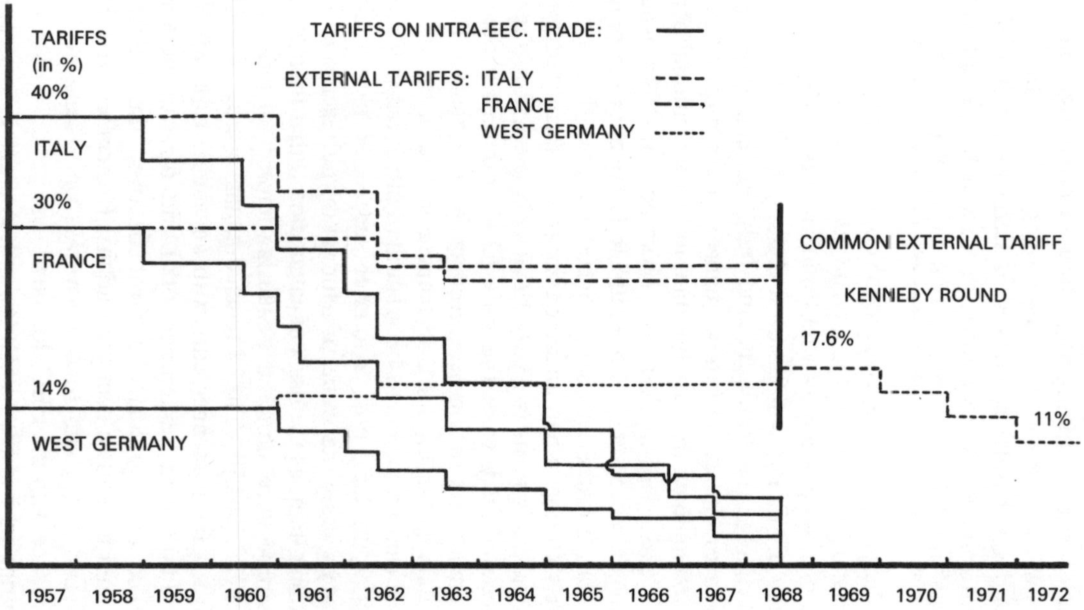

TARIFFS ON INTRA-EEC. TRADE:

EXTERNAL TARIFFS: ITALY
FRANCE
WEST GERMANY

TARIFFS
(in %)
40%

ITALY

30%

FRANCE

14%

WEST GERMANY

COMMON EXTERNAL TARIFF

KENNEDY ROUND

17.6%

11%

1957 1958 1959 1960 1961 1962 1963 1964 1965 1966 1967 1968 1969 1970 1971 1972

*Sources:* Motor vehicle trade associations.

19

products. They were introduced gradually in accordance with the following schedule for the EEC countries: 40 per cent of the whole concession on 1 July 1968, and 20 per cent in January of each of the years 1970, 1971 and 1972.[8] The 20 per cent reduction accompanying the Dillon Round was included in the new concessions and corresponded to the first tariff cut effected on 1 July 1968. For passenger cars, the Kennedy Round resulted, consequently, in a reduction of the common external tariff from 17.6 per cent in 1968 to 11 per cent in 1972.

As regards quantitative restrictions, the countries engaged in negotiating the Rome Treaty had already removed them on more than 80 per cent of their total imports in 1955 as a result of the OEEC negotiations on a Europe-wide free-trade area.[9] According to the Rome Treaty, the EEC countries were not allowed to impose any new quotas in their mutual trade but only to eliminate the existing ones over a transitional period of eight years. This period was shortened in 1960 when the member states agreed on a complete removal of the remaining quantitative restrictions before 1 January 1962.[10]

West Germany had already removed its quantitative restrictions on car imports in 1956–1957.[11] By the end of the 1950s, France and Italy were the only EEC countries protected by quantitative restrictions. According to the Rome Treaty, a quota amounting to not less than 3 per cent of the Italian and French car output was to be granted to other member countries in 1959. In fact, both countries succeeded in reducing the quotas by using the value of national output exclusive of taxes and other items as the basis of calculation rather than quantities. (This procedure aimed at penalising imports of large German passenger cars.)[12] The French quotas were, nevertheless, abolished for passenger cars with an engine capacity of more than 3,000 cc in September 1959 and for cars of less than 3,000 cc on 1 January 1960.[13] In Italy the quotas were increased by 20 per cent for each EEC member on 1 January 1960 and 1961, and totally removed on 1 January 1962, in accordance with the EEC decision.[14]

By the end of the 1960s the customs union was completed for the passenger car markets, since customs duties and quantitative restrictions had been totally removed among the member countries and the common external tariff had come fully into operation.

## The European Free-Trade Association

The Stockholm Convention, which established the European Free Trade Association, was signed on 4 January 1960 and came into force on 3 May of the same year. It was confined to Austria, Denmark, Norway, Sweden, Portugal and Britain. A central concern for the founder-members was to establish among themselves a free-trade area for manufactured products. To realise this objective, the seven member countries eliminated trade barriers among themselves but let each member fix its own tariff on trade with third countries. As far as trade policy is concerned, this last aspect constitutes the main difference between the European Free-Trade Association and the European Economic Community.

Independent trade policies towards third countries are likely to result in large tariff disparities in trade with non-members. It may also lead to trade deflection, that is imports from non-member countries through the partner country that has the lowest customs duties. To prevent this form of trade, which if present invalidates the principle of independent trade policies towards third countries, the EFTA countries devised rules of origin that allow freedom of intra-EFTA trade only in industrial products originating in the free-trade area.

In a first stage, the EFTA members planned to get rid of internal tariffs over a ten-year transition period beginning in July 1960 and ending in January 1970. However, as in the EEC case, the dismantling of internal tariffs occurred at a faster rate than was planned from the outset, and the tariff-cutting process was already concluded on 31 December 1966 (see Figure 2.1). Figure 2.3 illustrates the dismantling of internal tariffs for passenger cars in two EFTA countries, Sweden and Britain.

Countries forming a free-trade area continue to have the power to fix their own tariffs on trade with non-member countries. This explains why substantial tariff disparities on trade with third countries existed among EFTA members at the end of the 1960s. The tariff rates prevailing prior to the start of the integration process remained in force in all the EFTA countries, except Britain, until the beginning of the Kennedy Round in 1968.[15]

Two facts explain the different profile of the British tariff policy prior to 1968. Firstly, in an effort to further the British application to join the EEC in 1961 and 1966, the British tariff

21

**Figure 2.3:** Tariff disarmament for passenger cars with EFTA

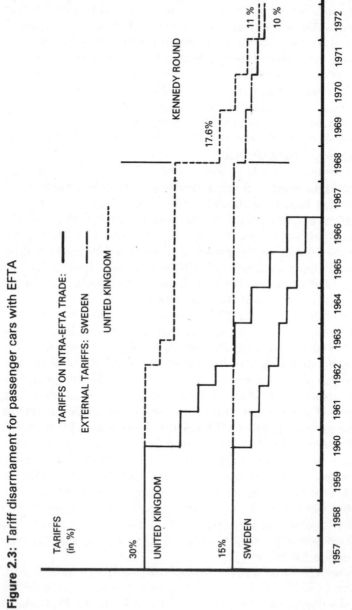

*Sources:* British Motor Trade Association and Swedish Board of Customs.

22

on trade with non-EFTA countries was adjusted downward towards the common external tariff of the EEC. Secondly, in order to cope with the huge deficit of the balance of payments, a 15 per cent temporary surcharge on most imports of manufactured products — including those from the EFTA countries — was introduced by the British government on 26 October 1964.[16] This import surcharge was, however, reduced to 10 per cent from April 1965 as a result of EFTA and GATT countries' criticisms and was completely removed on 30 November 1966.

As mentioned above, the Kennedy Round resulted in a tariff reduction which amounted to an average of approximately 35 to 40 per cent on industrial products and which extended over a five-year period, 1968–1972. On 1 January of each of the years of this transitional period, a tariff cut equal to 20 per cent of the total reduction was achieved in all the GATT countries adhering to the normal schedule. Britain as well as the EEC countries implemented the first two tariff cuts — 40 per cent of the whole reduction — on 1 July 1968 and then followed the normal schedule.

Concerning trade policy towards passenger cars, the Kennedy Round, along with the efforts of Britain to bring its tariff into line with the Common External Tariff of the EEC, contributed to a substantial reduction in the tariff disparity between Sweden and Britain (see Figure 2.3). By 1972 the two countries formed a kind of customs union since they had removed internal tariffs and had approximately the same tariff (10 per cent versus 11 per cent) on trade with third countries.

The Stockholm Convention devoted its longest article to the removal of quantitative import restrictions, although only a few quotas actually remained in force in the contracting countries when they decided to create a free-trade area in 1960. The quasi-absence of quantitative restrictions was mostly the result of the OEEC Code of Liberalisation that induced countries like Britain, Sweden and Switzerland to abolish most import quotas during the second half of the 1950s.[17] According to the Stockholm Convention, the remaining quotas should have been eliminated by 31 December 1969. In fact, the transition period was accelerated, and by December 1966 the great majority of the remaining quotas had been removed. No quantitative passenger car restrictions were operative in Britain and Sweden during the 1950s.[18]

The end of the 1960s saw the complete establishment of the

European Free-Trade Area and the beginning of the enforcement of the Kennedy Round. The main effect of the latter was to lower the separate external tariffs of the EFTA countries.

## TARIFF POLICIES IN THE 1970s: THE PAUSE

As outlined above in the case of passenger cars, the trend in protection was clearly downward during the 1960s and early 1970s. This rapid move towards more liberal trade was exceptional, and the tariff cuts that occurred in the following period were much less sizeable. Nevertheless, two events, the enlargement of the European Economic Community and the signing of free-trade agreements between the EEC and the remaining EFTA countries, strengthened the process of economic integration in Western Europe. They created an integrated economic area embracing both EFTA and the enlarged Common Market. This economic area came into force on 1 July 1977, when the last internal tariff cuts occurred.

In the next two sections, we will see how these two events established a free-trade area for passenger cars in Western Europe and how the trade negotiations of the Tokyo Round affected tariff policies towards third countries.

### The entry of Britain into the European Economic Community

The Treaty of Accession to the Common Market of Britain, Ireland and Denmark was signed in Brussels on 22 January 1972 and came into force on 1 January 1973.[19] Its main purpose was to create an enlarged customs union with nine members. To achieve this objective, the participating countries first devised the gradual elimination of tariffs between the old Six and the three new members. The next step was to adjust the latter's external tariffs to the common external tariff of the EEC. These two processes were completed after a transition period stretching from 1973 to 1977.

The gradual elimination of internal industrial tariffs among the members of the enlarged Community followed the pre-established timetable and was accomplished in five phases at 20 per cent (see Table 2.2). Table 2.2 also illustrates the adoption

**Table 2.2:** EEC tariff policy, 1973–1977

| | Tariff elimination within the enlarged EEC and between the EEC and EFTA countries (%) | Alignment to the Common External Tariff for the new EEC members (%) |
|---|---|---|
| 1 April 1973 | 20 | — |
| 1 January 1974 | 20 | 40 |
| 1 January 1975 | 20 | 20 |
| 1 January 1976 | 20 | 20 |
| 1 July 1977 | 20 | 20 |

*Source.* Taber (1974), p. 68.

in four phases of the Common External Tariff by the three new members.

Figure 2.4 illustrates the elimination of the internal tariff on imports of passenger cars between the original EEC countries and Britain. As a result of the Kennedy Round and British trade policy during the 1960s, the tariffs imposed on third-country exports were the same in the EEC and Britain prior to the membership of the latter. By implication, no alignment towards the Common External Tariff was necessary for Britain.

The British Preferential Tariff Rate (i.e. the rate imposed on imports from the Commonwealth) was relinquished after a four-year transition period which brought it to the level of the Common External Tariff. This increase especially affected exports from countries such as Canada, Australia, New Zealand and South Africa, which benefited from Commonwealth preferences prior to Britain's entry into the EEC.[20]

The trade negotiations concluded in April 1979 and known as the Tokyo Round resulted in further tariff reductions on trade with non-member countries. The industrialised countries agreed to lower tariffs over the next eight to ten years by 33 to 38 per cent on manufactured products.[21] In view of the rather low tariffs existing in 1979, this percentage reduction meant very small changes in tariff protection towards third countries. Moreover, a certain number of products concerning competing exports from developing countries and Japanese exports were exempted from the normal tariff-cutting process by the EEC in the Tokyo Round trade negotiations.[22] Passenger cars were one of the manufactured products that were exempted by the EEC. A final tariff of 10 per cent was imposed by the EEC on passenger car imports from third countries. The negligible tariff

**Figure 2.4:** EEC, British and Swedish tariffs for passenger cars, 1972–1987

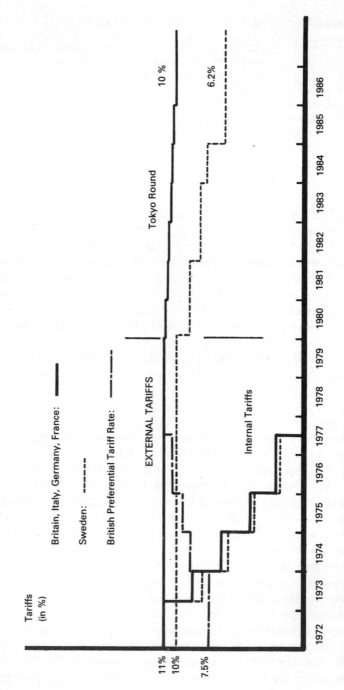

*Sources:* Motor vehicle trade associations and Swedish Board of Customs.

reduction (from 11 per cent to 10 per cent) was phased in over a seven-year period and is expected to be completed in 1987.

## The free-trade agreement between the EEC and Sweden

On 22 July 1972 free-trade agreements were concluded between the EEC and the remaining EFTA countries. These agreements, which became effective from 1 January 1973, provided for the progressive achievement of free trade for industrial products in an enlarged, unified, West European area.[23] The transition period followed the same stages as those that applied to Britain's entry into the EEC (see Table 2.2, column 1). The nature of the association, a free-trade area, implies that the EEC as a whole and the non-applicant EFTA countries retained the power to fix their own tariffs on trade with countries that did not belong to the enlarged free-trade area.

Figure 2.4 shows the elimination of tariffs on imports of passenger cars between Sweden and the EEC. It also illustrates the reduction of the tariff levied on third countries by Sweden which, contrary to the EEC, applied the Tokyo Round tariff reduction. This was achieved through the use of the formula

$$\text{Post-Tokyo Round Tariff} = \frac{(16 \times \text{pre-Tokyo Round Tariff})}{(16 + \text{pre-Tokyo Round Tariff})}$$

and resulted in a gradual decrease in the Swedish tariff rate from 10 per cent in 1979 to 6.2 per cent in 1985. The 6.2 per cent tariff rate means that Sweden has been less tariff-protected towards third-country exports than the other West European car-making countries over the last five years (see Figure 2.4).

In addition to tariff elimination, four aspects of the free-trade agreement are worth noting for they might have some influence on trade between the EEC and Sweden. First, all duties that had the same effect as tariffs were relinquished during the transition period. Second, all remaining quantitative restrictions were removed on 1 January 1973. Third, a rule of origin was devised to prevent trade deflection, which could have occurred because of tariff disparities between Sweden and the EEC. Finally, all agreements between firms or restrictive practices that prejudice the free flow of trade between Sweden and the EEC and hence

27

distort competition, were prohibited.

One of the main results of the Tokyo Round of negotiations has been that of bringing non-tariff barriers into the focus of attention. In the next section, we will survey the different non-tariff barriers that impede the free flow of passenger car trade and see whether their use has increased since the removal (or drastic reduction) of traditional protective measures.

## NEW PROTECTIONISM

In discussing non-traditional obstacles to trade, the Tokyo Round concentrated more particularly on public subsidies to domestic firms, technical and administrative obstacles to trade and government preferences granted to domestic producers. There exists, however, a much wider variety of non-tariff measures, the main effect of which is, either by design or by accident, to distort and hamper free trade. These measures vary greatly from country to country and from industry to industry. In this respect, we may expect the use of non-tariff protective measures, such as technical standards, to be more common in highly differentiated industries because the room for such measures increases with the number of characteristics of the product.

In this section, we will take up only those non-tariff measures that are regarded as the most trade-distorting for passenger cars, namely quantitative import restrictions, discriminatory purchase taxes, technical and administrative obstacles and public subsidies to private firms. We will omit a certain number of non-tariff measures that are considered to have only limited trade-distorting effects. Government preferences given to domestic suppliers of cars is one example of such non-tariff measures where the effects are limited because most passenger cars are purchased by private persons or firms.

### Quantitative restrictions and managed trade

Quantitative restrictions have become a favourite instrument of trade policy over the last decade. They constitute the most representative non-tariff measure of what is known as new protectionism. Their main effect is to create a scarcity of imported products and, thus, to increase the prices charged for these products by a given percentage which corresponds to a tariff equivalent. Quantitative restrictions can take several forms. They can be unilaterally imposed by the importing countries (traditional import quotas) or bilaterally negotiated by countries or firms ('voluntary' export restraints or orderly marketing arrangements). In the latter case, it is likely that they are accepted by the exporting countries (or firms) because they are backed up by the threat of import quotas. The experience of the passenger car industry provides a good illustration of the different sorts of quantitative restrictions that have appeared in world trade in recent years.

A bilateral agreement between Italy and Japan limits annual imports of motor vehicles in each market to 2,200 units, of which 1,700 are passenger cars.[24] This agreement, which was originally a voluntary export restraint, was initiated by Japan as early as 1955 when Japanese producers feared competition from Fiat. However, since the mid-1960s, it can be regarded as a quota because it has been included since that time in the list of import quotas published each year in the Italian *Official Journal* (*Gazzette Ufficiale*).[25] Two facts should be noted about the Italian import quota. Firstly, it survived the removal of Italian quantitative restrictions on passenger car imports at the beginning of the 1960s, since Italy did not apply the GATT's most-favoured-nation principle. Secondly, the Italian quota is officially approved by the EEC.[26] This latter fact is all the more surprising since the EEC is said to form a customs union and, thus, we expect the countries belonging to it to have the same trade policy towards third countries.

It must be emphasised that the Italian import quota only became operative at the beginning of the 1970s, when exports from Japan turned out to be successful in the West European markets (see Table 2.3 and compare the import penetration rate in Italy with the other European car-producing countries). Since the early 1980s, the Italian market has also been protected by quantitative restrictions concerned with passenger car exports from state-trading East European countries. Italian import licences permit only 2,650, 1,500 and 500 passenger cars originating in the Soviet Union, Czechoslovakia and Romania, respectively.[27]

France is protected against Japanese exports by a severe 'voluntary' export restraint (VER) that limits the share of

**Table 2.3**: Japanese passenger car import penetration, 1968–1984 (as a percentage of new car registration)

|      | France | Germany | Italy | Sweden | Britain | (1)  | (2)  |
|------|--------|---------|-------|--------|---------|------|------|
| 1968 | 0.6    | 0.1     | a     | 0.1    | 0.2     | 2.1  | 1.8  |
| 1970 | 0.2    | 0.1     | a     | 0.7    | 0.4     | 4    | 5.3  |
| 1972 | 0.4    | 0.3     | a     | 2.8    | 2.9     | 9.7  | 10.9 |
| 1975 | 1.5    | 1.7     | a     | 6.5    | 9       | 16   | 14.2 |
| 1976 | 2.7    | 1.9     | 0.1   | 8.2    | 9.4     | 17.4 | 14.1 |
| 1977 | 2.6    | 2.5     | 0.1   | 10.6   | 10.4    | 19.5 | 15.1 |
| 1978 | 1.8    | 3.7     | 0.1   | 9.7    | 11      | 18.4 | 13.4 |
| 1979 | 2.2    | 5.6     | 0.1   | 10     | 10.8    | 18.8 | 17.6 |
| 1980 | 2.9    | 10.4    | 0.1   | 12.1   | 11.9    | 25.2 | 28.1 |
| 1981 | 2.6    | 10      | 0.1   | 13.7   | 11      | 24.5 | 28.5 |
| 1982 | 2.9    | 9.8     | 0.1   | 15.2   | 11      | 21.3 | 28.8 |
| 1983 | 2.7    | 10.6    | 0.1   | 15.2   | 10.7    | 23   | 30.6 |
| 1984 | 3      | 11.6    | 0.1   | 15     | 10.7    | 22.3 | 29.3 |

*Sources:* Motor Vehicle Manufacturers' Association of the United States (1982, 1984–1985); *L'Argus de l'automobile et des locomotions* (1985); Bilindustriföreningen (1985); Associazione Nationale fra Industrie Automobilistiche (1985); and Verband der Automobilindustrie (1985).
(1) Average market share in Belgium and the Netherlands.
(2) Average market share in Austria, Denmark, Norway and Switzerland.
ªLess than 0.1%.

Japanese passenger car producers to 3 per cent of the domestic market.[28] Opinions differ concerning the date of introduction of this VER. According to most authors, it was introduced in 1977 by the French Industry Minister, Giraud. According to other sources, the VER dates back to the mid-1960s and was introduced by Giscard d'Estaing, who was at that time Minister of Finance.[29] This confusion is symptomatic of the less transparent nature of VERs, as compared to that of tariffs. Whatever the actual date, the VER only became operative in the mid-1970s, when Japanese exports became highly competitive in Western Europe. During the last decade, French car manufacturers approached the trade department on several occasions to secure continuing protection from Japanese exports.[30] Table 2.3 shows that the VER has been successful, since it has maintained the Japanese market share at less than the alloted 3 per cent over the last eight years (with the exception of 1984).

Another country, Britain, benefited from an informal agreement that restricts the Japanese share of the British car market to 11 per cent.[31] This agreement is an orderly marketing arrangement. It was reached by the two motor vehicle trade associations working on behalf of the passenger car industries (the British Society of Motor Manufacturers and Traders and the Japanese Automobile Manufacturer Association) without formal involvement of the British and Japanese governments. As with France, secrecy surrounded the agreement, and the date of introduction of the quantitative restriction varies between 1975 and 1977, depending on the source.[32] Table 2.3 shows that this agreement has been effective. Between 1975 and 1978 it has drastically slowed down Japanese penetration and, since 1978, has maintained it at around 11 per cent of the British passenger car market.

Prior to June 1981, West Germany had no quantitative import restrictions. At this time, the Japanese car manufacturers gave German authorities an assurance that their car exports to West Germany would not rise by more than 10 per cent in 1981.[33] It was the visit to Tokyo of the German Minister of Economics, Otto Lambsdorff, on 9 June that 'persuaded' Japanese car producers to restrain their exports. The German action bypassed the Commission of the EEC which, a month earlier, had decided to negotiate with Japan on 'voluntary' export restrictions to the EEC.[34] The absence of reaction from the Commission was interpreted as a tacit approval of separate national trade policies towards third countries. Table 2.3 shows that the Japanese commitment effectively stopped the rapid increase in Japanese market penetration in West Germany during the second half of the 1970s.

Of the five West European car-making countries, only Sweden is not protected by any form of quantitative restriction for Japanese passenger car exports. There are, however, marketing agreements between Swedish and some continental firms that may have the same effects as quantitative restrictions. The most obvious example concerns the deal between Volvo and Renault in 1980 which, among other things, resulted in the takeover by Volvo of the distribution of Renault motor vehicles in Sweden. It is common knowledge that since then Volvo's distribution network has been unwilling to sell on the Swedish market the Renault cars which compete with Volvo's own passenger cars. It is likely that the agreement partly explains why the sales of Renault in Sweden dropped from an annual average of 8,300 units during the 1970–1979 period to an average of 2,800 units during the 1980–1984 period.[35]

31

Three main conclusions emerge from an analysis of quantitative restrictions for Japanese car exports to Western Europe. Firstly, quantitative restrictions appear to have gained a great deal of ground in passenger car trade over the last decade. The restrictions take different forms: unilateral protective measures in Italy, country-to-country agreements in France and West Germany and industry-to-industry arrangements in Britain. This increasing control of passenger car trade flows confirms the revival of protectionism over the last decade and is a good illustration of what has come to be called the 'new protectionism' and its less transparent nature.[36]

The second conclusion concerns the attitude of the European Community and the present nature of the integrated economic area that exists in Western Europe. As seen above, each EEC country has had its own trade policy towards Japanese car exports since the mid-1970s. This is officially (Italy) or tacitly (the other EEC countries) accepted by the Commission of the Common Market, although it is contrary to one of the basic requirements of a customs union, a uniform trade policy on trade with non-participating countries. As regards the form of international integration, this leads to the important conclusion that the EEC countries no longer form a customs union. Since the mid-1970s, the EEC has become *a de facto free-trade area.*

The policy of the EEC Commission to prevent trade deflection (for example, of Japanese car exports to Italy through Holland or Denmark) confirms the de facto conversion of the EEC into a free-trade area. As seen above, a free-trade area must be equipped with rules of origin in order to avoid trade deflection which, if present, invalidates the principle of independent trade policies towards third countries. A customs union, unlike a free-trade area, does not need to devise rules of origin, since a uniform policy on trade exists with third countries. Planned originally as a customs union, the EEC does not have formal rules of origin for preventing trade deflection, but the EEC Commission takes measures that actually have an equivalent effect.[37] These measures equivalent to rules of origin are based on Article 115 of the EEC Treaty, which authorises exceptions to the intra-EEC free movement principles for imports of products originating in third countries.[38] The recent use, on a larger scale, of Article 115 to prevent trade deflection gives some support to the above view regarding the de facto conversion of the customs union into a free-trade area in recent years.[39] Moreover, it is worth noting that the necessary consent of the EEC Commission to the use of Article 115 increases further the degree of bureaucratisation of EEC institutions.

It is interesting to note that it was only in January 1982 that the EEC Commission formally authorised Italy to prevent indirect imports of Japanese passenger cars under Article 115.[40] This formal authorisation is not necessary for other EEC countries, since Japanese producers restrain 'voluntarily' their car exports to these countries.

A recent episode provides further evidence of the difficulties entailed in the working of a free-trade area that is not equipped with formal rules of origin. In 1982 the Italian motor vehicle trade association (ANFIA) urged the Italian government to stop imports of the Acclaim car, produced by British Leyland under licence from Honda in Britain, on the pretext that it was a Japanese car which should be subject to the Italian import quota.[41] After some time and certain diplomatic incidents between Britain and Italy, the Commission rejected the Italian argument. It decided that the Acclaim car meets the 'made in the EEC' requirement and, consequently, could not be restricted under Article 115.[42]

The third conclusion to be drawn from the analysis in the present section is that the increasing management of trade flows illustrated above has resulted in increased cooperation between manufacturers. This relates to both producers of the same country (Japan) who have cooperated in order to allocate quotas and divide West European markets and to producers of different countries who have developed a 'gentleman's agreement' for competition in the import countries. This development can be regarded as an important step towards the formation of international cartels in passenger car trade. The secret marketing arrangement negotiated by the British and Japanese motor vehicle trade associations is the most illustrative episode of such a development.

## Trade restrictions: the hidden sales taxes

West European countries impose a wide variety of taxes on the purchase of new passenger cars. Although these taxes do not formally distinguish between vehicles produced in different countries, they may actually be discriminatory if they result in

33

higher prices for buyers of vehicles produced in some countries than for buyers of vehicles produced in other countries. Table 2.4 presents the taxes imposed on car purchases in the countries under study and the changes in these taxes over the last two decades.[43]

As illustrated in Table 2.4, tax harmonisation has so far resulted in the adoption of the same value-added tax system in all of the five countries. Substantial differences, however, exist between the rates of tax imposition on new car purchases. Moreover, as far as passenger cars are concerned, no trend towards harmonisation of these rates has occurred over time. Only two of the five West European car-making countries, Italy and Sweden, have tax systems that may distort international trade flows in passenger cars, since they distinguish between vehicles of different engine sizes and weights.

In Italy it is clear that taxes are used as a protective measure against foreign competition. Table 2.4 shows that the structure of the Italian tax system results in higher prices for buyers of vehicles of large engine size than for buyers of vehicles of low engine size. This discrimination against large cars is not very surprising since Italy, which has the lowest per capita income of the five countries examined, produces mostly passenger cars of low engine size. The political economy of tax changes over the last 25 years supports the view that the purchase tax is used as a non-tariff barrier to trade in Italy.

The removal of quantitative import restrictions and the drastic lowering of tariff protection at the beginning of the 1960s resulted in a sharp increase in passenger car imports to Italy. A Fiat-owned newspaper (at the time), *La Stampa,* initiated a violent press campaign against the excessively rapid growth of imports. It urged the Italian government to impose restrictive measures on trade in order to rescue the threatened domestic motor vehicle industry.[44] The anti-foreign car campaign turned out to be very successful. In February 1964 the Italian government introduced a new car purchase tax that increased according to cylinder capacity and total car volume and, thereby, discriminated against larger, mostly foreign-made passenger cars.[45]

The trade-distorting effects of the Italian tax structure were further intensified over the last 11 years. Between 1974 and 1985 the gap between the tax rates imposed on new cars of less and more than 2,000 cc increased actually from 12–18 per cent

**Table 2.4:** Taxes imposed on the purchase of a new car, 1960–1985

| Country | Tax | Amount of tax | Date of imposition |
|---|---|---|---|
| France | Value-added tax | 20% | < 1 Dec 1968 |
| | | 33% | ⩾ 1 Dec 1968 |
| West Germany | Commodity tax | 11.77%  (German cars) | < 1 Jan 1968 |
| | | 11%       (Foreign cars) | |
| | Value-added tax | 10% | ⩾ 1 Jan 1968 |
| | (all goods) | 11% | ⩾ 1 Jul 1968 |
| | | 12% | ⩾ 1 Jan 1978 |
| | | 13% | ⩾ 1 Jul 1979 |
| | | 14% | ⩾ 1 Jul 1983 |
| Italy | Commodity tax | 12.03%  (Italian cars) | < 1 Feb 1964 |
| | | 13.1%    (Foreign cars) | |
| | | n.a.[a] | < 1 Jan 1973 |
| | Value-added tax | 12% (<2,000 cc) | ⩾ 1 Jan 1973 |
| | | 18% (⩾2,000 cc) | |
| | | 12% (<2,000 cc) | ⩾ 9 Jul 1974 |
| | | 30% (⩾2,000 cc) | |
| | | 12%[b] | ⩾ 1 Jan 1978 |
| | | 30% | |
| | | 20% (<2,000 cc) | ⩾ 5 Aug 1982 |
| | | 38% (⩾2,000 cc) | |
| | | 18% (<2,000 cc) | ⩾ 1 Jan 1985 |
| | | 38% (⩾2,000 cc) | |

| Sweden | Commodity tax      plus | excise tax based on car weight (per kg) | |
|---|---|---|---|
| | (and VAT after 1969) | | |

| 4% | < 1 Jan 1962 | to < 31 Jan 1966: 1.1 SKr and an additional |
| 6% | ⩾ 1 Jan 1962 | 1.45 SKr for every full 50 kg over 1,600 kg |
| 9.1% | ⩾ 1 Jul 1965 | to ⩾ 1 Feb 1966: 1.55 SKr and an additional |
| 10% | ⩾ 1 Mar 1967 | 1.95 SKr for every full 50 kg over 1,600 kg |
| 14% | ⩾ 9 Feb 1969 | to ⩾ 20 Nov 1968: 1.9 SKr and an additional |
| 15% | ⩾ 1 Jan 1971 | 2.4 SKr for every full 50 kg over 1,600 kg |
| 12% | ⩾ 1 Apr 1974 | to ⩾ 6 Feb 1973: 2.3 SKr and an additional |
| 15% | ⩾ 16 Sept 1974 | 2.9 SKr for every full 50 kg over 1,600 kg |
| 17.1% | ⩾ 1 Jun 1977 | to ⩾ 1 Jan 1984: 3.2 SKr and an additional |
| 19% | ⩾ 8 Sept 1980 | 4 SKr for every full 50 kg over 1,600 kg |
| 17.7% | ⩾ 16 Nov 1981 | to ⩾ 15 Jun 1985: 4.8 SKr and an additional |
| 19% | ⩾ 1 Jan 1983 | 6 SKr for every full 50 kg over 1,600 kg |

| Britain | Purchase tax | 55% | < Jul 1961 |
|---|---|---|---|
| | | 45% | ⩾ Apr 1962 |
| | | 25% | ⩾ Nov 1962 |
| | | 27.5% | ⩾ Jul 1966 |
| | | 33.33% | ⩾ Mar 1968 |
| | | 36.66% | ⩾ Nov 1968 |

35

Table 2.4 continued

| Country | Tax | | Date of |
|---------|-----|---|---------|
| Britain | Purchase Tax | Amount of tax | imposition |
| | | 30% | ⩾ Jul 1971 |
| | | 25% | ⩾ Mar 1972 |
| | Value-added tax plus car tax | 23% | ⩾ Apr 1973 |
| | (car tax — 10% of five-sixths | 20.4% | ⩾ Jul 1974 |
| | of recommended retail price) | 24.58% | ⩾ Jun 1979 |

Sources: Information provided by the national motor vehicle trade associations. Several issues of *Motor Traffic in Sweden* (Bilindustriföreningen (1960–1985); Associazione Nazionale (1985); and Moneta (1962), p. 35.

Notes: <, before; ⩾, after.

[a]Not available, but the tax introduced in 1964 increased with engine size.

[b]From 1 January 1978, the lowest rate of tax imposition concerns diesel cars up to 2,500 cc.

to 18–38 per cent (see Table 2.4). The protectionist purpose of these changes cannot be denied. They further favour the small Fiat engines while they intensify discrimination against large imported passenger cars by increasing their local prices. The tariff equivalent of the indirect tax change in 1974 can be estimated at around 10 per cent. In view of their discriminatory nature, it is rather surprising that these changes did not result in any reaction from the Commission of the European Community.

An exception is the action engaged in by the Commission in 1985 against the introduction in Italy of different rates of value-added tax on diesel-engine motor vehicles of different cylinder capacities.[46] The main argument of the Commission was that no diesel cars in excess of 2,500 cc were produced in Italy and, accordingly, that Italy failed to respect the Treaty of Rome by applying the highest tax rate exclusively to motor vehicles originating in other member countries.

Sweden too has a purchase tax system that is trade-distorting, since it results in higher prices for some vehicles than for others (see Table 2.4). For example, the Swedish VAT and excise tax are equivalent to a percentage sales tax of 22.1 per cent on a 1980 Volkswagen Golf CLS, 22.3 per cent on a 1980 Saab 900 GLS, 24.9 per cent on a 1980 Volvo 244 DL and 20.1 per cent on a 1980 Mercedes 280 CE.[47] These examples indicate that, because of the weight–price relationship of the Swedish cars, the

36

tax imposed on the purchase of new cars in Sweden tends, in practice, to discriminate against Swedish passenger cars. The purpose of the differentiated Swedish tax system (on the basis of weight) cannot, therefore, be considered as protectionist, although the system is trade-distorting since it affects the relative prices of passenger cars.

To complete the picture, mention should be made of a French periodic tax which discriminates against vehicles manufactured in foreign countries.[48] This annual tax (*vignette*) is based on age and fiscal horsepower and ranges from FF 73 to FF 2,226. France also imposes a special annual tax for passenger cars with a power rating exceeding 16 fiscal hp, which varies from about FF 9,000 for cars under five years to FF 1,300 for cars between 20 and 25 years old. As noted by the EEC Commission, it is obvious that the French taxes discriminate against the bigger, more powerful imported passenger cars.[49]

The main conclusion that emerges from the analysis of the various taxes paid on the purchase of a new car and of their changes over time is that one country, Italy, has used the indirect tax instrument in order to achieve trade policy-related goals. This use has no equivalent in other West European car-producing countries. The analysis suggests that trade-distorting taxes exist only in France.

## Technical and administrative obstacles to trade

One of the main results of the Tokyo Round of trade negotiations was to bring into the focus of attention those technical and administrative rules and practices that create significant obstacles to international trade and have substantial trade-distorting effects. In view of their effects, these regulations undoubtedly constitute a form of non-tariff barrier. The first kind of regulations, technical hindrances to trade, refer generally to different technical national regulations that oblige producers to adapt their products in order to penetrate different national markets. The second kind of regulations refer to administrative practices and procedures that, in one way or another, discriminate against non-domestic producers.[50]

Different national technical requirements necessitate the adaptation of the product to different markets. They result in an extra adaptation cost that varies according to the country of origin and the manufacturer. This extra cost is not necessarily trade-distorting, since it can equally affect domestic and foreign firms. It is actually trade-distorting only if the production process is subject to economies of scale and if the extra adaptation of the production process somewhat prevents foreign producers from taking advantage of these economies. The larger these economies of scale, the more likely that technical regulations introduced by a country will negatively affect those foreign producers that export only limited quantities to this country. In other words, the smaller the market (country) protected by technical non-tariff barriers and the larger the economies of scale in an industry, the larger the tariff equivalent that exporters will have to bear in order to enter this market.

The existence of administrative provisions and practices does not require — contrary to technical provisions — an adaptation of the products and production processes. It is concerned with the obligatory procedures followed by exporters who want to enter the market. Administrative regulations may result in an administrative cost, such as an inspection fee, and/or uncertainty for exporters.[51] The first effect may be trade-distorting, since inspection fees — the amount of which is independent of the quantity sold — negatively affect firms that sell only a limited quantity, that is in most cases foreign firms. As regards the second effect, we may expect uncertainty to increase information costs for exporters and, consequently, to deter their entry. The information costs decrease with the output volume exported to the market protected by an administrative non-tariff barrier. Thus, the tariff equivalent of an administrative non-tariff measure, like technical provisions, is likely to be higher in small rather than large markets (countries).

*Technical obstacles to trade*

The more differentiated a product is, the greater will be the scope for different technical and administrative regulations among countries. Because of the differentiated nature of the passenger car product, a wide variety of motor vehicles standards existed, and still exist, among West European countries (such as different lighting and signalling equipment, noise levels and permissible levels of exhaust fumes). Even if incomplete, the evidence tends to show that technical standard disparity among West European countries increased up to the very end of the 1960s. For example, according to the West German firm

Volkswagen, one basic model could be exported anywhere in Western Europe in 1955, whereas no less than nine to ten variations of the basic model were necessary at the very end of the 1960s.[52] It is clear that the presence of different technical standards had a negative effect on the process of economic integration of passenger car markets in Western Europe by creating non-negligible obstacles between them.

Harmonisation of technical regulations (i.e. adoption of the same regulations by different countries) has been regarded as the best way to cope with this problem. As far as passenger cars are concerned, the international efforts to harmonise technical standards and eliminate the integration-retarding technical obstacles to trade have mainly occurred in two organisations, the United Nations Economic Commission for Europe (ECE; Working Party 29) and the EEC.[53]

Since 1960 the Economic Commission for Europe has designed 55 regulations that have sought to lay down international technical standards for most motor vehicle parts.[54] Not all have been accepted by the participating countries. Of the 55 proposals on motor vehicle standards, the five countries examined, West Germany, France, Italy, Sweden and Britain have only accepted 31, 41, 45, 37 and 38, respectively.

For its part, between 1970 and 1984 the EEC adopted about 70 directives concerned with motor vehicle standards (some of them were only revisions of previous standards).[55] These directives, which deal with such things as permissible sound level, exhaust system, steering equipment, safety belts and heating system, grant free access to every market of the European Community to vehicles that conform to EEC technical standards. Only three directives, related to windscreens, tyres and permitted towing weights, remain to be adopted. Their adoption will allow for the coming into force of an EEC-type approval, the main result of which will be to accept, throughout the EEC, a passenger car approved in any one EEC country and to suppress technical barriers between member countries.

However, the EEC-type approval may never come into existence. The three remaining directives have been blocked for several years as a result of the opposition of EEC car manufacturers and national governments (above all the French). The main reason behind their opposition is that third-country producers should not enjoy the advantages of the EEC-type approval system unless there is reciprocity from third countries on EEC passenger car exports.[56]

An important aspect of the harmonisation process in the EEC is that directives are only optional and that member countries can continue to apply their own national standards for products confined to the domestic market.[57] By implication, two sets of motor vehicle standards may cohabit in each EEC market. In view of the optional nature of the EEC standards, we can wonder, of course, to what extent they have been used as a substitute for national standards in the member countries and, in consequence, have become mandatory. A related question is to what extent car manufacturers comply with the EEC harmonised standards.

As regards the first aspect, a study of the Common Market covering 40 of the directives shows that, among the member countries examined in 1982, Italy had substituted the most (40) EEC standards for national standards, France less than half and West Germany mainly those concerned with environment protection purposes, that is ten at the most.[58] No indication of the British standards is provided in the study. Another study suggests, however, that great efforts have been made in Britain since 1978 in order to bring British technical provisions in line with the rest of the Common Market.[59]

Concerning the second question, the same EEC study shows that Italian and, to a lesser extent, Japanese car manufacturers comply with most of the EEC harmonised standards.[60] The larger implementation of EEC harmonised standards in Italy explains of course these results. Of the 40 EEC directives, about half — concerned mainly with environment protection and vehicle safety — were largely followed by the 20 car manufacturers studied. This rather low figure is surprising because car manufacturers should find it uneconomic to manufacture cars conforming to two sets of standards and, hence, to partly sacrifice the economies of large-scale production. A likely factor behind this reluctance towards the harmonisation process is strong home-consumer preferences for a certain number of product characteristics embodied in national standards and the fear among domestic firms of losing loyal domestic consumers.

As stated above, different technical regulations entail an adaptation cost for producers. By implication, we may expect the harmonisation of technical standards to entail cost savings. This is because firms do not need any longer to produce many varieties and styles of the same product, and the fewer the number of differentiated products manufactured in each plant, the lower are unit costs. An EEC study estimated the cost savings of the harmonisation measures adopted by the Common Market for passenger cars to be more than 10 per cent.[61]

One of the car-making countries under study, Sweden, has remained outside the harmonisation process as a result of its non-membership in the European Community. As a consequence, technical regulations in Sweden and in the EEC car-making countries are expected to differ. Table 2.5 illustrates the existing differences by comparing the Swedish regulations with the ECE regulations and the EEC directives (only those regulations that differ between the EEC and Sweden are reported).

The clear conclusion that emerges from Table 2.5 is that Swedish regulations are much more stringent than ECE regulations and EEC directives. Distinctly deviating regulations actually exist for exhaust emissions, brakes, permissible noise level, diesel exhaust, position of exhaust tailpipe, marking for the identification of vehicles, and so on (see Table 2.5). It should be stressed that several of these regulations have been introduced since the mid-1970s, that is just after the removal of traditional trade barriers between Sweden and the EEC. For example, exhaust emission regulations were introduced from 1976–1977 and further sharpened in 1981.

The widely different Swedish requirements imply that foreign car producers have to bear adaptation costs that should be substantial, given the small size of the Swedish market (and thus of the quantity exported to Sweden) and the large economies of scale in passenger car production.[62] For foreign car manufacturers, these substantial adaptation costs correspond to a high tariff equivalent which amounts to the gap between the average unit costs of the production for the home market (or a combined production for the home and most export markets) and of production solely for the Swedish market.

*Administrative obstacles to trade*

Administrative impediments to passenger car trade pertain principally to the inspection procedures exporters have to follow in order to have their cars accepted on foreign markets. These procedures are performed by national authorities who control whether the vehicle checked is in conformity with the national regulations in force in each country.

**Table 2.5:** Comparison of ECE regulations, EEC directives and Swedish regulations for passenger cars

| Regulation | ECE regulation no.–year/Series of amendments | EEC Directive year/no. | Swedish regulation |
|---|---|---|---|
| Whole vehicle type approval | Draft reg. WP29/R.254 | 70/156[a] 78/315 78/547 80/1267 | BoF 53[a] |
| Exhaust emission by gasoline engines | 15–04 | 70/220[a] 78/665 | F140 and A10[b] (A10 is mandatory since 1985 year models) |
| Exhaust smoke by diesel engines | 24–02 | 72/306 | F19 and F20[b] |
| Exhaust tailpipe-routing requirements | | | BoF 08[a] (positioned on the left side as opposed to the practice in other countries) |
| CO in passenger compartment | | | Type inspection[b] manual 8.2–19 |
| Measuring of fuel consumption | 15–04 Annex 9 | 80/1268[a] | The directions of National Board for Consumers' Policies[b] KOVVFS 1979:11 |
| Measuring of engine power; gasoline engines | 15–04 Annex 9 | 80/1269[a] | |
| Prevention of fire risks | 34–01 | 70/221[b] | ECE (BoF 07) (mandatory with respect to plastic fuel tanks. Special requirements concerning the fastening of fuel lines and electrical wiring) |
| LPG equipment | Draft reg. GRPE/R.46/Rev.1 | | BoF 07[a] |
| Tyres | 30–02 | COM (76)[a] 712 | ECE (BoF 03) (special requirements regarding snow tyres, studded tyres and recapping) |
| Total weight | Draft reg. WP29/R.127 | R/683/78 (ECO 63) | BoF 54[b] |

| Braking system | 13–04 | 71/320[a] | BoF 05[a] |
|---|---|---|---|
| | | 79/489 | (F18–1971) |
| Compressed air tanks for braking systems | | 111/1583/80 | BoF 05[b] (F18–1971) |
| Steering system; steering forces | Draft reg. WP 29/GRRF/R.72 and R.77 | 70/311[b] | |
| Speedometer | 39–1978 | 75/443[a] | ECE (BoF 18) |
| Body; external projections | 26–01 | 74/483[a] 79/488 | BoF 27[b] |
| Body; interior fittings | 21–01 | 74/60 78/632 | BoF 10 (F8–1968)[b] (special requirements with regard to so-called vanity mirror in sun shades) |
| Body; glazing | 43–1980 | R/976/78[a] (ECO 88) | BoF 10[a] (laminated windshield is mandatory) |
| Protection shield for taxicab driver | | | BoF 57[b] |
| Seat belt anchorages | 14–01 | 76/115[a] 82/318 | ECE (BoF 24) |
| Child-restraining devices | 44–01 | | BoF 24[b] |
| Securing of load | Draft reg. WP29/R.37 | | BoF 10[b] |
| Communication system; Direction indicators | 6–1967 | 76/759[a] | ECE (BoF 13) |
| Parking lamp | Draft reg. WP29/R.202 | 77/540[a] | |
| Lighting and light signalling devices | 48–1981 | 76/756[a] 82/244 | BoF 13[a] |
| Driver's field of vision | Draft reg. WP29/R.43 WP29/R.236 | 77/649[a] 81/643 | BoF 10[b] |
| Windshield wipers, windshield washers | Draft reg. WP29/R.36 | 78/318[a] | BoF 15 and 16[b] (F4 and F5–1968) |
| Defrosting and demisting devices | Draft reg. WP29/R.44 | 78/317[a] | BoF 17[b] (F6–1968) |
| Control symbols | Draft reg. P29/R.1/Rev. 3 | 78/316[a] | BoF 11[b] (F1–1968) |
| Tachograph | | 1463/70 2828/77 | BoF 18[b] |
| Kilometre counter | | | RSN directions[b] |

Table 2.5 continued

| Regulation | ECE regulation no.–year/Series of amendments | EEC Directive year/no. | Swedish regulation |
|---|---|---|---|
| Anti-theft devices | 18–01 | 74/61[a] | ECE (BoF 11) |
| Vehicle | | 76/114 | BoF 52[b] |
| identification | | 78/507 | (marking required both in front and rear portions) |
| Cadmium ban | | | SFS 1979:771 Code of statutes of the National Environment Protection Board, SNFS 1981:5, PK:13[b] |
| Asbestos ban | | | Code of statutes of the National Board of Industrial Safety, AFS 1981:23[b] |

*Source:* Bilindustriföreningen (1983), pp. 10–15.
[a]Certain deviations.
[b]Distinctly deviating requirements or other scope of requirements. All others: requirements agree.
Swedish regulations: BoF and F (Road Safety Office's vehicle regulations); A (National Environment Protection Board's regulations); RSN (National Tax Board's regulations).

Complete harmonisation in the EEC countries should greatly simplify administrative procedures, since only one administrative operation valid throughout the Common Market will be necessary once the EEC-type approval is adopted. However, as mentioned above, the complete EEC-type approval system will not come into being in the near future, and it is likely that it will remain for years in its present stage. One of the main reasons behind this suspension of the harmonisation process in the EEC is the fear of some member-states and car manufacturers of losing national administrative control over third-country imports. It should be noted that the determinant role played by car producers and their trade associations in working out the ECE regulations and EEC directives — in the attempts to get rid of the technical and administrative barriers to trade that protect them from foreign competition — throws some doubt upon the chances of success for the ongoing harmonisation process.[63] Nevertheless, it cannot be denied that the various

EEC harmonisation measures adopted until now have brought about a reduction of the administrative non-tariff barriers within the Common Market.

Among the countries under study, Sweden has the most stringent administrative regulations.[64] In this country the inspection procedure actually applies to basic passenger car models as well as to versions of the basic models, whereas it applies only to basic models in other West European car-producing countries. Moreover, every new model-year version is checked in Sweden, even if it has nothing new. The inspection fees to be paid by car manufacturers are rather low. In 1983, they amounted to SKr 5,600 for basic models and SKr 2,800 for versions of the basic models. These administrative procedures negatively affect car producers that capture only a limited share of the small Swedish market, that is mainly foreign producers. This is because inspection fees are independent of the quantity sold and, thus, the smaller the quantity sold by foreign producers on the Swedish market, the larger the tariff equivalent of inspection procedures borne by them.

The presence of another administrative impediment to trade, uncertainty, has been pointed out in Sweden.[65] Uncertainty ensues, principally, from unwritten directives of the Swedish Motor Vehicle Inspection Company, which are not available to car manufacturers and relate, for example, to the mounting of brake lines. Such unwritten rules undoubtedly create uncertainty for exporters. Once more, we may expect small exporters to be more inhibited than large firms by such a non-tariff barrier, because small firms have more difficulty obtaining information on the relevant unwritten requirements and administrative practices.

*Conclusions*

Four main conclusions can be drawn from a detailed examination of the various technical and administrative non-tariff barriers in passenger car trade. Firstly, one country, Sweden, is much more protected than other West European car-producing countries by technical and administrative barriers to trade. This depends partly upon the fact that Sweden is a small country and that technical and administrative barriers to trade are more effective — resulting in a higher tariff equivalent — in smaller than in larger countries.

Secondly, the study tends to show that West Germany is the

EEC country that is most reluctant to substitute harmonised ECE and EEC regulations for national ones, and Italy is the country that has made most progress along the road of harmonisation.

Thirdly, there exists a close relationship between technical and administrative obstacles to trade: the more stringent (deviating) the former, the greater the scope for severe administrative controls at the grass-roots level. Furthermore, administrative barriers are much less sizeable than technical trade barriers in terms of tariff equivalents.

Finally, the analysis raises the question of the political economy of standard harmonisation, of the role of firms and pressure groups (especially trade associations) in the decision-making process. It actually shows that the complete harmonisation of technical regulations and the removal of most technical and administrative barriers to trade in the EEC were hampered by the action of passenger car manufacturers and some member-states. Furthermore, it detects a shift in the centre of decision-making with regard to the international harmonisation process from the UN ECE working group in the 1960s to the EEC harmonisation organisation over the last decade. Both facts reflect the greater incentives (gains) for EEC manufacturers to organise in order to capture business from non-EEC producers through 'favourable' technical standards than to organise with non-EEC producers to work out worldwide standards that increase the degree of competition.

### Trade-distorting subsidies to the passenger car industry

Government subsidies to domestic industries were another source of concern for the countries that participated in the Tokyo Round. They can be regarded as non-tariff distortions since they protect or favour, in one way or another, domestic producers *vis-à-vis* foreign suppliers and harm the exports of non-subsidising countries.

Public subsidies to trade-exposed industries are always trade-distorting but are not always trade-impeding. On the one hand, public subsidies can result in an increase in the country's export supply if used to subsidise exports. In this case, public subsidies are trade-distorting since they discriminate against non-subsidised foreign exports, but they are also trade-promoting since they result in an increase in the volume of international trade. On the other hand, public subsidies can result in a decrease in the subsidising country's import demand schedule if they bring about a downward shift in the supply curve and an increase in domestic production. In this second case, public subsidies are still trade-distorting, since they discriminate against foreign non-subsidised producers, but they are now also trade-impeding. A subsidy protects domestic producers much as a tariff would, since it increases the price they receive. Note, however, that a public subsidy affects domestic production and imports but not consumption, because it does not change the price paid by consumers. The effect on imports of a subsidy is, therefore, less than that of a tariff, which changes the producer price by the same amount. If the subsidised firms cannot now discriminate between the domestic and foreign markets, public subsidies are still trade-distorting but they may have only a limited net effect on the volume of international trade.

It is often argued that the volume of public subsidies to domestic firms has increased substantially, firstly during the period since the Second World War as a result of the wider involvement of governments in Western economies and secondly, since the mid-1970s as a result of enormous economic changes and ambitious adjustment policies.[66] This conclusion is in most cases impressionistic because the scope for public subsidies is difficult to assess accurately for two related reasons. Firstly, governments are not anxious to make exhaustive studies that may reveal to what extent they subsidise their own industry and thus run the risk of retaliatory measures from countries that are discriminated against. Secondly, trade-distorting subsidies are difficult to estimate because they take different forms, are highly complex and, moreover, are often hidden (subsidised rates of interest, regional aids, public participation in the equity of firms, state export guarantees, etc.).[67] In this respect, it should be added that the presence of state-owned firms in some countries further increases the difficulties of measurement since it blurs the boundary between the private sector and government.

## National subsidy policies

The experience of the West European passenger car industry is highly illustrative of the wide variety of forms taken by public subsidies within and between countries and of the difficulties of measurement faced by economists who attempt to estimate their scope and impact in a comparative cross-country perspective. It is likely that, before the mid-1970s, public subsidies to West European car manufacturers were limited to state-owned firms and the ailing British industry because their main causes, economic difficulties and the resulting industry pressures, were absent before this date. The possibility that public aid was modest before 1975 is supported by the fact that it was only from the *Fifth EEC Report on Competition Policy*, concerned with the year 1975, that national aid to the EEC motor vehicle industry was mentioned and had thus become a source of EEC concern.[68]

In West Germany, much of the government assistance provided to the motor vehicle industry takes the form of tax rebates and accelerated depreciation for fixed assets.[69] These tax benefits are generally granted for capital investments made in certain regions, such as West Berlin, or aimed at reducing air pollution and industrial waste. Moreover, one of the West German car manufacturers, Volkswagen, benefited from regional aid (DM 210 million) to solve its redundancy problem in 1974.[70]

In Sweden, as in West Germany, public assistance to the car industry takes the form of tax benefits. Swedish companies can actually build up untaxed reserves of up to 50 per cent of their annual pre-tax income and use them with the approval of the Swedish government to invest in new equipment and machinery or to set up new plants. After five years, Swedish companies may use 30 per cent of the reserves without special approval from the government. Such reserves correspond to tax rebates and have no equivalent in other West European countries. They have been used to a limited extent by Swedish car manufacturers during the last decade. However, the two Swedish firms, Volvo and Saab, will each have at their disposal no less than SKr 12.5 billion of these investment reserves in order to set up two new plants in Sweden during the second half of the 1980s.[71]

One of the two Swedish producers, Volvo, benefited — and still benefits — from substantial direct aid from the Dutch government through its Dutch subsidiary, Volvo Car BV. This aid takes two forms: first, capital injection, which occurred in connection with the increase in the shareholding of the Dutch government in Volvo Car BV (from 25 per cent to 45 per cent in 1977 and from 45 per cent to 70 per cent in 1981); second, grants or debt write-offs, which were accorded to Volvo Car BV by the Dutch government in three stages, £72 million between 1977 and 1980, £30 million between 1980 and 1984 and around £108 million between 1984 and 1986.[72] These grants undoubtedly represent a high level of subsidisation since they corresponded, for example, to around 14 per cent and 11 per cent of the turnover of Volvo Car BV in 1977 and 1978, respectively.[73]

In Italy government aid mainly takes the form of loans at lower interest rates than the ones prevailing on the private capital market and of regional development aid programmes aimed officially at helping depressed areas such as the Mezzogiorno.[74] State-owned Alfa Romeo has been the main recipient of the Italian public subsidies. It has benefited from both low-interest loans and direct public money. The second Italian manufacturer, Fiat, also benefited from public subsidies. For example, it received L 135,798 million (around £59 million) in investment grants between 1981 and 1983. Most estimates of the level of subsidisation in Italy should, nevertheless, be considered as tentative due to the well-known overlapping of the private and public industrial sectors in this country.[75]

In France and Britain state-owned passenger car firms are subsidised in a more direct manner through public equity injections. Table 2.6 gives both the absolute size of the French and British government contributions to capital funds and their relative size as related to the turnover of the firms concerned. It shows that the state-owned firms have been the recipients of considerable sums of public money over the last decade. British Leyland has been much more subsidised than Renault if one takes into account the volume of public subsidies related to turnover. It is the completion of a restructuring programme intended to facilitate the future privatisation of British Leyland which is the official explanation of the huge public funds (around £2.2 billion) poured into the state-owned car manufacturer by the British government between 1975 and 1983. As a result of the reservations put forward by the EEC Commission, the British government decided not to give more public money to British Leyland and to withdraw its proposal to inject a further £100 million in 1984.[76]

State-owned Renault benefited too from low-interest subsidised loans (9.25 per cent) granted by the French Industrial Modernisation Fund (FIM) in 1984 and 1985 in spite of the reservations of the EEC Commission.[77]

Over the last decade, state aid in both Britain and France has

**Table 2.6**: French and British public subsidies in the form of capital injection to state-owned motor vehicle manufacturers (in millions of francs and pounds and as a percentage of turnover; in 1980 £1 ≈ FF 9.8)

| Year | Renault (as a % of turnover) | | BL (as a % of turnover) | |
|------|------|------|------|------|
| 1962–1972 | FF 1,355 | (1.7%) | — | — |
| 1973 | — | — | — | — |
| 1974 | — | — | — | — |
| 1975 | FF 320 | (1.75%) | £200 | (10.7%) |
| 1976 | — | — | — | — |
| 1977 | FF 350 | (1.2%) | — | — |
| 1978 | FF 175 | (0.5%) | £449 | (14.6%) |
| 1979 | FF 425 | (1%) | £149 | (5%) |
| 1980 | FF 250 | (0.5%) | £450 | (15.6%) |
| 1981 | — | — | £520 | (18.1%) |
| 1982 | FF 1,020 | (1.55%) | £260 | (8.5%) |
| 1983 | FF 700 | (0.95%) | £181 | (5.3%) |
| 1984 | FF 1,050 | (1.5%) | — | — |
| 1985 | FF 4,166 | (4.7%) | — | — |

*Sources:* Subsidies: Le Pors and Prunet (1975), De Carmoy (1978), Bhaskar (1984) and *Le Monde* (1985). Turnover figures: Renault Company Reports (only the passenger car division, amounting to 70–75% of the Renault's industrial group turnover, is considered in Table 2.6); British Leyland information provided by the Society of Motor Manufacturers and Traders.

also been provided to privately-owned car manufacturers. In Britain, most private manufacturers have benefited in one way or another from public subsidies over the last decade.[78] Ford received various regional grants that amounted to £158.5 million between 1976 and 1983 (around 0.7 per cent of its turnover).[79] Another subsidiary of a US company, Vauxhall (General Motors), was given £25.5 million in state aid for regional and industrial purposes between 1979 and 1983 (around 0.6 per cent of its turnover). In 1975, three years before it was taken over by Peugeot–Citroën, Chrysler UK obtained a grant amounting to £72.5 million, a low-interest loan of £55 million and a guarantee of £35 million.[80] Between 1978 and 1982, the same firm, now called Talbot UK, received £58 million from the British government (around 2 per cent of its turnover). Another example of Britain's extensive subsidisation of the car industry is the grants provided to the Japanese firm Nissan at the beginning of the 1980s.[81] These grants covered about one-third of the total cost of setting up a new Nissan plant in Britain.

The privately owned Peugeot–Citroën obtained financial assistance from the French government on two occasions. The first was in 1974 when Citroën benefited from a low-interest loan of FF 1,000 million (9.75 per cent) granted for a 15-year period.[82] The loan was, nevertheless, repaid within a two-year period. The second occasion was in 1983 when the company obtained FF 700 million in the form of low-interest loans and regional grants to modernise some of its plants in France.[83]

*EEC subsidy policy*

The introduction of EEC subsidy policy into the study complicates, for two main reasons, the above account of the extent of government subsidies to the West European passenger car industry. First, EEC subsidy statistics refer to the countries benefiting from the aid but not the companies. Moreover, in some cases, statistics do not even provide the name of the recipient country (as, for example, the statistics of the European Social Fund). Second, EEC subsidies take six different forms and, thus, it can be rather difficult to obtain an overview of their precise scope. The available material may, nevertheless, provide a rough picture of their extent compared to national government subsidies. Most EEC subsidies to the motor vehicle industry have been granted officially for regional and social reasons.[84]

Regional aid to the motor vehicle industry amounted to 290 million European Units of Account between 1975 and 1980 (around £190 million; in 1978, £1 ≈ 1.5 EUA). In 1981 and 1982, the same aid amounted to 29.5 million European Currency Units (around £18.5 million).[85] The main recipients of EEC regional aid, which has been shared out according to the extent of regional problems in the EEC countries, have been in order of importance, Italy, France, West Germany, Britain and the Netherlands. In 1981–1982, for instance, the passenger car industries in Italy, France, West Germany, Britain and the Netherlands received regional aid totalling £7.8, £6, £4.5, £0.7 and £0.5 million, respectively. Another instrument of the EEC regional policy is the loans granted by the European Investment Bank (EIB). For example, Italy benefited from such loans amounting to about £50.4 million in 1981–1982.[86] It should be emphasised that the trade-distorting effects of the EIB loans are limited, since they are generally granted on the basis of prevailing market conditions.

EEC social aid, which may have trade-distorting effects,

consists of so-called reconversion loans combined with interest subsidies. They are granted by the European Coal and Steel Community (ECSC) for job creation in depressed areas and amounted to 435 million EUA (around £290 million) for the motor industry in the whole EEC between 1975 and 1980.[87] However, the level of subsidisation, which corresponds to the volume of interest subsidies, accounts for only a limited share of these loans. For instance, interest subsidies to the automobile sector amounted to 247,000, 495,000 and 306,000 ECUs in France, Britain and West Germany in 1981–1982.[88] These sums corresponded to 8 per cent, 10.6 per cent and 14 per cent respectively, of the reconversion loans granted to these three countries during the same period.

Although important, EEC subsidies are much smaller than the national government subsidies provided to West European car manufacturers (compare, for example, the subsidies granted to Renault and British Leyland with the EEC figures). It does not, therefore, change the overall comparative picture that emerged from the above review of national subsidies. According to this picture, state-owned firms in Britain, France and Italy have been the main recipients of public money over the last two decades. The study suggests that France and Italy have made the greatest use of subsidies to car manufacturers if one considers the last two and a half decades. However, if only the last decade is taken into account, it is without doubt Britain that has had the highest level of subsidisation. This is because of the enormous sums of public money poured into the British motor industry during this period. The Dutch subsidiary of Volvo, whose main shareholder since 1981 is the Dutch state, has also been generously subsidised during the last decade. Finally, the analysis suggests that West Germany and Sweden have, to a much lesser extent, used public subsidies as non-tariff trade measures.

## SUMMARY AND CONCLUSIONS

In the present chapter, we have examined changes in trade policy over the last two and a half decades. We detected two sub-periods characterised by opposing trends. First, we provided evidence of a rapid liberalisation of passenger car trade up to the beginning of the 1970s. The liberalisation took the form of considerable tariff cuts. These were the result of the different steps taken on the road to the formation of an enlarged free-trade area in Western Europe and, to a lesser extent, the three worldwide Rounds of trade negotiations. Second, we illustrated the revival of protectionism since the mid-1970s, which confirms the reversal of the trend in trade policy. The revival took the form of various non-tariff measures that have emerged in most West European countries over the last decade. Various forms of quantitative import restrictions and marketing agreements are operative in all the West European car-producing countries. More stringent technical barriers have been introduced in Sweden. Trade-distorting tax changes have taken place in Italy. Finally, huge public subsidies have been provided to British, French and Italian car manufacturers.

One conclusion of the present chapter is that the emergence of non-tariff barriers in the passenger car industry gives some support to the political economy approach to protection. This is because the passenger car industry possesses the characteristics which, according to this theory, are required for an industry to obtain protection from abroad. The main required characteristics (a small number of firms, a large number of employees, i.e. large factories, a low rate of growth of output and a large proportion of unskilled personnel in total work force) as well as the way in which these increase the chance of receiving protection were presented at the beginning of the present chapter. The detailed analysis of the formation of non-tariff barriers at the passenger car industry level suggests that other characteristics play a significant role as well. First, the large public subsidies given to state-owned firms in France, Italy and Britain indicate that the presence of state-owned firms in an industry increases its chance of receiving protection from foreign competition. Second, the decisive role of the Italian and British motor vehicle trade associations in erecting non-tariff barriers confirms the importance of a high degree of institutional organisation of business interests in obtaining protection from abroad.

Another purpose of the analysis was to illustrate two processes of formation of non-tariff barriers in the wake of international integration. According to the first process, non-tariff barriers were expected to be raised just after the removal of tariffs as a result of the action of organised and threatened producers. Evidence provided in the present chapter confirms this shift from tariffs to non-tariff barriers. The indirect tax changes in Italy in 1964, the sharpening of technical barriers to trade in Sweden during the second half of the 1970s and the grant of huge public subsidies to the British industry during the last decade took place just after tariff abolition within the EEC and between the EEC and the original EFTA countries.

These measures as well as the measures introduced independently of tariff reductions — such as public subsidies in France and Italy and other tax changes in Italy — have hampered the free flow of trade within the tariff-unified economic area. They have raised new and substantial barriers among West European national markets and undoubtedly constitute disintegrating measures.

According to the second process of formation, non-tariff barriers were expected to ensue from the action of organised member producers at the supranational level to capture business from producers of non-member countries. An example of such action is the successful opposition of EEC car producers at the EEC level to the complete harmonisation of technical regulations. This should have removed national technical barriers to trade and made it easier for third-country exporters to penetrate the EEC market. Another example may be the EEC subsidies received by EEC producers, the main effect of which is to protect EEC producers against exports of non-member countries. Note, however, that the main non-tariff barriers, the quantitative restrictions directed towards Japanese exports, were not introduced by the Commission as a result of pressures from EEC producers acting jointly, but individually by member countries.

A last important result concerns the impact of non-tariff barriers on the form of international integration. In the 1960s the removal of internal tariffs among member countries and the introduction of a common external tariff meant that the EEC countries formed a customs union. The EFTA countries, on the other hand, formed a free-trade area since they removed internal tariffs but kept their own tariffs on trade with non-member countries. However, the introduction of very different quantitative restrictions — mostly directed towards Japanese exports — implies that the EEC countries have nowadays different trade policies on trade with non-member countries. Therefore, the EEC no longer constitutes a customs union but rather a free-trade area. The policy of the Commission of the EEC to prevent trade deflection confirms further this de facto conversion of the

Common Market into a free-trade area. As far as passenger car markets are concerned, both the EEC and the EFTA countries constitute an enlarged free-trade area. The presence of non-tariff barriers within the tariff unified economic area indicates moreover that it is a rather imperfect free-trade area.

## NOTES

1. See Anderson and Baldwin (1981); Baldwin (1982), pp. 263–86.

2. 'The larger the trade-creating effects, that is, the greater the need to reallocate resources in the wake of tariff abolition, the greater will be the resistance to the union among various highly concentrated and vocal producer interests of the member countries. The gains from trade creation, on the other hand, lie in the future and are likely to be diffused among numerous firms and among the consumers at large. Thus trade creation is on balance a political liability. Trade diversion implies, on the contrary, that concentrated producer groups of the member countries will be able to capture business away from their present competitors in nonmember countries. These effects will therefore endear the customs union to the interest groups concerned and will provide some badly needed group-support for a union' (Hirschman, 1981, p. 271).

3. On trade policy prior to the beginning of the integration process, see Kock (1969), Chapter 4; Curzon (1965), Chapter 4.

4. Maxcy and Silberston (1959), p. 13.

5. Wemelsfelder (1960), pp. 94–104.

6. In view of the tariff rate imposed by Benelux (24 per cent) the Common External Tariff should have been higher if the basic rule had been followed.

7. Curzon (1965), pp. 99–100; Nême and Nême (1970), pp. 62–63.

8. United Nations (1968), p. 37; Nême and Nême (1970), pp. 380–81.

9. Frank (1961), p. 11; Kock (1969), pp. 139–45.

10. Nême and Nême (1970), pp. 39–41.

11. See OEEC (1957), pp. 91–92.

12. Frank (1961), pp. 254–58.

13. Information provided by the French Motor Vehicle Trade Association.

14. Busch (1966), p. 183; Ouin (1964), p. 262.

15. In 1960 the level of tariffs for manufactured products was rather low — about 5 per cent — in the Scandinavian countries and Switzerland and relatively high — 15 per cent or more — in Britain and Austria. See Frenger, Jansen and Reymert (1979), p. 33.

16. Curzon (1974), pp. 215–21; Coombs (1976), p. 113.

17. Middleton (1975), pp. 14–24; Curzon (1965), pp. 155–65;

Kock (1969), pp. 139–45.

18. It should be noted, however, that severe quantitative restrictions, directed toward passenger car producers in all GATT countries (including EFTA suppliers), still existed in two EFTA countries, Finland and Portugal, during the second half of the 1960s. See EFTA (1968), p. 6; EFTA (1969), p. 172.

19. On the enlargement issue, see Swann (1984), pp. 27–48.

20. See Stigelin (1973), p. 165.

21. Kreinin and Officer (1979), pp. 543–72.

22. A list of the products exempted by the EEC is given in Cable (1983), p. 42.

23. Dahlström and Söderbäck (1972), pp. 11–32; EFTA (1980), p. 15.

24. See Salvatore (1985), p. 6; *Le Monde* (1982).

25. See *Le Monde* (1982).

26. Bronckers (1983), p. 66.

27. *Official Journal of the European Communities* (1982e).

28. Bronckers (1983), pp. 66–67.

29. See for example *Le Monde* (1984b); *Newsweek* (1981).

30. See for example *The Economist* (1983a), p. 62.

31. Bronckers (1983), p. 68; *Financial Times* (1982b).

32. According to *The Economist*, yearly arrangements between the two trade associations have existed since 1975. See *The Economist* (1982c), pp. 82–85.

33. See *The Economist* (1982c), p. 84; Bronckers (1983), pp. 67–68.

34. See Bronckers (1983), pp. 67–68. In June 1981, probably as a result of the Commission planned action (threat) towards Japanese exports, Japan too decided to cut back car exports to Belgium and Luxembourg and to freeze exports to Holland.

35. It should be noted that the Volvo–Renault deal is in opposition to one of the aspects of the free-trade agreement between Sweden and the EEC which prohibits, explicitly, any agreements between firms prejudicing the free flow of trade and distorting competition (see in the present chapter, pp. 27–28). The figures on Renault sales were collected in different issues of *Motor Traffic in Sweden* (Bilindustriföreningen (1960–1985)).

36. A practical implication of the less transparent nature of new protective measures is that empirical studies of trade policy must, to a much larger extent than before, rely upon non-official sources such as newspapers or magazines.

37. See Vogelenzang (1981), pp. 169–96; Bronckers (1983), pp. 71–74.

38. For the rules of application of Article 115, see Van Dartel (1983), pp. 99–123.

39. An updated list of products originating in third countries and subject to control under Article 115 is available in *Official Journal of the European Communities* (*OJ*) (1985c).

40. *Official Journal of the European Communities* (*OJ*) (1982b). Since September 1982, the authorisation of the Commission concerns

also motor vehicles originating in the Soviet Union, which are in free circulation in other member countries, but surprisingly not vehicles originating in Czechoslovkia and Romania. See *Official Journal of the European Communities* (1982d, 1983, 1985b, 1985e).

41. On this episode, see *The Economist* (1982b), p. 53; *Financial Times* (1982a); *Financial Times* (1982c).

42. A formal rule of origin concerned with passenger car trade actually exists between the EEC and EFTA and requires that the non-EEC or -EFTA materials incorporated should not exceed 40 per cent of the value of the finished cars if no tariffs are to be imposed on trade between the two West European trading blocs. *Official Journal of the European Communities* (1982e).

43. It should be noted that other minor taxes are imposed on the purchase of new passenger cars in some of the countries studied. In West Germany, Italy and France, there are registration fees which amount to 0.1–0.2 per cent, 0.1 per cent and 0.6–0.9 per cent of the price, respectively. In Sweden there is a car-scrapping charge that amounts to 200 SKr.

44. This episode is related in detail in *Business Week* (1965), pp. 90–94.

45. In April 1964 the Italian government took a more drastic measure in order to curb imports by obliging car importers to pay foreign exchange within 30 days of importing instead of 360 days. See *Business Week* (1965), p. 94.

46. See *Official Journal of the European Communities* (1985d).

47. On the weight and price of passenger cars in Sweden, see *Jan Ulléns Bilfakta* (1980).

48. For a review of periodic taxes imposed in EEC countries, see *Official Journal of the European Communities* (1986).

49. *Official Journal of the European Communities* (1982c, 1986).

50. Definitions of technical and administrative hindrances to trade are discussed in depth in Slot (1975), Chapter 1; Middleton (1975), Chapter 5.

51. See Slot (1975), pp. 62–63.

52. See Baldwin (1971), p. 145.

53. On the various international organisations, see Bilindustriföreningen (1968), pp. 5–11; Slot (1975), Chapter 6.

54. The details of the ECE regulations and the date of their eventual acceptance is available in Bilindustriföreningen (1983), p. 8.

55. A detailed list of the EEC directives with their date of adoption is available in Commission of the European Communities (1984b). This list does not include a recent directive which relates to the permissible sound level and the exhaust level of motor vehicles and which was adopted in September 1984 and came into force on 1 January 1985. See *Official Journal of the European Communities* (1984).

56. See *Official Journal of the European Communities* (1982a); Commission of the European Communities (1983b), pp. 7–8; BEUC (1981), p. 14.

57. On the role of directives versus regulations as instruments of harmonisation, see Dashwood (1981), pp. 7–17.

58. See Commission of the European Communities (1983b), pp. 18–23.
59. See Husbands (1981), pp. 79–80.
60. Commission of the European Communities (1983b), p. 20.
61. Commission of the European Communities (1981b), p. 68.
62. Estimates of scale economies in passenger car production will be provided in Chapter 4.
63. The process of laying down a directive in the EEC (actors, procedure, etc.) is described in Slot (1975), pp. 94–98. Concerning the working-out of ECE regulations, see Bilindustriföreningen (1968), pp. 5–8.
64. Bilindustriföreningen (1968), pp. 6–7.
65. Ibid., p. 7.
66. See for example Malmgren (1977), p. 1; Ohlin (1978), p. 21.
67. For the problems that arise out of the concept of subsidy, see Malmgren (1977), pp. 18–22; Lundgren and Ståhl (1981), pp. 145–46; Carlsson (1983), pp. 2–3, 6–7.
68. See the first five EEC *Reports on Competition Policy*, Commission of the European Communities (1972–1977); Warnecke (1978), pp. 147–49, 164–65.
69. See Bhaskar (1984), pp. 52–58.
70. See De Carmoy (1978), p. 51.
71. See *Affärsvärlden* (1986), pp. 29–31.
72. See Commission of the European Communities (1981a), p. 144; Bhaskar (1984), p. 89.
73. For figures on Volvo Car BV's turnover in 1977 and 1978, see *Volvo Company Report* (1979).
74. See Bhaskar (1984), pp. 59–68.
75. On Italian state capitalism, see Curzon (1981), pp. 65–69; Prodi (1974), pp. 45–63.
76. *The Economist* (1985a), pp. 66–68; Commission of the European Communities (1985), pp. 155–56.
77. Commission of the European Communities (1985), pp. 155, 162–63.
78. Bhaskar (1984), pp. 74–78.
79. Figures on Ford, Vauxhall and Talbot UK turnover were provided by the Society of Motor Manufacturers and Traders.
80. See Commission of the European Communities (1976), p. 84.
81. Bhaskar (1984), p. 78.
82. Commission of the European Communities (1976), pp. 83–84.
83. Bhaskar (1984), pp. 47–48.
84. See Commission of the European Communities (1981b), p. 37; Bhaskar (1984), pp. 31–41.
85. Commission of the European Communities (1983b), Annex 27, Table 27a.
86. Ibid. (1983b), Annex 27, Table 27b.
87. Commission of the European Communities (1981b), p. 37.
88. Commission of the European Communities (1983b), Annex 27, Table 27a.

# 3

# Trade Effects of Trade Policy

The preceding chapter contained a review of the trade policy measures that were introduced over the last two and a half decades. The aim of these measures was either to bring markets near each other or to move them away from each other. In other words, their purpose was either to integrate or disintegrate an economic area made up of several national markets. Little or nothing was said about the real integration (interpenetration) in terms of trade flows of West European passenger car markets and industries. Nor was it discussed whether these trade flows can be related to the trade policy measures. The main purpose of the present chapter is to concentrate on these issues.

The chapter is divided into two parts. The first part illustrates, for the passenger car markets and industries, the tendency for West European economies to become more open to international trade and more integrated with each other. It also attempts to see whether any changes have occurred over the last decade. To what extent the changes in openness can be ascribed to changes in trade policy is the subject of the second part. The main concern there is to measure the trade effects of the abolition of traditional trade policy instruments as well as of the introduction of non-tariff barriers. A related concern is to isolate these effects from the effects of other factors such as changes in income and changes in the competitiveness of the domestic industry.

## CHANGES IN OPENNESS

Over the last two and a half decades, there has been a clear-cut tendency for West European economies — as for the world as a whole — to become more open to international trade. Trade has grown at a rate faster than output. This tendency has been particularly striking for the manufacturing sector.[1] Roughly the same picture emerges from a study of changes in the openness of the British, French, West German, Italian and Swedish passenger car markets and industries over the last 30 years.

Two measures of openness can be used to evidence this point. The first, the share of imports in registration of new passenger cars, expresses the degree of import penetration in a market. The second, the share of exports in domestic production, tells us how much an industry is engaged in international trade. Both measures are used in the following sub-sections, which are devoted to an analysis of changes taking place on the import and export sides.

**Import penetration**

Figure 3.1 plots the ratio of imports to domestic consumption in the five West European passenger car markets under study over the past three decades. On the basis of this figure, a certain number of points can be made about the comparative level and the trend of import penetration.

If the whole period 1954–1984 is considered, Figure 3.1 conveys a picture of a rather rapidly growing import penetration in the British, French, German and Italian passenger car markets and a constant penetration in the Swedish market. The latter market experienced the highest degree of openness of all during the whole period, with a peak in 1958. Its all-time low was attained during the 1967–1971 period. No clear-cut tendency towards greater or lesser openness emerged from the Swedish market and, as a result, the level of import penetration in Sweden was more or less the same in 1984 as at the beginning of the period examined.

Prior to the start of the integration process at the very end of the 1950s and beginning of the 1960s, the passenger car markets of the four largest West European nations were nearly closed to imports. As is discernible from the first observations in Figure 3.1, import penetration was limited in West Germany, France, Italy and Britain during the 1950s and the early 1960s. Imports captured actually less than, or about, 5 per cent of the passenger car markets in West Germany up to 1958, in France

**Figure 3.1:** Import penetration, 1954–1984 (imports in units as a percentage of domestic consumption)

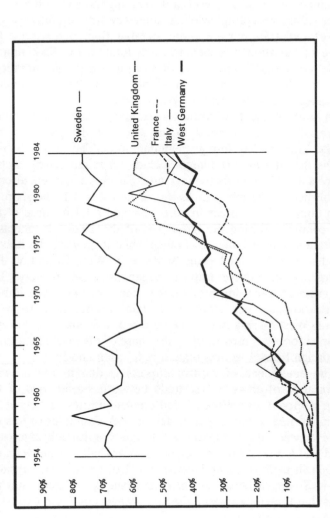

*Sources:* Motor Vehicle Manufacturers' Association (1984–1985 edition); Associazione Nazionale (1985); Verband der Automobilindustrie (1985); Bilindustriföreningen (1985).

and Italy up to 1961 and in Britain up to 1965.

The profile of the rate of import penetration in Britain differs somewhat from other countries' rates. It grew more slowly during the 1960s, escalated much more rapidly up to 1977 and remained more or less constant at a higher level afterwards. After 1975, excepting Sweden, inter-country discrepancies in import penetration were more sizeable than before, but the range of variation was, nevertheless, limited. In 1984 imports made up about 77 per cent of the passenger car market in Sweden, 56 per cent in Britain, 48 per cent in Italy, 51 per cent in France and 46 per cent in West Germany.

In four of the five countries examined, the above import figures do not correspond to the share of the passenger car market captured by foreign manufacturers. The reason behind this is that the import figures include what are called captive imports, that is imports by passenger car manufacturers already established in the market. As shown in Table 3.1, the share of such imports in total car imports changed a lot in three of the five countries during the latter part of the 1970s. It increased substantially in Britain and France while it grew moderately in Sweden and remained roughly stable in West Germany. The emergence of captive imports began later on in Italy. The presence of such imports implies that 'competitive' import penetration is much lower in Britain, France and, to some extent, West Germany than is indicated in Figure 3.1. Foreign competition — as measured by the share of the market captured by foreign firms — is thus highest in Sweden and Italy.

The emergence of captive imports is due to the growing importance of cross-border trade between subsidiaries of the same company established in different countries or between a parent company and its subsidiary abroad. Examples of this are trade between the German, British and Spanish subsidiaries of Ford and General Motors (Opel and Vauxhall), or between the French firms Renault and Peugeot–Citroën and their subsidiaries in Spain, or between Volvo and Peugeot–Citroën and the firms that they took over in the mid-1970s, DAF and Chrysler–Europe, respectively.

An important consequence of the emergence of captive imports is the development of a new form of trade in differentiated products in Western Europe — intra-industrial intra-firm trade. This new form of trade means that firms are both importers and exporters of similar products, in our case

**Table 3.1:** Captive imports as percentage of total imports

|      | France | West Germany | Italy | Sweden | Britain |
|------|--------|--------------|-------|--------|---------|
| 1973 | 9[a]   | 12[a]        | 0     | 0      | 4.6     |
| 1979 | 16.5   | 10.5         | 0[b]  | 7.5    | 42.5    |

Sources: Sweden: Bilindustriföreningen, Motor Traffic in Sweden (1974, 1980). France, West Germany and Italy: L'Argus de l'automobile et des locomotions (1974, 1980) and Associazione Nazionale (1985). Britain: Maxcy (1981), pp. 221–22.

[a]Domestic sale statistics for Ford, Peugeot–Citroën and Renault do not differentiate home-made from foreign-made passenger cars. The figures for West Germany and France were estimated from the car models sold by these three firms on the German and French markets and produced by them in Belgium, Spain and Britain.

[b]Since 1983, captive imports (imports from Fiat's subsidiary in Brazil) amount to 4–6.5 per cent of total imports in Italy.

passenger cars. Another consequence is that a non-negligible part of the growth of intra-European trade in passenger cars over the last decade can be ascribed to the development of this new form of trade.

**Export involvement**

In Figure 3.2 the ratio of exports to domestic production is plotted to highlight the export involvement of the five passenger car industries under study. The figure covers the period 1954–1984. It does not at first sight show any obvious trends, as was the case with import penetration. It displays, nevertheless, a certain number of interesting features.

Figure 3.2 provides evidence of various patterns of export involvement. Sweden, France and West Germany exhibit an increasing export–domestic production ratio if the whole period 1954–1984 is considered. This increase is more marked in Sweden and in France than in West Germany. Furthermore, Italy does not display any clear-cut tendency towards greater or lesser export involvement over the last three decades. Finally, Figure 3.2 illustrates a slowly declining degree of export involvement in Britain.

The peculiar profile of the British trend dates back to the beginning of the 1950s. About 66 per cent of the production

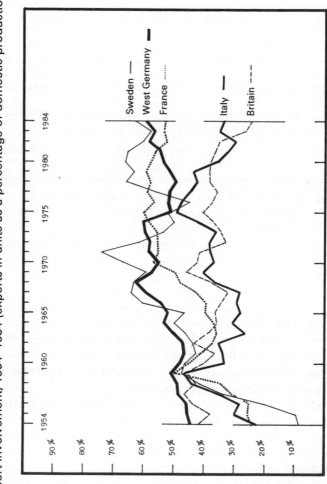

**Figure 3.2:** Export involvement, 1954–1984 (exports in units as a percentage of domestic production)

Sweden ——
West Germany ▬
France ⋯⋯⋯
Italy ——
Britain – – –

90 %
80 %
70 %
60 %
50 %
40 %
30 %
20 %
10 %

1954   1960   1965   1970   1975   1980   1984

*Sources:* See Figure 3.1.

64

was exported in 1950 while the figure was as low as 42 per cent in 1954.[2] It should be noted that this tendency towards less British export involvement over the last 30 years is not peculiar to the passenger car industry. As pointed out by several studies, the same tendency can be observed in the whole British manufacturing sector.[3]

Four other aspects of Figure 3.2 are worth noting. Firstly, the share of production that was exported increased rapidly just prior to the start of the integration process in the countries that were least export-oriented in the mid-1950s, namely Sweden, France and Italy. Secondly, the export involvement of all the countries examined was roughly similar in 1959, the year of the start of the integration process in Western Europe. Thirdly, Sweden, West Germany and France have been the most successful passenger car exporters since the mid-1960s. Finally, a decline over the last decade in the proportion of exports to production can be observed in Italy, Britain and, to a much lesser extent, France.

A decrease in export involvement can be observed for all the countries under study between 1959 and 1962–1963. This decrease may be the result of the structure of the export–production ratio ($R = X/P$). Actually, the ratio varies if exports ($X$), imports ($M$) or consumption ($C$) changes, since $P = (C - M + X)$. The partial derivatives of the $X/P$ ratio with respect to exports, imports and consumption are

$$\frac{\partial R}{\partial X} > 0, \quad \frac{\partial R}{\partial M} > 0, \quad \frac{\partial R}{\partial C} < 0.$$

If imports or exports rise, the export–domestic ratio rises while the opposite happens if registration of new passenger cars goes up. The growth of passenger car imports (see Figure 3.1) and exports (see Figure 3.3) suggests that the decrease in export activity during the earlier part of the 1960s originated in a rapid increase in consumption, that is in the number of new passenger cars registered (see Figure 3.4).

The rapid growth of new car registration after 1962–1963 slowed down the upward effect of increasing imports and exports upon the export–production ratio. This explains why the upward trend in export involvement in West Germany and France is less pronounced than the upward trend in car exports

65

**Figure 3.3:** Exports of passenger cars, 1954–1984 (indices, 1959 = 100)

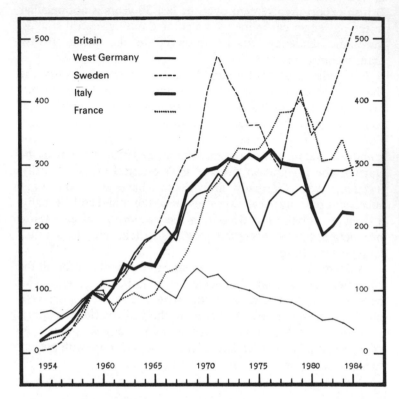

*Sources:* See Figure 3.1.

from these two countries (compare Figure 3.2 with Figure 3.3).

A striking feature of Figure 3.4 is the tremendous increase in new car registration in Italy from the start of the integration process up to the beginning of the 1970s. This increase explains why the Italian industry became less and less engaged in international trade during this period (see Figure 3.2). Sweden, on the other hand, exhibits a rather stagnating passenger car market over the whole period. The main reason behind this contrast is different per capita income levels in Italy and Sweden and the existence of a strong relation between income per capita and demand for new cars. The lower the income per capita, the faster the rise in car purchases that will result from an increase in the income level, and vice versa.[4]

**Figure 3.4:** New car registration, 1954–1984 (indices, 1959 = 100)

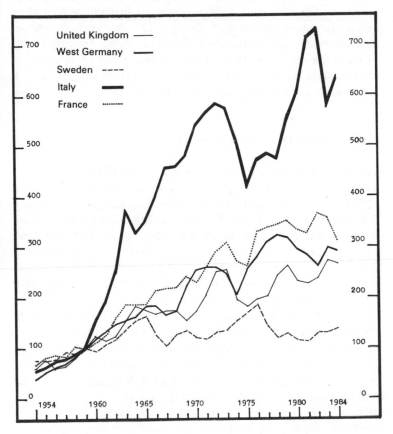

*Sources:* See Figure 3.1.

The main conclusion that emerges from the above analysis is that changes in passenger car trade over the last three decades have resulted in increased trade exposure of West European car markets and industries. Substantial differences exist, however, among the five countries examined. On the import side, apart from Sweden, a tremendous increase in the openness of the passenger car markets could be observed during the 1960s and the first half of the 1970s. Apart from France, a pause in internationalisation through growing import penetration took place during the last decade. At the end of the period examined,

67

imports (including captive imports) accounted, nevertheless, for more than 45 per cent of the domestic market in all five countries. On the export side, the analysis provides evidence of rather divergent patterns of change. On the basis of export performances, three countries, Sweden, West Germany and France, appear to be the winners in the game of changes in international trade and integration, whereas Britain and, to a much lesser extent, Italy, appear to be the losers.

## THE EFFECTS OF TRADE POLICY

Trade in passenger cars has grown at a rate faster than output since the start of the integration process at the very end of the 1950s. This is the main factor behind the changes in openness that were illustrated in the first section. The main purpose of the second section is to see to what extent changes in trade flows can be ascribed to changes in trade policy. Trade policy is defined here in its broadest sense and includes tariff as well as non-tariff trade barriers. Trade flows are influenced by other factors as well. Another purpose is thus to examine other explanatory factors, such as income and the competitiveness of the industry, and to assess their role in changing trade flows.

We will make use of regression analysis and consider trade flows from the point of view of the importing country.[5] The reason for this is that the use of explanatory variables drawn mainly from the importing country reduces considerably the difficulties associated with data collection. The empirical results obtained should, nevertheless, be conclusive as regards the impact of trade policy on trade flows, since the imports of one country are the exports of other countries.

### The time-series model and the data

The model considered here attempts to explain the number of passenger cars imported — the share of demand captured by imports — by a combination of variables representing trade policy, income and domestic industry competitiveness. The model is specified in logarithmic form in order to obtain elasticities. It can be expressed by the following equation:

$$\log M = \alpha_1 + \alpha_2 \log Y + \alpha_3 \log T + \alpha_4 \log S$$

$$+ \alpha_5 Q + \alpha_6 NTB \qquad (3.1)$$

where $M$ is passenger car imports in quantities; $Y$ is the real gross national product; $T$ is the weighted tariff variable; $S$ is the competitiveness variable; $Q$ is a dummy variable representing the quotas in the 1950s; and $NTB$ is a dummy variable representing non-tariff barriers for certain years. It is likely that the effects of tariff reductions on imports vary with the tariff level. These effects should be sizeable when the tariff level is high but smaller when it is low. To capture this idea, a slightly different specification of the above model with a tariff variable equal to the square of log $T$ (and a tariff coefficient equal to $\alpha_7$) will also be tested.[6]

The volume of passenger car imports is likely to increase with the level of real economic activity and income in the importing country. We expect thus a positive sign for the income elasticity $(\alpha_2 > 0)$. This should vary from country to country because, at least for part of the period examined, passenger cars were in different phases of the product life cycle in the different countries. The real GNP data were obtained from the *Yearbook of National Accounts Statistics* (New York: United Nations, 1957–83) and for recent years from *OECD Main Economic Indicators*, 1982–86 (Paris: OECD).

A reduction of import duties is expected to lower the relative prices of imported passenger cars and, as a consequence, to further imports. The tariff elasticity is thus likely to be negative $(\alpha_3 < 0)$. Our tariff variable was constructed in such a way as to reflect both the composition of imports and the date of the tariff cuts. The tariff variable was weighted to reflect the relative importance of imports from EEC (or EFTA) countries and non-EEC (non-EFTA) countries. Only the average shares for the whole period examined were considered to avoid possible simultaneous biases (imports affecting the tariff variable through the composition of imports). The data on the share of EEC, EFTA (including Britain) and other countries was taken from the yearly issues of the *OECD Foreign Trade Statistical Bulletins*, 1958–86 (Paris: OECD). This weighting scheme implies that the tariff variable principally reflects tariff policy towards imports from original EEC countries, since an average of 85–95 per cent of imports in the countries studied come from these countries. Moreover, for calculation purposes, calculation of $(\log T)^2$, 1 was chosen as the lower bound of the tariff variable. The construction of the tariff variable also takes into account the fact that tariff cuts did not always occur at the beginning of the year. If, for example, the tariff cut occurred in the middle of a year, the average of the pre- and post-tariff levels was taken. The sources of tariff data are given in Table 2.1 and Figures 2.2 and 2.3.

The great majority of empirical studies of West European integration deal exclusively with the demand side and ignore the role of supply conditions in member countries.[7] Trade is a function of variables drawn from several countries. Thus, the allowance for supply conditions in trading countries undoubtedly improves the specification of trade models and the reliability of the integration studies. Our model introduces a proxy variable, the purpose of which is to reflect the competitiveness of domestic supply and to express its ability to meet changes in demand.[8] A decline in the competitiveness of the domestic industry is expected to entail a rise in imports, because on such occasions domestic products are less able to compete with imported ones, and vice versa. A negative correlation is thus likely to exist between the competitiveness variable and imports ($\alpha_4 < 0$). Our proxy variable for country $i$ ($i = 1, \ldots, 5$) is equal to the ratio of the passenger car exports from that country to the sum of exports from the five car-making countries under study: $S_i = X_i/\Sigma X_i$ ($i = 1, \ldots, 5$). From 1965, the competitiveness variable for West Germany, Sweden and Britain has been adjusted in order to take into account Japanese passenger car exports to Western Europe. These exports were almost zero in 1965 and, consequently, no prejudicial break in the variable resulted from the operation. From that year, the competitiveness variable is expressed as $S_i = X_i/\Sigma X_j$ ($j = 1, \ldots, 6$, where $6$ = Japanese exports to Western Europe). The competitiveness variable was not adjusted for Italy and France, because these countries are protected against Japanese exports by nearly prohibitive quantitative restrictions. The sources of the export data are given in Figure 3.1.[9]

$Q$ is a dummy variable that allows for the existence of quotas at the end of the 1950s and the early 1960s in France and Italy.[10] The dummy variable takes on the value of 1 if there is a quota and 0 if not. The dummy variable for France takes on the value of 1 in 1958 and 0 thereafter. The reason for this is that the French quotas were, first, enlarged at the very beginning of 1959 and then removed in September of the same year for cars of more than 3,000 cc and in January 1960 for other cars. The dummy variable for Italy takes on the value of 1 in 1958, 1959 and 1960 and 0 thereafter. The year 1961 was selected as the year of quota removal, although Italian quotas were only abolished on 1 January 1962. The reason for selecting 1961 was that the Italian quotas were increased by 20 per cent for each EEC member in January 1960 and 1961. A negative sign is expected for the quota variable, because a move from 1 to 0, as a result of the suppression of quotas, should entail a rise in imports ($\alpha_5 < 0$).

*NTB* is a dummy variable that tries to capture the effects on imports of some of the non-tariff barriers examined in Chapter 2. The *NTB* variable takes on the value of 1 if there are non-tariff barriers and 0 otherwise. The introduction of non-tariff barriers is expected to negatively affect imports ($\alpha_6 < 0$). Several non-tariff barriers were considered.[11] The first is the decision of Japanese car producers to limit the growth of their exports to West Germany in 1981–1982. The second concerns Italy in 1964–1965 and 1974–1975 when trade-distorting indirect tax changes occurred. Two-year periods were taken because of the response lag of trade flows to changed market conditions.[12] The third is the orderly marketing agreement that has restrained Japanese exports to Britain since 1975. Note that this dummy may also capture the effects of the huge public subsidies given to the main British producers since the mid-1970s. The fourth concerns the much more stringent technical non-tariff barriers that have been introduced in Sweden since 1977.

Neither the Italian nor the French quantitative restrictions imposed on Japanese exports were taken into account. The reason for this is that they have restricted Japanese exports to a negligible share of their domestic passenger car markets over the *whole* period examined. No dummy variable can therefore capture their import effects in time-series analysis.

It should be added that the effects of these quantitative restrictions on the volume of total imports may be limited, although their impact on the composition of imports cannot be denied (see Table 2.3). A source-specific quantitative restriction in a country belonging to either a customs union or a free-trade area may actually 'leak'. It may result in an increase in imports from partner countries, which still benefit from free access, and leave the volume of total imports relatively unchanged. Increased exports from the discriminated third country to the unprotected partner countries are likely to replace, in partner countries, the share of production exported to the member country, protected by a source-specific restriction. These trade flows correspond to what is called indirect trade deflection. They cannot be eliminated by rules of origin. The argument also pertains to the orderly marketing arrangement existing between the British and Japanese motor vehicle trade associations since 1975.

Empirical evidence tends to support the argument that source-specific restrictions 'leak'. Between 1975 and 1981 the share of the Italian and French car markets captured by German exporters (originating in a country unprotected by a source-specific quantitative restriction prior to 1981) increased from 11.2 and 10.4 per cent to 16.2 and 16.3 per cent.[13] During the same period, the Japanese share of the German market increased from 1.7 to 10 per cent.[14] Further evidence is provided by the British passenger car market, where the share captured by German exporters grew from 12.3 per cent in 1977 to 16.1 per cent in 1981. Although convincing, these figures should be interpreted with care, because they are influenced by other factors, such as the competitiveness of the West European car manufacturers and their pricing policies.

Finally, another dummy variable $D(1960)$ is used for Britain in 1960. Its purpose is to avoid distorting the regression estimates by capturing the positive effects on imports of strikes and of the inability of British firms to forecast the sharp increase in new car registration in 1960.[15]

## Regression results

The above model was used to explain British, French, Italian, Swedish and West German imports of passenger cars during the 1958–1984 period. Two different specifications were tested. The first one conforms exactly to the original model while the second one introduces the slightly different tariff variable, equal to the square of log $T$, to capture the idea that the tariff elasticity increases with the tariff level. In the case where log $T$ is used the estimated elasticity is constant. In the case where $(\log T)^2$ is used the tariff elasticity is $2\alpha_7(\log T)$. The regression results yielded by these two specifications are presented in Table 3.2 with $t$-statistics within parentheses.

Multicollinearity between the independent variables does not seem to constitute a problem for the countries under study, with the exception of Britain. For this country, a high degree of multicollinearity between some of the explanatory variables probably explains the very high income elasticity (+5.5!) estimated with the first specification. Note that a more reliable elasticity (+3.2) is obtained for Britain with the second specification.

Not surprisingly, imports are very responsive to changes in the level of economic activity. All the estimated income coefficients are actually of the expected signs and significant at the 5 per cent level, except for Sweden with the second specification. The results obtained with the first specification imply that a 1 per cent increase in real economic activity resulted in a 1 per cent, 3.6 per cent, 1.6 per cent and 1.6 per cent increase in the number of passenger cars imported in Sweden, France, West Germany and Italy, respectively. These results are similar in sign and roughly similar in order of magnitude to those obtained with the second specification, except for Italy and Britain. According to the second specification, the income elasticities amount to +2 and +3.2 in these two countries (see Equations 3.6 and 3.12). Such results seem more reliable given the level of income per capita prevailing in Italy and Britain. The size of the income elasticity varies greatly from country to country. The relatively high income elasticity in some of these countries reflects that, at least for part of the period examined, passenger cars were in the growth phase of the product life cycle.

All the tariff coefficients are of the right sign. According to the first specification, they are only statistically significant at the 5 per cent level in West Germany and Italy and at the 10 per cent level in Britain. The tariff elasticities differ in order of magnitude from country to country. They can be interpreted to mean that a 10 per cent decrease of the tariff level led, other things being equal, to a 4.6 per cent, 3.1 per cent and 2.5 per cent increase in the volume of imports in West Germany, Italy and Britain, respectively.

The second specification produces tariff coefficients that are of the right sign and statistically significant at the 5 per cent level in France, West Germany, Italy and Britain. The results

**Table 3.2:** Estimation of the effect of trade policy, income and domestic industry's competitiveness upon passenger car imports, 1958–1984

### France

(3.2)  $\log M = -3.958 + 3.632 \log Y - 0.313 \log T - 2.288 \log S - 0.984\ Q$
           (0.554)  (3.803)       (1.185)       (5.385)     (4.165)
           $R^2(\text{adj}) = 0.871$                  $SEE = 0.213$

(3.3)  $\log M = -4.211 + 3.488 \log Y - 0.099\ (\log T)^2 - 1.945 \log S - 0.797\ Q$
           (0.856)  (4.534)       (1.748)       (4.908)     (3.474)
           $R^2(\text{adj}) = 0.864$                  $SEE = 0.205$
           Mean Tariff Elasticity $= -0.245$ (mean $\log T = 1.238$)

### West Germany

(3.4)  $\log M = -0.232 + 1.639 \log Y - 0.465 \log T + 0.475 \log S - 0.23\ NTB$
           (0.072)  (3.669)       (3.82)        (1.677)     (1.833)
           $R^2(\text{adj}) = 0.978$                  $SEE = 0.158$

(3.5)  $\log M = 1.835 + 1.75\ \log Y - 0.156\ (\log T)^2 - 0.211 \log S - 0.147\ NTB$
           (0.663)  (5.562)       (5.203)       (0.884)     (1.311)
           $R^2(\text{adj}) = 0.985$                  $SEE = 0.138$
           Mean Tariff Elasticity $= -0.279$ (mean $\log T = 0.894$)

### Italy

(3.6)  $\log M = 5.852 + 1.638 \log Y - 0.315 \log T - 1.275 \log S - 1.847\ Q$
           (0.975)  (2.144)       (2.123)       (2.208)     (7.108)

           $-0.112\ NTB$
           (0.779)
           $R^2(\text{adj}) = 0.975$                  $SEE = 0.272$

(3.7)  $\log M = 3.199 + 2.014 \log Y - 0.089\ (\log T)^2 - 1.185 \log S - 1.085\ Q$
           (0.544)  (2.713)       (1.819)       (1.882)     (5.581)

           $-0.203\ NTB$
           (0.75)
           $R^2(\text{adj}) = 0.848$                  $SEE = 0.272$
           Mean Tariff Elasticity $= -0.212$ (mean $\log T = 1.191$)

### Sweden

(3.8)  $\log M = 7.529 + 0.999 \log Y - 0.06\ \log T - 0.588 \log S - 0.349\ NTB$
           (2.867)  (1.996)       (0.449)       (2.268)     (1.867)
           $R^2(\text{adj}) = 0.975$                  $SEE = 0.137$

(3.9)  $\log M = 6.505 + 1.184 \log Y - 0.636 \log S - 0.291\ NTB$
           (4.359)  (3.735)       (2.696)     (2.31)
           $R^2(\text{adj}) = 0.977$                  $SEE = 0.135$

(3.10)  $\log M =$  8.059 + 0.893 log $Y -$ 0.028 (log $T)^2 -$ 0.559 log $S -$ 0.335 $NTB$
                  (2.462)  (1.415)      (0.531)          (2.006)          (2.19)
                  $R^2$(adj) $=$ 0.976                    $SEE =$ 0.137
                  Mean Tariff Elasticity $= -0.199$ (mean log $T =$ 1.657)

Britain

(3.11)  $\log M =$  $-$ 22.445 + 5.489 log $Y -$ 0.248 log $T -$ 0.144 log $S -$ 0.052 $NTB$
                  (3.558)   (6.21)       (1.434)        (0.418)          (0.187)

                  + 0.749 $D$(1960)
                  (3.628)
                  $R^2$(adj) $=$ 0.933                    $SEE =$ 0.212

(3.12)  $\log M =$  $-$ 6.554 + 3.201 log $Y -$ 0.161 (log $T)^2 -$ 0.372 log $S -$ 0.371 $NTB$
                  (1.045)   (3.562)      (3.544)           (1.62)           (1.726)

                  + 0.821 $D$ (1960)
                  (3.931)
                  $R^2$(adj) $=$ 0.98                     $SEE =$ 0.194
                  Mean Tariff Elasticity $= -0.621$ (mean log $T =$ 1.928)

---

The equations are estimated with the ordinary least squares (OLS) method and corrected for serial correlation with the Cochrane–Orcutt procedure. The critical value of the $t$-statistic (in parentheses) at the 5 and 10 per cent level with a one-tailed test are $t(22) =$ 1.717 and 1.321. $R^2$, coefficient of multiple determination; $SEE$, standard error of the regression.

*Variables:* $M$, passenger car import variable; $Y$, income variable; $T$, weighted tariff variable; $S$, competitiveness variable; $Q$, quantitative restrictions in Italy and France at the end of the 1950s and beginning of the 1960s (for France 1958 $=$ 1 and 0 otherwise and for Italy 1958, 1959 and 1960 $=$ 1 and 0 otherwise); $NTB$, non-tariff barrier variable (for West Germany 1981 and 1982 $=$ 1 and 0 otherwise; for Italy 1964, 1965, 1974 and 1975 $=$ 1 and 0 otherwise; for the United Kingdom 1975–1984 $=$ 1 and 0 otherwise; for Sweden 1977–1984 $=$ 1 and 0 otherwise); $D$(1960), dummy variable (for the UK 1960 $=$ 1 and 0 otherwise).

mean that the tariff elasticity is dependent upon the tariff level and that the lower the tariff level the smaller the impact on imports of a tariff change, and vice versa. For example, they tell us that tariff elasticities were equal to −0.673, −0.823 and −0.657 in France, West Germany and Italy prior to the beginning of the integration process in 1958, while they were equal to −0.482, −0.569 and −0.459 in 1965.[16] While this second specification is theoretically more satisfactory than the first, the $t$-statistics are significantly higher only in the cases of France, West Germany and Britain. The higher German elasticity — compared to France's or Italy's — suggests, moreover, that cross-country differences between the tariff elasticities are not only explained by differences in tariff levels. The reason for this is that the former country had a lower tariff level prior to the start of the integration process.

Two other aspects of the results are worth noting, the relatively high tariff elasticity in Britain and the absence of tariff effects in Sweden. According to the second specification, the British tariff elasticity amounted to $-0.67$ in 1973. The rapid growth of captive imports following Britain's entry into the EEC in 1973 (see Table 3.1) probably explains this high tariff elasticity. The reason for this is that firms already established in Britain with sales networks, repair facilities and better information about the market at their disposal could more easily increase their market share and imports in the wake of tariff abolition.

The absence of tariff effects in Sweden may have its origin in the much greater importance of non-tariff barriers — principally technical trade barriers — during the whole period examined but, also, in the presence of a certain number of 'market imperfections'. It is most probably a combination of these two kinds of factors that explains the absence of trade effects of tariff abolition within EFTA in the 1960s and between Sweden and EEC countries during the 1970s.

Actually, the share of British manufacturers in Swedish imports fell from an average of 19.5 per cent during the 1956–1959 period to an average of 14.6 per cent during the 1965–1967 period in spite of tariff removal within EFTA.[17] The decline of the British motor industry and the allocation since the 1950s of the Swedish market to the German subsidiaries (Opel and Ford) of two American-owned firms (General Motors and Ford), rather than to their British subsidiaries (Vauxhall and Ford-Dagenham), which accounted for about 40 per cent of the British car output at the beginning of the 1960s, explain why removal of tariffs within EFTA had no trade-creating effects in Sweden.[18]

The export policy of EEC manufacturers may explain the absence of import effects of the enforcement of the free-trade agreement between Sweden and the EEC in the mid-1970s. Actually, EEC suppliers facing two opening markets, the British and the Swedish, might have preferred the former, which is much larger and still growing, to the latter, which is small and stagnating (see Figure 3.4). Another reason is the high technical barriers in Sweden, which imply a costly adaptation of the products for EEC suppliers.

The structure of the Swedish sales network is a market characteristic that might have prevented tariff cuts from having their expected import effects. Several Swedish dealers sell motor vehicles of different foreign car manufacturers originating in different trading blocks.[19] Such dealers may not want to favour the products of one of the foreign firms at the expense of the others even if it benefits from tariff reduction. The distribution of Volkswagen cars by a company which is majority-owned (two-thirds) by one of the Swedish car manufacturers, Saab, may have the same effect. These characteristics of the dealer system create an atmosphere inimical to price warfare and vigorous competition. Their presence probably helped to prevent the enforcement of the free-trade agreement between Sweden and the EEC from affecting Swedish imports.

The results of Table 3.2 show that the coefficients of the competitiveness variable are of the right sign and statistically significant at the 5 per cent level in France, Italy and Sweden. In Britain the coefficient is of the right sign but significant only at the 10 per cent level. In West Germany the coefficients of the competitiveness variable are not statistically significant and, moreover, of the wrong sign in one of the two specifications. The results confirm that the competitiveness of the domestic industry substantially affected imports, at least in some of these countries. It indicates that a 1 per cent decrease in the share of West European exports resulted in a 1.9, 1.2, 0.6 and 0.4 per cent increase in the volume of imports in France, Italy, Sweden and Britain, respectively.

The results for West Germany, however, cast some doubt on the ability of our proxy variable to reflect accurately competitiveness in differentiated industries. An example may illustrate this point. Passenger cars are mainly produced with reference to the domestic demand, that is to satisfy home market tastes.[20] These tastes are mainly shaped by the level of per capita income. As a consequence of this, countries with a higher per capita income — like West Germany — mostly produce higher-quality cars. If now, as a result of an increase in per capita income, a shift in consumer demand towards higher-quality cars occurs in such countries, we expect a substitution of domestic for imported cars to take place. The reason for this is that domestic manufacturers are more able to meet this new demand because they benefit from longer runs of production in higher-quality cars and are already accustomed to the market. Although such a change is synonymous with improved competitiveness for the domestic industry on the home market, it is not captured by our proxy variable.

Not surprisingly, the suppression of import quotas in Italy and France at the end of the 1950s and beginning of the 1960s led to a significant rise in imports. The larger size of the Italian coefficient may be due to the fact that import quotas were more restrictive than in France; these were abolished at a later date (1961 as compared with 1959).

In regard to non-tariff barriers, the regression results of Table 3.2 are less conclusive. The sign of the coefficients of the $NTB$ variable is the expected one in most cases. However, their size indicates that the impact of non-tariff barriers on passenger car imports was rather limited. In West Germany the coefficient of the $NTB$ variable, the purpose of which is to capture the effects on imports of the Japanese export restraint in 1981–1982, is of the right sign but statistically significant at the 5 per cent level in only one of the two specifications. In Italy the coefficient of the $NTB$ variable, the purpose of which is to reflect the trade-distorting indirect tax changes in 1964–1965 and 1974–1975, bears the right sign but is not statistically significant. In Sweden the $NTB$ variable, which reflects the sharpening of technical barriers to trade after 1977, is of the right sign and statistically significant in the two specifications. In Britain the coefficient of the $NTB$ variable, expressing the orderly marketing agreement between the British and Japanese car industries as well as the huge sums of public subsidies received by the home industry, is of the right sign but statistically significant at the 5 per cent level in only one case.

All this suggests that non-tariff barriers had some effects but that these effects were limited. It also shows that the effects of non-tariff barriers differ from country to country and that their exact estimation is rather difficult. This depends partly upon the use of dummy variables, which only approximate to the import effects of non-tariff barriers and can capture other events that occur at the same time. A likely reason behind the low coefficients of the $NTB$ variable is that the introduction of non-tariff barriers mostly influenced the composition of imports, leaving their volume relatively unchanged. For example, the trade-distorting changes in the structure of the Italian tax system in 1974 might have favoured imports of cars of less than 2,000 cc at the expense of larger cars without significantly changing the volume of Italian car imports. The same argument can be put forward for Swedish technical barriers that mainly discriminate against foreign firms enjoying a small share of the Swedish passenger car market or, as mentioned above, for the British marketing agreement.

## SUMMARY AND CONCLUSIONS

This chapter has concentrated on changes in trade flows (in relation to the passenger car markets and industries) and the factors behind these changes since the start of the integration process at the very end of the 1950s. Emphasis has been laid on the impact of trade policy because our main purpose has been to highlight the trade effects of integrating and disintegrating measures.

In the first section we provided evidence of the increased trade exposure of West European car markets and industries since the start of the integration process. An interesting aspect of the results concerns the emergence of captive imports and intra-firm intra-trade during the last decade. As illustrated by the British example in the second section, this new form of trade was greatly furthered by the dismantling of tariffs between the original EEC and EFTA countries and the formation of an enlarged free-trade area in Western Europe.

The rapid tariff liberalisation of trade up to the mid-1970s has resulted in a growing integration of West European passenger car markets. Most of the tariff effects took place in Italy, France and West Germany during the 1960s and in Britain during the 1970s. This and the fact that EFTA had very limited trade effects substantiate one of the basic propositions of integration theory, namely the superiority in terms of trade creation and welfare of a union between countries with competitive industries to a union between countries with complementary industries.[21]

The estimation of the impact of tariff policy indicates that the trade effects of tariff cuts diminish with the level of the tariff. This and the low level of tariffs prevailing since the mid-1970s imply that the role of tariffs is very limited nowadays. Among other things, this means that the trade effects of the Tokyo Round tariff cuts were negligible in view of the low tariff rates in force before the implementation of the Tokyo Round.

Among the car-making countries examined, one country, Sweden, shows very different trade patterns. We suggested that it is the importance of non-tariff barriers that explains the absence of tariff effects and the peculiar profile of import development in Sweden. Further, we put forward the role of a certain number of 'market imperfections' that had trade-impeding effects. All these factors taken together indicate that the Swedish passenger car market is to a limited extent integrated into the West European economic area.

A final conclusion concerns the trade effects of the various non-tariff barriers, the emergence of which stopped the rapid movement towards freer trade. Some of the non-tariff barriers (public subsidies, technical barriers in Sweden and trade-distorting indirect taxes) discriminate against third as well as partner countries. An important result of the analysis is thus that the emergence of non-tariff barriers has brought about a certain disintegration of the West European economic area.

## NOTES

1. For an illustration, see Batchelor, Major and Morgan (1980), pp. 28 and 38, Tables 2.4 and 3.5, and Beenstock and Warburton (1983), pp. 130–39.
2. Figures on British car exports and production at the beginning of the 1950s are available in Maxcy and Silberston (1959), pp. 223 and 226.
3. See Batchelor, Major and Morgan (1980), p. 48.
4. On cross-country evidence, see United Nations (1983), pp. 4–10.
5. For the use of regression analysis to explain trade flows, see Mayes (1981), Chapter 7.
6. This procedure is suggested by Maddala (1979), p. 115.
7. See for example Balassa (1975), pp. 79–118, and EFTA (1969).
8. On the importance of the inclusion of supply variables in empirical analyses of trade flows, see Mayes (1978), pp. 10–12 and Mayes (1981), pp. 273–80.
9. Data on Japanese exports to Western Europe are available for 1965–1973 in *Motor Traffic in Sweden* (Bilindustriföreningen, 1965–1974), for 1973–1983 in *World Motor Vehicle Data* (Motor Vehicle Manufacturers' Association, 1984–1985 edition), and for 1984 in *Tatsachen und Zahlen* (Verband der Automobilindustrie, 1985).
10. See Chapter 2, p. 20.
11. On the *NTB* in West Germany, Italy, Britain and Sweden, see

Chapter 2, pp. 30–31, 34–36 and 41–44.

12. On the different lags in international trade, see Junz and Rhomberg (1973), pp. 412–13.

13. Figures collected in *L'Argus de l'automobile et des locomotions*, special issues on motor vehicle statistics (1976, 1978 and 1982).

14. See Chapter 2, Table 2.3.

15. See Turner, Clark and Roberts (1967), pp. 110–12.

16. These tariff elasticities are somewhat higher than those derived from previous more aggregated studies. See Prewo (1980), pp. 88–90.

17. Based on figures collected in *Foreign Trade Statistical Bulletins* (OECD, 1956–1967).

18. See EFTA (1968), pp. 2–6.

19. For example, Förenade Bil AB sells BMW and Honda, Philipsons Automobil AB sells Datsun, Mercedes-Benz and Talbot, Olle Olsson Bilimport AB sells Rover and Mazda, etc. For the structure of the Swedish dealer, see the yearly issues of *Motor Traffic in Sweden* (Bilindustriföreningen, 1960–1985).

20. See Hocking (1980), pp. 504–19.

21. For a presentation of this proposition of integration theory, see Södersten (1978), pp. 361–63.

# 4

# Foreign Competition, Public Policy and Market Structure

The main purpose of the present chapter is to analyse how international economic integration and public policy have influenced the structures of the passenger car markets in West European car-producing countries. The focus is on market structure, mainly because market structure and its change over time are expected to reflect the state of competition and, thus, to affect firms' pricing policies and consumer economic welfare.

Market structure is defined by the market share distribution of firms within the individual national markets. Large price disparities still exist for similar passenger car models between member countries of the enlarged West European free-trade area (i.e. the EEC plus EFTA). Chapter 7 will illustrate them in detail. Their existence justifies the analysis of competition at the national level because it indicates that national markets still form independent economic entities and that there is not a fully unified passenger car market in Western Europe.

As pointed out by Harry Johnson, the main limitation of aggregated studies is that they 'treat both industrial and international trade problems as if production and competition were homogeneous activities undifferentiated by the facts of technology and the practices of governments'.[1] The case-study approach avoids this bias because it takes into account, on the one hand, the underlying technology of the production process and its impact on economies of scale and the number of firms and, on the other hand, the policy of government.

The impact of international integration on competition should also be differentiated by the facts of technology and public policies. This impact is expected to vary from industry to industry and from country to country. Differences in underlying technologies, economies of scale, product characteristics and firms' behaviour account for the first type of variation. Different institutional environments, government policies and, here too, firm conduct account for the second type. How this complex of factors interacts with international integration to explain changes in market structure is the subject of this chapter.

A central concern is to test the U-shape hypothesis on the relationship between international integration and market concentration.[2] This hypothesis tells us that the opening up to trade has two main effects. First, it gives rise to import prenetration and a move towards a more competitive market structure. Then, at some point, it gives rise to takeovers and mergers, an increase in concentration and a return to less competitive market structures. Public policy may further this increase in concentration through its impact on takeover and merger activity. Another purpose is thus to analyse government practices. Both integration and government policy influences on competitive conditions depend upon the way economies of scale constrain the ability of firms to survive. A first purpose of the present chapter is therefore to estimate the extent of economies of scale in the passenger car industry.

The chapter is arranged in three parts. The first concerns economies of scale and their role in the ability of firms to survive. It begins with a presentation of the underlying technology of the production process in the passenger car industry and the extent of economies of scale on the production side. It also gives some insights into the extent of multi-plant economies of scale. A related question, explored thereafter, is how the characteristics of the product and firm policy can relax the scale constraint faced by manufacturers. The way economies of scale affect the survival ability of firms depends upon which phase of the product life cycle the industry finds itself in. Another aspect examined in this first part is thus the changing impact of economies of scale upon the ability of firms to survive.

In the second part, we analyse the impact of foreign competition and international integration on market structure. Two effects are examined. The first corresponds to the way foreign entry influences market structure. The second is concerned with the impact of increased foreign competition on the exit of firms that suffer from small-scale disadvantages. These two effects have opposite impacts on competitive conditions and market

83

concentration. The first one should result in a move towards more competitive market structures while the second means a move towards less competitive market structures. A question that we will try to answer is whether the experience of the passenger car markets conforms to these two effects, which explain the U-shaped relationship.

Public policy played an active role in several of the passenger car mergers. This involvement may be the result of a shift in public policy from trade to industrial policy in the wake of international integration. The active government role suggests that public policy should be included in the analysis because it explains in part the U-form of the relation between the opening up to trade and market concentration. In the third part, we focus on those aspects of public policy, such as merger and anti-trust policies, which are expected to shape market structure. We present their role in large-scale mergers in the West European motor vehicle industry. The interacting role of economies of scale, international integration and firm policy in large-scale mergers is also investigated in this section.

As suggested in Chapter 2, when non-tariff barriers were examined, public assistance to the passenger car industry is very likely because of the characteristics of this industry (large in terms of employment and votes, presence of state-owned firms, small number of firms, highly organised firms, etc.). Public assistance can take the form of merger assistance and institutional barriers to exit. Another aspect investigated in the third section is the official logic of public policy in merger operations as compared to the actual line of reasoning. In other words, an attempt is made to see whether the motive of industrial policy was to favour the emergence of technically efficient firms more able to meet the trade liberalisation challenge or to rescue ailing firms more able to obtain merger assistance.

It should be noted that the U-shape hypothesis as well as the merger assistance issue are of great importance for the outcome of integration. The former has welfare implications. It suggests that the eventual welfare losses to consumers due to increased concentration may wipe out the welfare gains to consumers of increased imports. The latter has efficiency implications. Public assistance to maintain the life of ailing firms erects institutional barriers to exit and impedes resource mobility between the countries of the integrated area.

## ECONOMIES OF SCALE IN THE PASSENGER CAR INDUSTRY

The way unit costs of production change with the size of a firm (or a plant) constitutes economies of scale. Firms achieve the lowest possible production costs for a certain output level, which corresponds to what is usually called minimum optimal scale (MOS) or minimum efficient scale (MES). Production at a scale below the MES output level implies small-scale disadvantages and is viable only if prices charged by efficient firms are above long-run costs and/or the product is differentiated. Economies of scale thus constitute one of the determinants of the ability of firms to survive.

Economies of scale in the passenger car industry arise at both the production (plant) and firm levels. The four production processes necessary to make a passenger car (pressing or stamping; casting of the engine; machining of the engine, gear boxes, etc.; and final assembly) give rise to technical or production economies of scale.[3] On the other hand, selling, management, advertising, research and development, spreading of risk and so on give rise to firm or multi-plant economies of scale.[4] Both kinds of economies of scale seem to be very large in the passenger car industry.

### Technical economies of scale

Table 4.1 presents the main results of various studies that have attempted to identify and measure technical economies of scale in the passenger car industry. Except for Rhys's study (1972a), all of them are engineering estimates that have isolated the different production processes to identify scale economies.[5] Pressing, the process of shaping car bodies, entails the largest economies. It determines the optimum production level for the whole production process. According to most estimates, the MES for body pressing corresponds to an annual production of 500,000 to 1 million passenger cars. Note that only the lower bound of the minimum efficient scale is given in Table 4.1.

Two features of the studies suggest that the MES figures should be interpreted with some care. First, according to all of the studies, there is no clear point at which costs increase (diseconomies of large scale) or cease to fall. This is one of the

**Table 4.1:** Technical economies of scale in the passenger car industry

|     | MES annual output | Country | Source | Year |
| --- | --- | --- | --- | --- |
| 1. | 600,000 | USA | Bain | 1951–1954 |
| 2. | 300,000 | W. Germany | Busch | 1958 |
| 3. | 400,000 | W. Germany | Müller and Hochreiter | 1965 |
| 4. | 500,000 | W. Germany | Jürgensen and Berg | 1967 |
| 5. | 400,000 | USA | White | 1969 |
| 6. | 500,000 | UK | Pratten | 1969 |
| 7. | 300,000 | W. Germany | Raisch | 1969–1970 |
| 8. | 600,000 | UK | Rhys | 1970 |
| 9. | 400,000 | USA | Toder | 1974 |
| 10. | 750,000 | UK | Central Policy Review Staff | 1974 |
| 11. | 500,000 | — | DAFSA | 1980 |

*Sources:* 1. Bain (1956), p. 78. 2. Busch (1966), p. 131. 3. Müller and Hochreiter (1975), p. 273. 4. Jürgensen and Berg (1968), p. 36. 5. White (1971), p. 39. 6. Pratten (1971), p. 149. 7. Raisch (1973), p. 71. 8. Rhys (1972a), p. 88. 9. Toder (1978), p. 133. 10. Central Policy Review Staff (1975), p. 23. 11. Commission of the European Communities (1981b), p. 7.

reasons behind the variation observed among MES estimates in Table 4.1. Actually, each estimate selected for the MES output a point after which the decline in costs was regarded as relatively insignificant. For example, according to Pratten, the MES is 'the minimum optimal scale above which any possible subsequent doubling in scale would reduce total average cost by less than 5%'.[6]

The second feature emerges from the difficulties of measurement of economies of scale in the passenger car industry because of the various models produced by the same firm. Some of the models are similar and use interchangeable components. Others are different and are not produced on the same assembly line. It is therefore difficult to measure accurately economies of scale in such an industry. For some components, the relevant output may be the whole production of the firm while, for others, it may be only the output of a particular model. The MES estimates quoted in Table 4.1 avoid this problem by concentrating on one basic model with some variations. An exception is Pratten's study, which provides an estimate of scale economies for one model (see Table 4.1) and another one for a range of models that consists of three basic bodies with variants

**Table 4.2:** Estimates of costs and scale for a range of models

| Output per year | Index of costs |
|---|---|
| 100,000 | 100 |
| 250,000 | 83 |
| 500,000 | 74 |
| 1,000,000 | 70 |
| 2,000,000 | 66 |

*Source:* Pratten (1971), p. 142.

and five basic engines (see Table 4.2). This second estimate shows that the MES is much larger (1 million units) once the calculation takes into account more than one model.

A question that arises now is whether the long-run average cost curve facing motor car manufacturers, and hence the MES, has changed during the past two and a half decades. Two factors explain the MES level and its change over time: relative factor prices and technology. The increase in the relative cost of labour observed since the beginning of the 1960s has probably favoured more capital-intensive methods of production, less divisible equipment and a larger minimum efficient scale. On the other hand, the introduction of robots and more automated production methods over the past decade has reduced the minimum efficient scale for the final assembly process. The reason for this is that it makes possible the assembly of several models on the same assembly line.[7] According to a recent study, production of 500,000 units is, nevertheless, still considered necessary to reach the minimum average cost in the production of engines.[8]

## Multi-plant economies of scale

The assessment of studies of the minimum efficient scale suggests that technical economies of scale are very large in the passenger car industry. Substantial small-scale disadvantages exist for firms producing less than 500,000 units per year. This figure may be even higher if firm (or multi-plant) economies of scale are taken into account. Several studies shed some light on the nature and magnitude of scale economies at the firm level.

About three years are required before a new model appears on the market. Once on the market, the new model can turn out to be a failure if consumer tastes have changed during the three years. There is thus a risk inherent in passenger car production. According to a study by Lawrence White, passenger car manufacturers should produce about 800,000 units a year split between two makes in order to safeguard themselves against such failures and to survive in the long run.[9]

Marketing constitutes another multi-plant activity that gives rise to substantial scale economies. The reason for this is that the minimum fixed cost of building up a marketing system and a dealer network may be very high. Statements made by the chairman of a large West European passenger car company suggest that a minimum production of 1.6 million units per year is required to support a marketing and after-sales-service organisation.[10]

Research and development is another important source of scale economies at the firm level because large firms can spread the R&D costs over their enormous output. A good example is given by General Motors, which spent $500 million on development of its X-car in the late 1970s.[11] Spread over an expected output of 5 million cars over a six-year period, the development cost per unit will amount to $100. A West European manufacturer building a similar car at a volume of 1 million would have to charge $500 to recover its development costs.

The main conclusion that emerges from an examination of the long-run average cost curve facing the passenger car industry is that there are large economies of scale and that firms producing less than 500,000 units per year face substantial small-scale disadvantages. Further, empirical evidence on multi-plant economies suggests that large economies of scale exist at the firm level in marketing and R&D but that only rough estimates can be provided because of measurement difficulties.

The extent of scale economies affects the survival ability of firms. Thus, it can be regarded as a constraint faced by passenger car manufacturers. Three factors may help to ease this scale constraint: product differentiation, firm behaviour and technological changes.

## Product differentiation and scale constraint

In the great majority of industrial markets, the nature of consumer demand is not for a single product — which could be produced in one long run — but for a differentiated set. Further, as per capita income grows so does the differentiated nature of consumer demand.[12] The presence of product differentiation in a market means that the products are not regarded as perfect substitutes by consumers. The latter are willing to pay more for one product than for another. By reducing price responsiveness among consumers and diverting rivalry into non-price forms, product differentiation helps to keep alive less-than-efficient firms that have to charge higher prices because of small-scale disadvantages.

The degree of product differentiation of the passenger car product is high since each manufacturer designs his or her own models and model variants. The heterogeneity of consumers' preferences between countries implies that this degree varies a great deal from country to country and that different product characteristics exist in different car-producing countries. Table 4.3 illustrates the high degree of product differentiation in the West European passenger car industry and its change over time. It shows that product differentiation has remained more or less

**Table 4.3**: Product differentiation in the passenger car industry

| Year | W. Germany | France | Italy | Sweden | Britain | Total |
|------|-----------|--------|-------|--------|---------|-------|
| | | Number of models | | | | |
| 1962 | 24 | 18 | 16 | 4 | 46 | 108 |
| 1970 | 28 | 23 | 21 | 5 | 46 | 123 |
| 1980 | 30 | 28 | 22 | 6 | 44 | 130 |
| | | Number of models/production (in millions) | | | | |
| 1962 | 11 | 13 | 18 | 31 | 37 | — |
| 1970 | 8 | 9 | 12 | 18 | 28 | — |
| 1980 | 8.5 | 9.5 | 15 | 25.5 | 48 | — |
| | | Number of variants | | | | |
| 1962 | 61 | 55 | 36 | 8 | 80 | 240 |
| 1970 | 116 | 101 | 50 | 11 | 85 | 363 |
| 1980 | 230 | 153 | 91 | 27 | n.a. | 501 |
| | | Number of variants/production (in millions) | | | | |
| 1962 | 29 | 41 | 41 | 61 | 64 | — |
| 1970 | 33 | 41 | 29 | 39 | 52 | — |
| 1980 | 65 | 52 | 63 | 115 | n.a. | — |

*Sources:* Estimated from *L'Argus de l'automobile et des locomotions* (1962, 1970, 1980), and Society of Motor Manufacturers & Traders (1967–1983).

constant in terms of models but has increased in terms of model variants, except for the British industry. The rapid rise in income per capita in Western Europe over the past two and a half decades has resulted in an increased demand for variety. This has been satisfied mainly by trade liberalisation and the growing availability of imported passenger car varieties in each national market. A complementary factor, illustrated in Table 4.3, is the increased variety of model variants produced by West European firms.

Product differentiation, which originates with the consumers, may help, through another channel, to keep alive firms that are non-efficient from the point of view of scale economies. In differentiated markets, consumers are not easily persuaded to change from one product to another. The loyalty of consumers towards products of established sellers raises a barrier to entry and signifies higher costs (penetration costs) for firms that attempt to break into the market. By blocking entry and limiting competition, product differentiation may thus permit established small firms to charge a higher price and survive in spite of small-scale cost disadvantages.

### Firm behaviour and scale constraint

Firms have several means at their disposal to reduce the MES constraint they face. First, they can adapt their product policy. For example, they can extend the model life and achieve economies of scale over time. They can also specialise in higher-quality products for which the price elasticity is lower and prices usually much higher than marginal costs.[13] Another appropriate product policy can be to simultaneously reduce the number of models and increase the number of variants. Such a policy permits the firm both to reap economies of large scale and satisfy the increasingly differentiated nature of consumer demand. Table 4.3 indicates that, except for British car manufacturers, this corresponds to the product policy adopted by passenger car manufacturers in the wake of international integration during the 1960s.

Second, by means of co-production ventures, passenger car manufacturers can distribute the MES output among several firms. An example of such co-production ventures concerned with technical economies of scale is the Peugeot–Volvo–Renault cooperation to manufacture an engine since 1974. Another example is the large number of agreements between West European passenger car manufacturers, the purpose of which is to launch common research programmes and to benefit from R&D economies of scale.[14] Public aid to finance R&D activities can also be a means used by car manufacturers to relax the R&D scale constraint.[15]

**Technological change and the scale constraint**

As illustrated in Chapter 1, the passenger car industry has benefited from an extended maturity phase. The main characteristics of such a phase are stability of technology of the production process, highly standardised products and competition based on costs.[16] These characteristics explain why products that have reached the maturity phase of the 'normal' life cycle usually shift to lower-cost sources of supply. They also explain why economies of scale determine firm survival ability during this phase of the product life.

It seems clear that the radical changes in technology and in the social organisation of the production process observed in the passenger car industry since the end of the 1970s have greatly altered the maturity phase. New product technologies and organisational innovations in the production process combined with consumer preferences for very different passenger car mixes may imply a process of 'dematurity' for the industry.[17] The existence of a 'dematurity' phase has far-reaching implications for industry and market structures. It suggests that scale requirements have been replaced by innovations in technology and product design as the driving forces for the ability of firms to survive. Moreover, less competition based on costs means that there is not likely to be a shift to lower-cost sources of supply. Consequently, the motor vehicle industry should remain located in industrial countries in the foreseeable future.

The main conclusions that emerge from an analysis of economies of scale in relation to firm survival ability in the passenger car industry are threefold. First, the influence of economies of scale on the ability of firms to survive was very important during the 1960s and the first half of the 1970s. Second, the presence of a high degree of product differentiation as well as firm behaviour have relaxed the scale constraint faced by West European car manufacturers. Third, economies of scale seem to have lost their determining role for firm survival ability over the past few years as a result of the radical innovations in the passenger car production process and design. All this should be kept in mind when one attempts to examine the impact of integration and public policy on market structure.

## FOREIGN COMPETITION AND MARKET STRUCTURE

A necessary starting point when analysing the relation between foreign competition and market structure is to see what the latter looked like before the start of the integration process. Several empirical studies of the Canadian and West European economies address this question and show that high tariff protection permits small, inefficient firms to survive.[18] This outcome can be the result of different factors. First, large firms in sheltered industries may choose to lose a share of the market to small, sub-optimal firms in exchange for higher prices. Second, consumers, by demanding differentiated products, may increase production fragmentation and, hence, production on a scale less than optimal if the market is not large enough to bear several efficient producers. Third, all the factors that inhibit price competition make production on a small scale viable and keep non-efficient firms alive.[19] Examples of such factors are government intervention, managers' preference for a quiet life and fear of being branded as monopolists and thus of losing protection against imports. All this suggests that the markets of sheltered economies very often consist of a few large firms and several smaller firms — fringe firms — whose production of brand varieties on a small scale is not competitive in international markets.

The typical pattern of sheltered markets is confirmed by the structure of passenger car markets in West European car-producing countries during the 1950s, that is prior to the start of the integration process. In West Germany, for example, there were three large firms, Volkswagen, Opel and Ford; some medium-sized firms such as BMW, NSU and Auto-Union; and several very small fringe firms such as Lloyd, Goliath, Borgward, Vidal, Heinkel, Bayerische Auto-Werke, Maico and

Victoria-Werke.[20] The same pattern could be observed in France with four large firms; Citroën, Peugeot, Renault and Simca; one medium-sized firm, Panhard; and several fringe firms such as Facel, Velam, Vespa, Talbot, Delahaye-Delage, Rovin and Salmson.[21] Sweden was the only West European car-producing country that had experienced a significant import penetration (see Figure 3.1). This country thus presented a different pattern, with only two domestic medium-sized firms, Volvo and Saab, three large importing firms, Volkswagen, Opel and Ford, and several fringe importing firms.[22]

How did the process of international integration that started at the very end of the 1950s and beginning of the 1960s affect the structure of the passenger car markets in the five countries under study? Two effects can be expected, a foreign entry effect and an exit effect. Both effects should be considered in order to accept or reject the U-shape hypothesis on the relationship between integration and market concentration.

### Foreign entry and market structure

Studies in industrial economics show that the extent of entry barriers affects the number of firms in a market, their share and thus market structure. The usual sources of entry barriers are economies of scale, product differentiation and absolute cost advantages for established firms, which arise from factors such as patent protected production, lower interest charges and favourable location. Higher barriers deter entry and bring about oligopolistic market structures. Low barriers promote entry and competitive market structures.

Tariffs and all forms of obstacles to trade also form entry barriers. They result in a cost that is borne by firms that attempt to enter the market, but not by firms that are already established. The reduction of trade barriers should have the same effects as reducing the usual entry barriers — promotion of new entry and more competitive market structures. Further-more, foreign entry should occur at a much faster pace for two reasons. First, foreign firms face neither the economies of scale nor the absolute cost disadvantage barriers to entry. Second, they already benefit from a well-established brand image abroad.

The different features of market structures prior to the

93

beginning of the integration process and a certain number of market characteristics, such as the presence of US subsidiaries in different West European countries and imports by leading domestic car manufacturers, suggest that the relationship between foreign entry and market structure (and concentration) may not be so simple in West European passenger car markets. Actually, foreign entry can affect market structure in three different ways.

The first is the most likely since we are concerned with producing countries that were highly protected up to the beginning of the 1960s. The gradual removal of tariff barriers results in the entry of foreign firms that capture continually growing shares of the domestic market. This process leads to the erosion of the market position of dominant domestic firms. In this first case, foreign entry undoubtedly favours the emergence of more competitive market structures.

The second case arises when imports are controlled directly by a leading manufacturer in a country. As illustrated in the preceding chapter (see Table 3.1), such imports (called 'captive imports') have grown rapidly in West European passenger car trade since the mid-1970s. In such a case, 'foreign' entry has the opposite effect on market structure because a removal of tariff barriers and an increase in captive imports enlarge — other things being equal — the market share(s) of the leading firm(s) and increase the level of market concentration.

The third case arises when importing firms dominate the domestic market and is more likely in non-producing than in producing countries. In such a case, an increase in imports — other things being equal — may enlarge the dominating firms' market shares and may bring about less competitive market structures. In our sample, the pattern concerns only Sweden because imports amounted to about 70 per cent of the market prior to the start of the integration process, and three importing firms (Opel, Volkswagen and Ford) captured a substantial share of the Swedish passenger car market.

Apparently, one cannot reach strong conclusions about the foreign entry effect on market structure. Yet it seems probable that the integration of West European economies led to more competitive market structures in car-producing countries. This should hold despite the fact that importing firms belong to the oligopolistic group or that domestic producers make substantial imports.

## Firm exit and market structure

High tariff protection permits small inefficient firms to survive through its upward effect on prices. A reduction in tariff protection exerts an opposite effect on prices in the domestic market and is likely to drive small-sized firms out of business. Firms suffering from insurmountable small-scale disadvantages may either disappear or be absorbed by larger firms. They may also merge in order to reap economies of scale and reduce competition among domestic firms. The different alternatives indicate that the process of international integration may give rise at some point to an increase in concentration and a return to less competitive market structures.

Does this pattern fit with the structural changes in the passenger car markets following from the integration of West European economies? Two different steps could be noticed. First, there was the demise of very small (fringe) car manufacturers in West Germany, France and Italy at the end of the 1950s and beginning of the 1960s. For example, the great majority of West German and French fringe car manufacturers simply disappeared during this period. Second, there was takeover of medium-sized firms during the second half of the 1960s. Table 4.4 illlustrates the wave of takeovers involving

**Table 4.4**: Takeovers in the West European passenger car industry between 1960 and 1970

| Year of acquisition | Acquired firm | Size ('000) | Acquiring firm | Size ('000) | Country |
|---|---|---|---|---|---|
| 1965 | Panhard | 31.6 | Citroën | 350 | France |
| 1966 | Auto-Union | 75 | Volkswagen | 1,200 | W. Germany |
| 1966 | Jaguar | 19.5 | BMC | 660 | Britain |
| 1967 | Rover | 30 | Leyland | 110 | Britain |
| 1968 | Glas | 28 | BMW | 56 | W. Germany |
| 1968 | Autobianchi | 36 | Fiat | 1,101 | Italy |
| 1969 | NSU | 111 | Volkswagen | 1,369 | W. Germany |
| 1970 (late 1969) | Lancia | 37 | Fiat | 1,307 | Italy |

*Sources:* Takeovers: Bloomfield (1978), Dunnett (1980), Ensor (1971), Fontaine (1980), Raisch (1973) and Rhys (1972b). Production figures: L'Argus de l'automobile et des locomotions, yearly issues 1962–1970.
Only medium-sized firms are concerned (5,000–120,000 cars per year).
The production figures refer to the average production during the three years preceding the takeover.

medium-sized firms in the passenger car industry between 1960 and 1970.

In view of the large economies of scale in the passenger car industry, it is clear that the acquired firms suffered from substantial small-scale disadvantages when trade was liberalised, all the more so because of the highly constraining nature of scale requirements for firm survival ability during the 1960s. All the takeovers involving medium-sized firms took place when tariffs on internal trade were removed within the EEC and EFTA. A similar wave occurred in other industrial sectors in most West European countries for probably the same reasons during the same period.[23]

Except for Saab in Sweden, no medium-sized passenger car firm survived the 1960s wave of takeovers (medium-sized firms are defined by a 5,000–120,000 yearly production). The 15 per cent tariff rate imposed on continental competitors up to the mid-1970s, the absence of trade effects of international integration (illustrated in Chapter 3) and the presence of high non-tariff barriers might have facilitated Saab's survival in Sweden. Two complementary factors are, firstly, the change of product policy of the firm during the second half of the 1970s — specialisation in higher-quality passenger cars — and, secondly, a recent co-production deal with the Lancia division of Fiat that allowed it to escape the scale constraint.

Another striking feature of the 1960s wave of exit and takeovers is the survival in Britain of very small independent firms. As stated above, these were driven out of business in the continental countries at the very beginning of the integration process. Two main factors may explain this survival of small specialised domestic firms such as Bristol, Morgan, Aston-Martin, Lotus, Rolls-Royce and Reliant. The first factor is the high tariffs that faced potential continental competitors and the resulting low import penetration in Britain up to the beginning of the 1970s. The second factor is the demand from British consumers for differentiated exclusive cars, probably as a result of an uneven income distribution. The presence of these firms, which still exist, explains partly the high level of product differentiation noticed in the British passenger car industry (see Table 4.3).

The integration of West European economies provoked a wave of takeovers in the passenger car industry during the second half of the 1960s. This undoubtedly affected market structures and had an upward effect on market concentration. The limited size of the firms involved in takeover operations suggests, however, that this effect was weaker than the foreign entry effect. A tentative conclusion is that the U-shape hypothesis on the relationship between integration and market concentration can be rejected if only the 1960s wave of takeovers is considered. The foreign entry and exit effects will be estimated in the next chapter. Then a more definite answer concerning the relevance of the U-shape hypothesis for the passenger car markets will be provided.

A by-product of the analysis concerns the efficiency effects. Efficiency gains from trade liberalisation and international integration flowed as much from domestic as from foreign tariff cuts. The former resulted in the rationalisation of domestic industry by the suppression or absorption of small, inefficiently producing firms. The latter induced firms to expand through exports and to improve technical efficiency by producing at a more efficient scale. Table 4.2 provides a rough estimate of the cost-saving gains that could be achieved through increased firm size (see also Table 1.2 on increased firm sizes). Both effects correspond to one of the so-called dynamic effects of international integration, the technical efficiency effect.

The next section will focus on the role of the institutional environment and the practices of government in bringing about large-scale mergers that alter market structures. This role has been influenced by the process of international integration and should also be analysed before we can accept or reject the U-shape hypothesis.

## PUBLIC POLICY AND MARKET STRUCTURE

There are a broad range and diversity of government policies that alter market structure: for example, anti-trust and competition, environment, research and development, trade. Most of them affect the market structure indirectly through their effects on market shares. For example, public preferences awarded to large domestic producers of products purchased by the government increase large domestic firms' market shares and, hence, market concentration. Similar consequences can be expected as a result of technological policy, the aim of which is to promote research and development activity in an industry and which results in public subsidies accorded preferably to large firms (picking-the-winners strategy). In the present section, the indirect effects of public policy on market structure will not be examined. We will concentrate on the direct effects of an active public policy of encouraging mergers and takeovers in the industrial sector.

In the period following the Second World War, most West European governments devoted a lot of attention to industrial policy and to the promotion of competitive industrial firms. The opening up to trade at the beginning of the 1960s resulted in increased competition from abroad for domestic firms and contributed further to government tolerance towards mergers and takeovers. These were regarded as the best means of making European industry efficient and able to meet the trade liberalisation challenge.

The fact that large firms, on average, export larger shares of their production than small ones is another argument put forward to justify the positive government attitude towards mergers and takeovers. Two reasons are generally advanced to explain why large firms are more successful exporters.[24] First, risks associated with export activity (as, for example, political events affecting foreign markets and fluctuations in exchange rates), transportation costs and the fixed cost to set up a distribution network abroad give rise to multi-plant economies of scale. Consequently, large firms are likely to be more successful exporters because they can spread such risks and costs over a much larger output. Second, firms that possess some degree of market power in their domestic market are better equipped to promote exports by charging a lower price abroad than at home.[25] The larger the firm, the easier it is to overcome adversity in the domestic market and thus the greater is its likely market power and its ability to discriminate between domestic and foreign markets. The scale economies and discrimination gains arguments suggest that governments can improve an industry's export performance by encouraging existing producers to amalgamate through mergers.

## Western European merger policies

Two kinds of measures can be introduced by governments to prompt industrial firms to merge or to take over smaller firms in the same line of business. The first category comprises all the measures that lower the cost of acquiring another firm or of merging, while the second includes those that increase the expected returns from concentration of production.

Three main instruments have been used by West European governments to bring down acquisition or merger costs: fiscal incentives, monetary facilities and merger agencies. Fiscal incentives have been the most widespread. In France, for example, the 1965 and 1967 merger laws meant the abolition of the old merger taxes and the allocation of fiscal advantages to firms reorganising industry in conformity with the plan.[26] Another example is Sweden, where tax exemptions have been granted by governments when the proposed merger (or takeover) was expected to serve the 'public interest'.[27] Certain aspects of the West German corporation tax have created a similar favourable climate for mergers in West Germany, where it is profitable to merge because it results in lower corporate taxes.[28]

The second policy instrument related to acquisition costs is the granting of monetary facilities in the form of credits or cheap loans to some firms in order to help them to purchase other firms. This instrument has been particularly employed in Britain, France and, to a lesser extent, Italy.[29] In the latter two countries, the use has been greatly facilitated by the existence of large public and semi-public credit institutions.

The third instrument is of a more interventionist nature since it consists of the creation of public merger agencies. Their role is to assist the reorganisation of industries by seeking out merger partners and promoting 'happy marriages'. Such agencies economise on the search for merger candidates by providing quickly and gratuitously information on the 'most suitable' partners. Among the five countries under study, two, Britain and France, have experienced such an active merger-fostering policy.[30]

Of course, the different instruments are not exclusive to each other, and some countries have used more than one of them to promote the formation of large firms. For example, the British 'marriage bureau' (the Industrial Reorganisation Corporation, which was created early in 1966 and ceased to exist in 1971) had at its disposal substantial funds which were preferentially allocated to firms involved in IRC-initiated merger situations.[31] Table 4.5 illustrates the similarities and differences with respect

**Table 4.5:** Merger policy in West European car-producing countries

| Country | Tax incentives | Monetary facilities | Merger agency |
|---|---|---|---|
| West Germany | + | | |
| France | + | + | + |
| Italy | + | + | |
| Sweden | + | | |
| United Kingdom | | + | + |

*Sources:* Based on Walsh and Paxton (1975), Mueller (1980), Rydén (1972), Stoléru (1969), Vernon (1974) and Blackaby (1978).

to merger policy between the five countries under study. It indicates that France and, to a lesser extent, Britain and Italy, have had the most active pro-merger public policies over the past two and a half decades.

As stated above, mergers and takeovers can also be encouraged by public measures that act upon the returns from concentration operations. Such indirect measures are of two sorts. The first consists of all the various forms of barriers to entry — such as tariffs, quantitative restrictions and technical and administrative hindrances — which are set up in order to forestall entry. These measures have a positive effect on returns from merger activity because they enable firms to raise their prices without attracting new entrants. Some of the indirect measures are trade-impeding and cannot be used freely to promote this or that merger because governments have bound their trade policy in successive rounds of multinational trade negotiations or membership in the EEC or EFTA. However, the fact, well illustrated in Chapter 2, that governments still have discretionary powers as regards a certain number of non-tariff trade-impeding measures indicates that this merger-promoting instrument is not completely obsolete.

The second kind of public policy that fosters merger activity through its impact on returns from concentration operations is competition policy. Actually, a lenient policy towards price-fixing agreements or unfair selling prices (above marginal costs) has a positive effect on returns from concentration of production because it enables firms to charge higher prices. Although all national legislation in Western Europe prohibits agreements between firms that have as their object price-fixing or restriction of production or allocation of markets, public policy, with the exception of Britain and to a certain extent West Germany, has been very tolerant of non-competitive business practices.[32] The opening up to trade of West European economies during the 1960s means that firms benefiting from dominant positions or concerted practices cannot totally escape the free play of international market forces and set their 'own' prices. The implications are that returns from further merger activity are lower in an open than in a closed economy and that a permissive competition policy is a less effective merger-promoting instrument in an economy subject to international competition.

The conclusion that emerges is that both kinds of policy instruments that affect returns are less successful in promoting mergers and takeovers in an internationally integrated economy. This explains why, as a result of the opening up to trade of Western economies, merger policy has tended to shift from a policy based principally on instruments that affect returns to a policy that gives greater place to instruments that affect costs or, in other words, from trade policy to industrial policy. This shift is illustrated by, on the one hand, the removal of tariffs and quantitative restrictions during the 1960s and, on the other hand, the introduction of tax facilities for merging firms and the creation of merger agencies during the same period. Note also that the argument applies more particularly to countries like France, Britain and Italy.

## Anti-trust policy

Up to now, we have examined public measures whose goal is to enhance merger activity and concentration of production. Yet, this is not the whole story. There are also anti-trust policies, the purpose of which is to prevent the growth of firms to dominant positions by impeding mergers between large firms.

Although many West European countries have rather tight anti-trust legislation, little has been done to enforce them.[33] Among the countries under study, only two, Britain and West Germany, have an effective apparatus to enforce the anti-trust laws. In Britain, a Monopolies and Mergers Act passed in 1965 gives a Monopolies Commission the right to investigate mergers in the private sector of the industry and to prohibit or dissolve mergers regarded as harmful to the 'public interest'.[34] This apparent tightness of the British anti-trust legislation was, however, not followed by a strict enforcement. Only 20 merger proposals — among 798 initially considered — were referred to the Monopolies Commission, and of these only 15 were not completed (i.e. less than 2 per cent).

In West Germany the 1957 Act against Restraint of Competition was amended in 1973 to better control merger activity. Furthermore, an independent Monopolies Commission was created and empowered to prohibit mergers that may lead to dominant positions.[35] Yet the new legislation does not seem to have had the expected effects on merger activity since a new amendment advocating a tighter merger control was submitted to the West German Parliament in 1978.[36] Thus, the experience of the two countries with the tightest merger control laws in Western Europe strongly indicates that their effects on merger and takeover activity have been very limited.

The same conclusion emerges from studies of the EEC competition policy towards mergers.[37] Although Article 86 of the Rome Treaty prohibits 'concentration operations made by companies in a dominant position to the prejudice of the consumer', competition policy towards mergers has been almost non-existent at the EEC level. Actually, only one merger case was tried on the basis of Article 86 between 1958 and 1981. Moreover, this merger case concerned a US company, Continental Can, and the decision of the European Community Commission was reversed by the European Court of Justice and the merger was completed in 1971.[38] In 1973 the Commission of the EEC proposed a merger regulation act to strengthen merger control. The proposal has not yet been implemented. The reason for this is the priority given to industrial policies that promote adjustment since the mid-1970s and the resulting greater powers accorded to the directorate-general for industrial affairs at the expense of the directorate-general for competition policy. The EEC competitive policy towards mergers has thus remained more or less an empty threat.

The main conclusion to be drawn from the analysis of public policy towards mergers is that all the countries considered have had a positive attitude towards mergers and concentration of production. Yet some difference in the degree of public involvement in merger activity between the five countries could be observed as a result of difference in views about government role in industrial affairs. One main argument justifies the positive public attitude: the perceived beneficial effects of mergers in the form of increased efficiency are more important than the harmful and more uncertain anti-competitive effects.

A second conclusion concerns the inability of anti-trust laws to deter large-scale mergers. Three reasons explain this development. First, there is the preferential treatment accorded to pro-merger industrial policies in Western Europe. A second reason may be the departure from the merger-control law that each country grants if the merging firms can show that the merger is in the 'public interest' or, to use the EEC formulation, in the 'common interest of the Community'. Thus, government decisions are likely to reflect mainly producers' opinions. This is because of the low costs of lobbying activities (few producers involved) in relation to the benefits for producers (higher prices, quieter life, rent-yielding position, etc.) compared to the high costs in relation to the benefits for consumers in obtaining information about a merger and in resisting it. The third reason pertains to the non-implementation of the EEC competition policy, which is partly the result of divergence of opinion between member states over merger policy.

## Public policy and merger activity in the passenger car industry

How did the above merger policies affect merger activity in the West European passenger car industry? Several takeovers involving small and mid-sized West European car manufacturers took place during the second half of the 1960s (see Table 4.4). As suggested in our discussion, these takeovers were the result of increased competition from abroad, which forced out inefficient small-scale car producers. A common feature is that they were not promoted by an active public merger policy, although tax incentives might have played a role. The absence of government intervention is, however, not the rule if one considers the whole period under study. An analysis of mergers involving larger passenger car producers demonstrates that the role of government policy is not a negligible matter. Two countries among the five under study, Britain and France, experienced a merger-promoting public policy that greatly re-shaped the passenger car market structures.

Before turning to a detailed analysis of government-initiated mergers in these two countries, it should be noted that several government-inspired merger proposals were not realised because of the involved firms' unwillingness to amalgamate their production. For example, the British government unsuccessfully tried to persuade two British car manufacturers, BMH (British Motor Holdings) and Leyland, to take over Rootes in 1967 before it was absorbed by Chrysler.[39]

Another example is the attempts of the Italian government to promote a merger in 1975 when British Leyland put into liquidation its passenger car assembly plant in Milan. The proposed merger between the Leyland Italian subsidiary, Innocenti, and Fiat or Alfa-Romeo did not take place and the assembly plant was taken over by an independent car manufacturer, De Tomaso, with the help of the Italian government and its industrial rescue agency GEPI (Gestioni Epartci Pazioni Industriali).[40] The rescue operation means that the Italian government owns a majority share in Innocenti, but De Tomaso runs the company and has an option to acquire the GEPI share.

*Britain*

As mentioned above, the creation of the Industrial Reorganisation Corporation (IRC) in 1966 had significant repercussions for merger activity in Britain. The experience of the British motor industry during the 1960s lends much support to this point. Instead of being passively in favour of mergers and takeovers, as was actually the case for the mergers between British Motor Corporation and Jaguar-Daimler in 1966 and between Leyland and Rover in 1967, the British government became heavily involved in promoting the merger between Leyland and British Motor Holdings (BMC plus Jaguar) in 1968.

To bring about the merger, the British government made use of two merger policy tools, direct intervention and allocation of monetary facilities. On the one hand, discussions between the heads of the two companies were organised under the auspices of the IRC and the Prime Minister to convince them of the necessity of the merger.[41] During the negotiations, the IRC pro-merger attitude was backed by a study of the Ministry of Technology, which stated that the two firms were too small to survive as independents and that only a merger would give them a chance to exploit all available economies of scale. On the other hand, the IRC accorded monetary facilities to the new company in the form of a £25 million loan on favourable terms.[42] All this illustrates that 'the government, with the help of the Industrial Reorganisation Corporation, played a very significant part in bringing about the merger between Leyland and British Motor Holdings'.[43]

The main argument used by the British government to ensure the merger was the following: only a larger motor vehicle manufacturer would be able to reap the fruits of economies of scale and to meet the growing competition from abroad. Two factors suggest that the argument is not as convincing as it appears at first sight. First, of the two firms involved, British Motor Holdings was the more favourably inclined to the merger. This was already a sizeable firm with a yearly production of more than half a million passenger cars (i.e. larger than many West European mass producers). For example, the average yearly production of the three biggest French firms — Renault, Citroën and Peugeot — amounted to less than half a million during the same period.[44] Second, a large firm like BMH could hardly be threatened at that time by import competition, which was very limited until the early 1970s because of the high tariff rates imposed on most imported passenger cars in Britain (see Chapter 2). This is borne out by the pre-tax profits of British Motor Holdings, which amounted to £15.4, 21.8, 50, 44 and 16 million in 1963, 1964, 1965, 1966 and 1967, respectively.[45]

In sum, the very active and persuasive role of the British government and the monetary facilities accorded to the newly formed British Leyland seem to have exerted a decisive influence on the decision of the two firms to merge in 1968. It should be added that the merger did not produce the expected efficiency effects and that British Leyland, faced with bankruptcy, was nationalised in 1975.[46]

It is often argued that the active merger and industrial policy in Britain in the 1960s drew its inspiration from the French experience.[47] We now turn to this example.

*France*

In addition to its extensive state participation in industry, the French government has been widely involved in private industrial affairs. As mentioned above, its main objective has been to promote mergers so as to constitute 'national champions' that could successfully meet foreign competition on the domestic and foreign markets. Mergers between French firms were therefore greatly encouraged, whereas foreign takeovers of French firms were deterred and restricted. The experience of the French passenger car industry is illustrative in this respect.

In 1969 the French government vetoed a deal that would have amounted to the takeover of Citroën by Fiat. It authorised the Italian firm to acquire only a 15 per cent share of the French company.[48] Three years later, in August 1971, public concern over the loss-making Citroën (see Table 4.6) led the French government to allow Fiat to increase its share holdings to 49 per cent. Fiat further attempted to obtain a majority in Citroën since it believed that Citroën could only survive as an integral part of a larger organisation. Fiat's efforts were rebuffed by the French government and, consequently, the Italian firm abandoned its share holdings in Citroën in 1973.

In France public merger policy has been the responsibility of the CIASI (Comité Interministériel pour l'Aménagement des Structures Industrielles). Its most common remedy used to rescue ailing firms has been to find a healthy firm in the same industry and to persuade it to take over the loss-making competitor. This remedy was used for Citroën, which faced bankruptcy in 1974 (see Table 4.6).[49] The CIASI selected a

**Table 4.6:** After-tax profits or losses (in millions of francs) and passenger car production (in thousands)

| | Citroën | | Peugeot | | Simca-Chrysler | |
|---|---|---|---|---|---|---|
| Year | Profits | Production | Profits | Production | Profits | Production |
| 1966 | + 22.2 | 452 | + 48.3 | 332 | + 40.6 | 327 |
| 1967 | + 11.8 | 419 | + 51.3 | 374 | + 11.9 | 276 |
| 1968 | − 174.8 | 384 | + 35.2 | 362 | + 31.8 | 350 |
| 1969 | − 63.4 | 426 | + 73 | 441 | + 36.6 | 388 |
| 1970 | − 377.8 | 471 | + 91.1 | 525 | + 10.8 | 403 |
| 1971 | − 40.9 | 578 | + 105.6 | 559 | + 91.1 | 484 |
| 1972 | + 137.9 | 649 | + 190.5 | 603 | + 98.3 | 534 |
| 1973 | + 231.9 | 659 | + 215.1 | 685 | + 153.9 | 560 |
| 1974 | − 999.2 | 599 | + 52.1 | 634 | − 71.8 | 444 |
| 1975 | − 304.4 | 624 | + 109.7 | 578 | − 110.6 | 449 |
| 1976 | + 297.6 | 657 | + 529.9 | 656 | + 214.6 | 483 |
| 1977 | + 359.3 | 715 | + 617.4 | 676 | + 47 | 477 |
| 1978 | + 597 | 708 | + 648 | 742 | − 91.5 | 431 |
| 1979 | + 202 | 713 | + 793 | 754 | − 426 | 381 |

*Sources:* Annual company reports (1966–1979); *L'Argus de l'automobile et des locomotions,* yearly statistical issue (1966–1980).

healthy company in the same line of business, Peugeot. The latter took over Citroën in two stages, 38 per cent in 1975 and 13 per cent in 1976, with the help of a cheap state loan of 1 billion francs. On that occasion, two instruments, merger agency and monetary facilities, were used by the French government.

It seems clear that the real motive for government intervention was to maintain employment by rescuing loss-making firms rather than to form a 'national champion' able to meet foreign competition by reaping all available economies of scale. Two reasons provide some support for this argument. First, Citroën was absorbed by a firm of about the same size which did not seem to have suffered from scale disadvantages prior to the mid-1970s (see Table 4.6). Second, the merger did not lead to economies of scale on the production side. Only multi-plant economies of scale were actually concerned, and the integration of R&D activities and some management tasks were the main effects of the merger.[50]

One factor behind Citroën's difficulties was international economic integration. Table 4.7 shows that Citroën's profitability

**Table 4.7**: Influence of foreign competition (import or tariff) on French firm profitability, 1960–1975

| | | |
|---|---|---|
| (4.1) Citroën: | Profitability = 3.861 − 0.283 $M/C$ <br> (1.402) (2.046) | $R^2 = 0.234$ |
| (4.2) | Profitability = −3.621 + 0.245 $T$ <br> (2.584) (2.031) | $R^2 = 0.231$ |
| (4.3) Peugeot: | Profitability = 2.071 − 0.021 $M/C$ <br> (4.53) (0.939) | $R^2 = 0.154$ |
| (4.4) | Profitability = 1.45 + 0.024 $T$ <br> (5.991) (1.236) | $R^2 = 0.188$ |
| (4.5) Simca-Chrysler: | Profitability = 1.044 − 0.009 $M/C$ <br> (0.719) (0.121) | $R^2 = 0.004$ |
| (4.6) | Profitability = 0.800 + 0.009 $T$ <br> (1.030) (0.135) | $R^2 = 0.004$ |

*Variables and sources:* Profitability: after-tax profits divided by turnover and multiplied by 100 (annual company reports, 1960–1975). $M/C$, rate of import penetration multiplied by 100 (see Figure 3.1). $T$, weighted tariff rate (see Chapter 3, pp. 69–70).

The equations are estimated with the OLS method and corrected for serial correlation with the Cochrane–Orcutt procedure. The critical values of the $t$-statistic (in parentheses) at the 5 per cent and 10 per cent level with a one-tailed test are $t(14) = 1.761$ and 1.345.

and thus its survivability were negatively and significantly affected by the growing import penetration and the tariff reduction process between 1960 and 1975. Unlike Citroën, the acquiring firm Peugeot and Simca-Chrysler were not affected by the process of international integration. The import and tariff coefficients of the equations concerned with Peugeot and Simca-Chrysler are of the right sign but not statistically significant. The similar size of Citroën and the acquiring firm Peugeot indicates that the difficulties of Citroën did not ensue from economies of scale but from market conduct (the firm's R&D policy, production of car models that are closer substitutes for foreign models, etc.). On the buyer side, it seemed to be the desire to improve its market position and the 'persuasive' arguments (among others, pecuniary) of the French government which decided Peugeot to purchase Citroën.

In August 1978 another important merger took place in France between Peugeot-Citroën and Chrysler-Europe.[51] The French firm acquired Chrysler's subsidiaries in France, Britain and Spain in exchange for $230 million in cash and a 15 per cent equity holding in the enlarged company. Opinions concerning the role of the French government differ. According to most authors, the French government was delighted at the announcement of the merger but did not play a direct role in its completion.[52] Other sources suggest, however, that it was the French government that encouraged Peugeot-Citroën to purchase Chrysler.[53]

Several reasons explain the large-scale takeover. On the seller side, it was the precarious financial situation of Chrysler in the United States, the need to find enormous sums of money to meet the Japanese and compact car challenges and the financial difficulties faced by the British Chrysler subsidiary — and to some extent the French subsidiary (see Table 4.6) — that lay behind Chrysler's decision to pull out of Western Europe. Chrysler's British subsidiary sustained an accumulated pre-tax loss of £93.3 million between 1974 and 1977.[54] On the buyer side, two motives seem to have decided Peugeot-Citroën to absorb Chrysler-Europe: the desire to reap further economies of scale and to obtain an improved market position, respectively. The already large pre-merger size of Peugeot-Citroën (see Table 4.6) and the fact that mergers do not yield, at least in the short run, production scale economies but only multi-plant economies cast some doubt on the first motive. The second motive seems more likely. According to the latter, the merger was expected to strengthen Peugeot-Citroën's market power by overcoming adversity in the domestic market and thus to create a potential for higher prices. A severe quantitative restriction towards Japanese passenger cars in France since the mid-1970s was probably expected to facilitate the realisation of this potential.

That the merger cannot be justified on efficiency grounds is confirmed by the performance of the newly formed firm after 1978. Its share of the French passenger car market amounted to an average of 34.5 per cent during the 1979–1984 period while the two merging firms, Peugeot-Citroën and Simca-Chrysler, captured together not less than on average 45 per cent of the French market during the 1975–1978 period.[55] Another indication of the worsening in performace after the merger operation is the substantial financial losses made by the newly formed firm (FF 6.751 million in after-tax losses between 1979 and 1984).[56]

The review of large-scale mergers in the West European passenger car industry shows that the higher degree of merger activity observed in France and Britain is, to a large extent, due to public policy. This finding is not surprising because, as illustrated above, these two countries had the most active public merger policy. A complementary factor in the French case is growing foreign competition. The U-shape hypothesis on the relationship between international integration and market concentration cannot therefore be rejected on *a priori* grounds for France.

An interesting aspect of the different large-scale merger cases is the absence of reaction from national and EEC anti-trust authorities. The different passenger car mergers were not referred to them, and the strict merger control laws remained an empty threat. An exception is the merger between Peugeot-Citroën and Chrysler-Europe which was referred to the Commission of the EEC and scrutinised for compatibility with Article 86 of the Rome Treaty. The Commission rejected the complaint, however, on the ground that abuse of dominant position was unlikely to follow from the merger, because of the competitive nature of the enlarged West European passenger car market.[57] The experience of mergers in the passenger car industry thus supports the view that anti-trust laws in Western Europe are unable to deter large-scale mergers.

## SUMMARY AND CONCLUSIONS

How did international integration affect market structure in the West European car markets? In this chapter, we have argued that the answer to the question depends upon industry-specific factors such as economies of scale, firm behaviour and public policy.

As regards the first set of factors, evidence provided here points to the large extent of economies of scale in passenger car production and marketing. This constitutes a severe constraint on the survival capacity of firms. Evidence suggests, however, that firms can escape the scale constraint through product differentiation and cooperation with other firms. Another result is that the impact of economies of scale on firm survivability changes over time according to where the industry finds itself in the technology cycle. The past decade's innovations in passenger car production mean a 'dematurity' phase for the industry. This new phase implies that the scale requirements have represented less of a constraint on firm survival ability over the past few years than they were during the 1960s and the first half of the 1970s.

The abolition of tariffs in the wake of integration has resulted in increasing competition from abroad. This has in turn brought about fresh entry and a move towards more competitive market structures. Increased competition may, however, have an opposite effect on market structures. It may drive out of business those firms that are inefficient from the point of view of scale economies and increase market concentration. Our findings suggest that this second effect was limited in the passenger car industry.

Increased competition from abroad may also encourage a pro-merger public policy and merger operations. Industrial policy has been more active since the start of the integration process. This judgement applies particularly to France, Britain and Italy. Large-scale mergers were experienced in the first two countries, which had the most active merger policies. Among other things, we found that increased foreign competition had exerted some influence on one of the mergers in France. This has implications for the relevance of the U-shape hypothesis on the relation between integration and concentration in the passenger car markets.

The tentative conclusion of this chapter is that the rapid rise

110

in import penetration has shaped more competitive market structures in spite of the reduction in the number of firms due to the exit of small and medium-sized firms. Thus, the U-shape relationship can be rejected for all countries except France. The next chapter will substantiate the overall competitive effect of international integration and estimate the contribution of each factor to changes in market structure over time. It will provide a more definite answer on the relationship between integration and market structure.

Another purpose of the chapter was to provide certain insights into the logic of public policy. Our findings cast a lot of doubt on the scale efficiency argument. Moreover, it questions the opportunities open to governments to obtain accurate information and an understanding of the future development of costs and markets in a particular industry. It is interesting to note that one of the reasons behind the failure of public and firm merger policy was a misunderstanding of the nature of the maturity phase and of the future changes in technology and design. It should be noted that the insignificance of economies of scale corresponds to the results of other studies concerned with a large number of industries.[58]

The desire to rescue ailing firms is a recurrent factor behind the state-promoted mergers in the motor vehicle industry. This is not surprising since the motor vehicle industry is a large employer, and the political benefits of rescuing a large firm should be great in terms of voting numbers. On the other hand, the political costs are likely to be low because the costs of a merger are spread over all taxpayers and consumers. Furthermore, the high degree of organisation of passenger car firms has probably facilitated lobbying efforts for merger assistance.

Another feature of the large-scale mergers is the belief of some firms that mergers are an effective means of firm reinforcement through market dominance. This feature has been illustrated in more aggregated studies.[59] It is somewhat surprising because the scope for higher prices is expected to be limited in integrated economies.

A final interesting feature of large-scale mergers is the absence of reactions of anti-trust authorities at the national as well as EEC levels. This finding lends more support to pessimistic views about the possibility of enforcement of West European merger control policies.[60]

**NOTES**

1. Johnson (1972), p. xiii.
2. There exist two aggregated studies concerned with the British economy on the U-shape hypothesis. Katrak (1980) and Utton and Morgan (1983), Chapter 4.
3. For a detailed description of the production process in the motor vehicle industry, see Pratten (1971), Chapter 14, or White (1971), Chapter 3.
4. See Scherer, Beckenstein, Kaufer and Murphy (1975), Chapter 7.
5. Most survival estimates of economies of scale in the passenger car industry tend to give results similar in order of magnitude to those of engineering estimates. For example, according to Weiss, the MES output amounted to 640,000 units per year during the 1941–1961 period. See Weiss (1964), p. 249.
6. Pratten (1971), p. 26.
7. Altschuler, Andersson, Jones, Roos and Womalk (1984), p. 182.
8. Ibid., p. 182.
9. White (1971), pp. 44–53.
10. Quoted by Mazzolini (1974), p. 3.
11. *Fortune* (1979), p. 132.
12. See for example, Greenaway and Milner (1986), pp. 91–92.
13. Empirical evidence suggests that the mark-up of prices over marginal costs in the US passenger car industry increases with product quality. See Bresnahan (1981), pp. 201–27.
14. For a history of the joint ventures in the passenger car industry, see United Nations (1983), pp. 54–63.
15. See for example, Bilindustrin (1978), p. 39, and *L'Avenir de l'automobile* (1976), p. 134.
16. For a description of the characteristics of the different phases of the product life cycle, see Wells (1972), p. 10.
17. See Clark (1983), pp. 103–49, and Altschuler *et al.* (1984), Chapter 8.
18. See for example, Eastman and Stykolt (1967), Auquier (1980) and Carlsson (1972).
19. Corden (1974), pp. 210–15, and Bain (1969), pp. 102–4.
20. Busch (1966), pp. 47–55.
21. Fontaine (1980), pp. 89–90.
22. Bilindustriföreningen (1960), *Motor Traffic in Sweden*, pp. 39–41.
23. See the studies on takeover activity in West Germany, France, Britain, Sweden and the Netherlands in Mueller (1980).
24. Pagoulatos and Sorensen (1980), pp. 305–27.
25. See for example White (1974), pp. 1013–20.
26. Jenny and Weber (1975), pp. 597–639.
27. Rydén and Edberg (1980), pp. 196–97 and Rydén (1972), pp. 156–58.
28. Reuss (1963), pp. 116–19.
29. Curzon Price (1981), Chapter 3, and Vernon (1974), p. 93.

30. Curzon Price (1981), Chapter 3, Vernon (1974), Chapters 5 and 6, and Maunder (1979), Chapters 5 and 7.

31. Maunder (1979), pp. 145–46.

32. See Walsh and Paxton (1975), Chapters 6 and 7; George and Joll (1975), p. 210.

33. Walsh and Paxton (1975), Chapter 7; OECD (1984b), pp. 11–49.

34. Utton (1975), pp. 95–121.

35. Cable, Palfrey and Runge (1980), pp. 99–132.

36. Cable et al. (1980), p. 117.

37. Markert (1975), pp. 67–90.

38. Ibid., p. 70.

39. Maxcy (1981), pp. 226–31.

40. See The Economist (1975), and the Financial Times (1981).

41. Dunnet (1980), pp. 98–106.

42. Ibid., p. 100.

43. W. Benn, Minister of Technology, quoted by Maxcy (1981), p. 228.

44. See Dunnet (1980), p. 100, and L'Argus de l'automobile et des locomotions, yearly statistical issues (1965–1970).

45. Dunnet (1980), p. 39.

46. A British study supports the view that the BL/BMH merger cannot be justified on efficiency grounds and that its actual logic is political. See Cowling, Stoneman, Cubbin, Cable, Hall, Donberger and Dutton (1980), pp. 170–90.

47. Franko (1979), pp. 31–50.

48. Moreaux (1979), pp. 6–11, and Wells (1974), p. 247.

49. Commission of the European Communities (1976), p. 83; Fontaine (1980), p. 91; Le Monde (1979).

50. Fontaine (1980), pp. 93–96.

51. Multinational Business (1978), pp. 1–8, and Le Monde (1979).

52. Multinational Business (1978), pp. 1–2, and Le Monde (1979).

53. Curzon Price (1981), p. 46, and Bhaskar (1984), p. 19.

54. For figures on Chrysler-Britain's losses, see Dunnet (1980), p. 37.

55. For figures on market shares, see L'Argus de l'automobile et des locomotions, yearly statistical issues (1976–1985).

56. After-tax profits of the newly formed firm are available in PSA (Peugeot-Citreön) Company Reports (1979–1985).

57. Commission of the European Communities (1979), pp. 105–6.

58. Mueller (1980), p. 302.

59. De Jong (1976), pp. 95–123, and George and Silberston (1976), pp. 124–42.

60. Scherer (1974), pp. 181–97.

# 5

# Changes in Market Structures and Their Determinants: Empirical Evidence

The purpose of this chapter is to analyse changes in market structure and their determinants. The analysis covers the period between the start of the integration process and the early 1980s. There are two reasons for the focus on market structure. First, market structure and its change over time are expected to express changes in competitive conditions. Thus, their analysis should shed some light on one of the so-called dynamic effects of international integration. Second, recent research in industrial economics has advocated emphasising market structure and its change over time in further empirical work.[1]

The present chapter is divided into two parts. The first is devoted to a detailed analysis of the structures of passenger car markets and their developments over the last two and a half decades. The analysis makes use of different measures that provide complementary information about concentration levels and trends. The main difference between the present analysis and previous analyses is that we will focus on concentration in well-delimited markets and not in industries. Another difference is the fairly long time period covered here.

In the second part, we will see to what extent the different determinants of changes in market structure over time are responsible for the actual changes. In particular, we will elaborate on the impact of international integration and public policy. One purpose will be to more definitely accept or reject the U-shape hypothesis on the relation between integration and market concentration. Further, it is expected that the fact that changes in market structure over time embody the impact of market conduct will shed some light on diverse elements of firm behaviour, such as pricing and product policies.

114

## CROSS-COUNTRY COMPARATIVE STUDY OF CHANGES IN MARKET STRUCTURES

The purpose of this part of the chapter is to estimate the level of market concentration and its change over time. The section is arranged in three parts. The first introduces the two measures used and briefy presents their advantages and shortcomings. The second discusses the data problems involved in measuring market structure and gives a short description of the data samples that occur in the study. There follows in the third section a cross-country comparative analysis of the changes that have taken place in the West European passenger car markets over the past two and a half decades.

### Market structure measures

The idea of concentration refers to situations in which it is possible for a limited number of firms to adopt a pattern of behaviour different from that of a purely competitive model, due to the fact that they control a large proportion of sales on a market. Market concentration measures should be able to depict such situations, or changes in these situations, which imply that a small number of firms are more or less able to depart from competitive behaviour. They should therefore reflect two major aspects of market structure, number and size inequality of firms.

There are many measures (Herfindahl, Rosenbluth, Linda, Entropy, Horvath, inequality indexes, etc.) available for the detection of non-competitive market conditions.[2] Most measures provide rather different pictures of market structure, although all of them consider it in terms of a range from pure competition to complete monopoly. Various weighting schemes explain the different responses of the measures to the same market conditions. Some of them attribute more weight to large firms. Others put more emphasis on small or medium-sized firms. Two measures were selected for the present study: the Herfindahl and Rosenbluth indexes.

Three reasons guided our choice. First, all inequality measures, such as the Gini coefficient and the Lorenz curve, were rejected because they fail to express one of the two main aspects of concentration, namely the number of firms. Second, we rejected those indexes, such as the concentration ratios, which *arbitrarily* truncate the index after the first four or eight firms or whatever. Third, the two indexes chosen were expected to largely complement each other in the amount of information they provide on prevailing market conditions.

The first selected measure, the Herfindahl index (sometimes called the Hirschman–Herfindahl index),[3] is equal to the sum of the squares of all the firms' market shares:

$$H = 1,000 \sum_{n=1}^{n} x_i^2$$

where

$x_i$ = market share of the firm $i$
$i$ = 1, 2, 3, ..., $n$
lower bound = $1,000/n$
upper bound = $1,000$

The squaring of market shares means that the Herfindahl index assigns greater weight to the largest firms in the market. This characteristic makes the $H$ index suitable for studies that want to investigate the role of big firms in competition.

The second selected index, the Rosenbluth index,[4] is equal to

$$R = 1,000 \bigg/ \left( 2 \sum_{i=1}^{n} i \cdot x_i - 1 \right)$$

where

$x_i$ = market share of the firm $i$
$i$ = 1, 2, 3, ..., $n$
lower bound = $1,000(3n^2 - 3n + 1)/n^3$
upper bound = $1,000$

The ranking device of the Rosenbluth index — ranks used as weights with the firms ranked in descending order — implies that the index is sensitive to changes in the distribution of small firms' market shares. The $R$ index is thus more suitable for studies that want to emphasise small firms' effects on competition. One factor behind this approach is that the extent of small

116

firm competition can be regarded as the best proxy for the degree of potential competition prevailing in a market.

## The data

The great majority of empirical studies on concentration focus on industry structure.[5] They are concerned with the shares of domestic production and ignore the role of imports and exports. Accordingly they tell us very little about the degree of competition prevailing in well-delimited national markets. Furthermore, their use as a tool for competition policy is open to criticism. The main reason behind the concern with industry structure is that most areas of activity lack consumption data or trade data properly linked to corresponding production data, such as exports and imports by firms.

The present work deals with market structure and the market share distribution of domestic and foreign firms within well-delimited natinal markets. The existence of data on registration of domestic as well as foreign new passenger cars in the five countries examined enables the avoidance of the frequent and substantial bias noticed in previous studies.

The data used to estimate market concentration and its change over time was derived from several sources. The first was the yearly statistical issues of *L'Argus de l'automobile et des locomotions* between 1961 and 1985. The second was the 1984–1985 edition of *World Motor Vehicle Data* (Motor Vehicle Manufacturers' Association, 1985). The third was data provided by the trade associations of the motor vehicle industry or available in their publications: *Motor Traffic in Sweden* (Bilindustriföreningen, 1960–1985), *Tatsachen und Zahlen* (Verband der Automobilindustrie, 1985) for West Germany and *Automobile in cifre* (Associazione Nazionale, 1985) for Italy. Fourth, as regards the British market during the first half of the 1960s, the data were collected from different issues of *Motor Business* (1960–1966). The data were available for West Germany between 1963 and 1984, for France between 1962 and 1984, for Italy between 1963 and 1983, for Sweden between 1960 and 1984, and for Britain between 1960 and 1983. The absence of data for three of the original EEC countries at the very beginning of the 1960s constitutes a serious shortcoming because substantial tariff cuts occurred

117

within the EEC during this period.

Our data sources give the number of passenger cars registered by make and model. Each make refers to a legally distinct firm. The patterns of control among firms are neglected. For example, Fiat and Ferrari are regarded as two different companies despite the fact that the latter was purchased by the former in late 1969.

To give economic meaning to the data and to take into account the fact that some firms are under the control of other firms, the data were rearranged according to the following criterion: When a firm possesses 50 per cent or more of another firm, the sales of both firms are consolidated. For instance, Rootes was considered as an independent firm up to 1967, though Chrysler held a 35 per cent share of it between 1964 and 1967. It was only after 1967, when Chrysler bought a majority in Rootes, that the sales of the two firms were consolidated. The same procedure was followed for the French firm Simca, only 25 per cent of which was owned by Chrysler before 1963.

In addition to the 1960s wave of takeovers (see Table 4.4) and the large-scale mergers examined above, two operations affected the patterns of control in the passenger car industry and our data during the period under consideration.[6] The first is the takeover of the Dutch firm DAF by Volvo in 1975. The second is the takeover of the Italian firm Innocenti by British Leyland in 1972. Note also that the nationalisation of British Leyland in 1975 did not affect our data sample, though this probably altered competitive conditions in the market.

Two exceptions were made to the 50 per cent rule. The first concerned the Dutch subsidiary of Volvo, Volvo Car BV (ex-DAF), 70 per cent of which came under the control of the Dutch government in 1981. The sales of Volvo Car BV have continued to be consolidated with Volvo since 1981 because it is clear that the parent company still decides the Dutch subsidiary's price policy and that the two firms cannot be regarded as competitors. The second exception concerned the Italian firm Innocenti. This was taken over by an independent car producer, De Tomaso, with the help of the Italian government, which owns a majority share in the firm.[7] The fact that De Tomaso runs the company and has an option to purchase the share of the Italian government motivates the non-consolidation of Innocenti with the state-owned Alfa-Romeo.

## Comparative study

Market structures and their changes over time in the five West European car-producing countries were estimated with the help of the two measures introduced above. The results are plotted in Figures 5.1 and 5.2. Several interesting findings emerge from these results.

The first finding concerns the level of concentration in the different countries. Both indexes provide evidence of a higher level of market concentration in Italy (and, after 1975, France) than in other West European car-producing countries. Differences are much less pronounced when the Rosenbluth index is considered. In view of the structure of the two indexes, such a disparity indicates that the countries examined are much more like medium-sized and small firms than large firms when it comes to the distribution of market shares. Of the countries considered, Sweden exhibits the lowest degree of market concentration. According to the Herfindahl and the Rosenbluth indexes, this amounted to about 150 during the whole period analysed. An interesting consequence of this first finding is a refutation of the argument: the smaller the market, the smaller the number of firms and the higher the level of concentration.

As suggested in Chapter 1, cross-country comparisons constitute a powerful test of the random-effect hypothesis in industrial economics.[8] This tells us that chance, not the extent of economies of scale in relation to the size of the market, explains the level of concentration. Our findings give some support to the random hypothesis. In the four largest countries, imports were very limited at the beginning of the 1960s. Hence, the very first observations for these countries in Figures 5.1 and 5.2 refer to rather closed economies. They show that concentration in West Germany and France was three times lower than in Italy, although their markets were only 1.3 and 1.15 times larger. Another illustrative example is the different concentration levels noticed in France and Britain, in spite of the fact that these two countries had passenger car markets of about the same size at the beginning of the 1960s.[9]

A striking finding concerns the changes in market structure over time. The figures for all the countries examined, except France, point to a downward trend in market concentration. The five indexes produce roughly the same picture of the downward trend. The trend is more pronounced in Italy (even

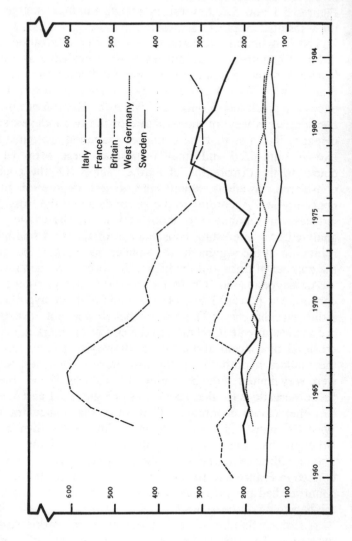

**Figure 5.1:** Changes in market structures in West European car-producing countries as measured by the Herfindahl index

120

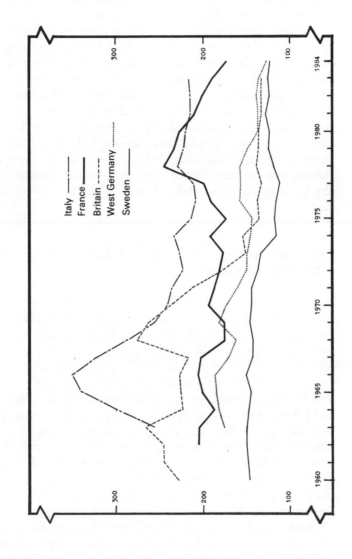

**Figure 5.2:** Changes in market structures in West European car-producing countries as measured by the Rosenbluth index

more with the *H* index) and Britain than in West Germany and Sweden. No clear trend can be noticed in France. This finding refutes the conclusion of a previous work concerned with the West European passenger car markets which stated that 'there is little doubt that, despite the rising incidence of imports on national markets, seller concentration has risen as well'.[10]

A final interesting finding is the low range of variation of the Swedish and, to a lesser extent, West German passenger car markets over the whole period studied. Such a low range of variation is the result of a slow erosion process of the dominant firms' market shares. In Sweden the same five firms (Volvo, Saab, Opel, Ford and Volkswagen) dominated the market over the whole period examined. Since the mid-1970s two other countries, Britain and to a lesser extent Italy, also show a low range of variation indicating small changes in the competitive conditions over time. France is the only country exhibiting non-negligible changes in market share distribution over the past decade.

## DETERMINANTS OF CHANGES IN MARKET STRUCTURES: EMPIRICAL EVIDENCE

Changes in market structure over time depend upon a complex of interacting factors involving the entry of firms (domestic or foreign), their growth (internal or external), their decline and their death (through exit or takeover). In Chapter 4 we concentrated on three factors, namely foreign entry, exit through takeover and external growth through merger. The reason for selecting these three factors is that they can be regarded as the main determinants of structural changes in markets characterised by high barriers to entry and a high degree of product differentiation. These two aspects explain the absence of influence — or the very limited influence — of two other factors, domestic entry and firm internal growth and decline, in passenger car markets. They justify the neglect of the latter in the empirical analysis. High barriers to entry explain the absence of domestic entry in the West European passenger car industry since the mid-1950s. The high degree of product differentiation combined with firm behaviour and the changing role of economies of scale over the product life cycle explain the loose relationship between the size of firms and their internal growth and decline. Another reason suggested by Richard Caves is that 'there is a strong tactical argument for putting the weight of further research efforts on these components of the identity that contribute most to explaining the variance of concentration'.[11]

## The models and the data

Using regression analysis we will adopt two rather complementary approaches. Both approaches take the Herfindahl and Rosenbluth indexes as the dependent variables. They attempt to see to what extent the variance of market structure over time can be ascribed to the entry of foreign firms (or its determinants in the second approach), to the exit of medium-sized firms and to large-scale mergers.

The first specification with imports as an explanatory variable is undoubtedly the most suitable for measuring the foreign-entry effect on market structure. The reason for having a second specification is that the use of imports as an explanatory variable in the first specification may result in a simultaneous equation bias. Specifically, measures of market structure that are assumed to be exogenous may themselves affect imports if they are a proxy for large firms' competitiveness: the larger the market shares of large domestic firms, the higher the measures of market structure and the lower the volume of import. However, the high explanatory power of the results obtained with the import specification and the fact that both specifications produce roughly the same results indicate that the first specification results can be regarded as reliable. The first approach can be expressed by the following equation:

$$\log H \,(\text{or } R) = \beta_1 + \beta_2 \log M + \beta_3 \, Tk + \beta_4 \, Mg \qquad (5.1)$$

Equation 5.1 splits up market structure changes into their component parts, foreign entry, death of small and medium-sized firms and large-scale mergers. The regressions must be viewed as identities rather than right–left causal relations. The behavioural forces behind the component parts were extensively analysed in Chapter 3 as regards imports and in Chapter 4 as regards the exit of small and medium-sized firms and large-scale mergers.

The presence of imports on the right-hand side of Equation 5.1 and its presence as a dependent variable in Equation 3.1 in Chapter 3 imply that the two equations form a recursive system.[12] Ordinary least squares (OLS) is an appropriate estimation procedure for each equation taken separately only if the error terms in Equations 3.1 and 5.1 are not correlated.[13] Equations 3.1 and 5.1 were estimated one at a time for each country examined. Simple correlation between the error terms amounted to 0.19, 0.13, 0.07, 0.06 and 0.06 for France, West Germany, Italy, Sweden and Britain, respectively. This low level of correlation suggests that Equations 3.1 and 5.1 can be estimated separately and that the regression results are reliable.

The import variable captures not only the foreign entry effect on market structure but also the destabilising effect of foreign entry on the distribution of market shares among domestic firms. Such an effect results from the fact that some domestic firms face more foreign competition than others because they produce brand models that are closer substitutes for foreign products.[14] As noted in Chapter 4, foreign entry is expected to promote more competitive market structures in spite of the presence of captive imports and dominant importing firms. Thus an increase in the volume of imports should lower the level of market concentration ($\beta_2 < 0$). The import variable is the same as used in Chapter 3.[15]

The 1960s wave of takeovers probably had a positive effect on the level of market concentration, since it resulted in the exit of medium-sized firms and the enlargement of large firms ($\beta_3 > 0$). The impact should be limited because of the rather small size of the absorbed firms.[16] To capture the effect of takeovers on market structures, a dummy variable taking on the value of 1 in the year of acquisition and 0 otherwise was used. The various takeovers are listed under Table 5.1. The exit of medium-sized firms was caused by an increase in foreign competition over a period of *several* years. The import variable in time-series studies does not capture this causal effect. The use of a dummy variable, the year of the takeover, seems therefore the most suitable method.

In Chapter 4, we analysed the determinants of the three mergers that occurred in the West European passenger car industry, namely Leyland and British Motor Holding, Peugeot and Citroën and Peugeot-Citroën and Chrysler-Europe.[17] Because of the large size of the firms involved in these mergers and their dominant position in the two domestic markets concerned, the merger variable is expected to have a substantial upward effect on the level of market concentration ($\beta_4 > 0$). The dummy variable used to capture this effect takes on the value of 0 up to the year preceding the merger and 1 thereafter. One reason motivates the adoption of a different procedure for mergers as compared with takeovers. The large size of firms involved in merger operations implies that these should alter market structure during the whole post-merger period and, thus, affect the intercept of the equation. Large-scale mergers may also influence foreign market structures. Merger variables in foreign countries turned out to be statistically insignificant and were omitted.

The second approach relates changes in market structure over time to changes in the determinants of imports (income, trade policy and domestic industry's competitiveness), to the exit of medium-sized firms and to large-scale mergers. The income, competitiveness, tariff and non-tariff barrier variables are the same as used in Chapter 3.[18] This second approach can be expressed by the following equation:

$$\log H \text{ (or } R) = \xi_1 + \xi_2 \log Y + \xi_3 \log S + \xi_4 \log T \\ + \xi_5 NTB + \xi_6 Tk + \xi_7 Mg \qquad (5.2)$$

The rapid rise in income noticed in Western Europe since the start of the integration process has resulted in a large increase in imports. This was extensively investigated in Chapter 3 in the case of passenger car imports. As suggested above, this increase in imports has probably brought about more competitive market structures. Thus a negative sign is expected between income and market concentration ($\xi_2 < 0$). The income effect is likely to vary greatly from country to country according to various influences of a change in income on imports, and to various influences of foreign entry on market structures. It should be added that the income variable may also capture the effect of a change in income upon the distribution of market shares among domestic firms.

An improved competitiveness should allow domestic firms to enlarge their market shares and restrain imports. As we are concerned with car-producing countries and as the largest firms in each market are domestic, a positive relation is expected between the competitiveness variable and market concentration ($\xi_3 > 0$).

A reduction in tariff barriers should increase the entry of foreign firms and bring about more competitive market structures despite the presence of captive imports and dominant importing firms. A positive correlation is expected between the tariff variable and market concentration ($\xi_4 > 0$). However, the correlation coefficient is likely to be hardly significant for the three original EEC countries. The reason for this is the lack of data on market structure for these three countries at the beginning of the 1960s, when substantial tariff cuts on EEC trade were implemented.

The introduction of non-tariff trade barriers blocks entry or renders it more difficult. Thus it is expected to have an upward effect on market concentration ($\xi_5 > 0$). The results of Chapter 3 suggest nevertheless that their effects on passenger car imports are limited because non-tariff barriers, such as source-specific quantitative restrictions and trade-impeding tax structures, 'leak'. They affect the composition of foreign entry but have only a marginal effect on its extent.

The takeover and merger variables are the same as those used in the first approach. Their effects on market structures should be similar in sign and order of magnitude ($\xi_6 > 0$ and $\xi_7 > 0$).

**Empirical results**

The results obtained with the two specifications are given in Table 5.1. The comments on the findings concern, first, the entry effect of international integration (and its determinants); second, the medium-sized firm exit effect; third, the large-scale merger effect.

The results obtained with the first specification show the importance of the rise in imports in shaping market structures. Furthermore, they point out the absence of large year-to-year shifts in market share distribution unexplained by changes in the international environment. The large rise in imports observed since the end of the 1950s gave rise to the decline in market concentration portrayed in the preceding section. The impact of import penetration on competitive conditions varies greatly from country to country. This explains the different market

# Table 5.1: Determinants of changes in market structure

### First Specification

| France | OBS: 1962–1984 |

(5.3)  $\log H = 8.152 - 0.235 \log M - 0.007\ Tk_1 + 0.315\ Mg_1 + 0.264\ Mg_2$
         (9.081)  (3.289)        (0.135)       (4.268)        (4.207)
         $R^2(\text{adj}) = 0.978$        $SEE = 0.062$        $DF = 18$

(5.4)  $\log R = 7.948 - 0.220 \log M - 0.009\ Tk_1 + 0.179\ Mg_1 + 0.181\ Mg_2$
         (10.375)  (3.602)       (0.209)       (2.698)        (3.232)
         $R^2(\text{adj}) = 0.985$        $SEE = 0.056$        $DF = 18$

| West Germany | OBS: 1963–1984 |

(5.5)  $\log H = 6.219 - 0.084 \log M + 0.056\ Tk_2 + 0.057\ Tk_3 - 0.052\ Tk_4$
         (12.468)  (2.230)        (1.199)       (1.089)        (0.989)
         $R^2\ (\text{adj}) = 0.985$        $SEE = 0.055$        $DF = 17$

(5.6)  $\log R = 6.256 - 0.087 \log M + 0.058\ Tk_2 + 0.081\ Tk_3$
         (13.49)  (2.483)        (1.222)       (1.711)
         $R^2(\text{adj}) = 0.985$        $SEE = 0.055$        $DF = 17$

| Italy | OBS: 1963–1983 |

(5.7)  $\log H = 9.751 - 0.295 \log M + 0.002\ Tk_5 + 0.05\ TK_6$
         (16.687)  (6.472)        (0.039)       (1.188)
         $R^2(\text{adj}) = 0.991$        $SEE = 0.05$        $DF = 17$

(5.8)  $\log R = 8.183 - 0.211 \log M - 0.007\ Tk_5 + 0.047\ Tk_6$
         (16.216)  (5.338)        (0.166)       (1.072)
         $R^2\ (\text{adj}) = 0.99$        $SEE = 0.051$        $DF = 17$

| Sweden | OBS: 1960–1984 |

(5.9)  $\log H = 5.916 - 0.083 \log M$
         (9.606)  (1.612)
         $R^2 = 0.989$        $SEE = 0.043$        $DF = 23$

(5.10)  $\log R = 5.742 - 0.057 \log M$
          (10.1)  (1.503)
          $R^2 = 0.986$        $SEE = 0.041$        $DF = 23$

| United Kingdom | OBS: 1960–1983 |

(5.11)  $\log H = 7.182 - 0.165 \log M + 0.024\ Tk_7 + 0.213\ Mg_3 + 0.07\ Tk_8$
          (17.353)  (4.784)        (0.437)       (2.339)        (0.914)
          $R^2(\text{adj}) = 0.982$        $SEE = 0.053$        $DF = 19$

(5.12)  $\log R' = 7.056 - 0.162 \log M + 0.013\ Tk_7 + 0.233\ Mg_3 - 0.001\ Tk_8$
          (11.546)  (3.242)        (0.172)       (1.754)        (0.0003)
          $R^2(\text{adj}) = 0.957$        $SEE = 0.076$        $DF = 19$

127

## Table 5.1 continued

### Second Specification

France           OBS: 1962–1984

(5.13) $\log H =$   $8.643 - 0.82 \ \log Y + 0.642 \log S + 0.082 \ Tk_1 + 0.235 \ Mg_1$
          (9.455) (4.269)      (4.242)      (1.335)      (3.845)

          $+ 0.24 \ Mg_2$
          (4.033)
          $R^2$(adj) $= 0.958$        $SEE = 0.062$        $DF = 17$

(5.14) $\log R =$   $8.857 - 0.797 \log Y + 0.522 \log S + 0.064 \ Tk_1 + 0.088 \ Mg_1$
          (11.381) (4.826)      (3.987)      (1.153)      (1.66)

          $+ 0.175 \ Mg_2$
          (3.391)
          $R^2$(adj) $= 0.955$        $SEE = 0.054$        $DF = 17$

West Germany           OBS: 1963–1984

(5.15) $\log H =$   $6.064 - 0.228 \log Y + 0.18 \log S + 0.042 \ Tk_2 + 0.081 \ Tk_3$
          (4.255) (1.636)      (1.016)      (0.901)      (1.786)
          $R^2$(adj) $= 0.989$        $SEE = 0.053$        $DF = 17$

(5.16) $\log R =$   $7.173 - 0.37 \ \log Y + 0.134 \log S + 0.052 \ Tk_2 + 0.09 \ Tk_3$
          (5.581) (2.984)      (0.834)      (1.233)      (2.143)
          $R^2$(adj) $= 0.989$        $SEE = 0.049$        $DF = 17$

Italy           OBS: 1963–1983

(5.17) $\log H =$   $10.107 - 0.657 \log Y - 0.007 \log S + 0.069 \ NTB$
          (5.935) (2.51)      (0.032)      (1.703)
          $R^2$(adj) $= 0.98$        $SEE = 0.075$        $DF = 17$

(5.18) $\log R =$   $8.119 - 0.389 \log Y - 0.078 \log S + 0.047 \ NTB$
          (5.954) (1.907)      (0.368)      (1.218)
          $R^2$(adj) $= 0.981$        $SEE = 0.069$        $DF = 17$

Sweden           OBS: 1960–1984

(5.19) $\log H =$   $6.695 - 0.399 \log Y + 0.023 \log T + 0.222 \log S + 0.09 \ NTB$
          (9.696) (3.057)      (0.596)      (3.126)      (1.557)
          $R^2$(adj) $= 0.750$    $DW = 1.911$    $SEE = 0.04$    $DF = 20$

(5.20) $\log R =$   $6.029 - 0.287 \log Y + 0.078 \log T + 0.181 \log S + 0.133 \ NTB$
          (9.096) (2.293)      (2.134)      (2.653)      (2.399)
          $R^2$(adj) $= 0.848$    $DW = 1.832$    $SEE = 0.039$    $DF = 20$

United Kingdom           OBS: 1960–1983

(5.21) $\log H =$   $11.7 \ \ - 1.056 \log Y + 0.084 \log T + 0.053 \log S$
          (4.06)   (2.444)      (1.808)      (0.459)

$$-0.164\ D(1960) + 0.243\ Mg_3 + 0.04\ Tk_7 - 0.073\ Tk_8$$
$$(2.649) \qquad (2.637) \qquad (0.666) \qquad (0.912)$$
$$R^2(\text{adj}) = 0.989 \qquad SEE = 0.051 \qquad DF = 16$$

(5.22)  $\log R =$  $12.297 - 1.201\ \log Y + 0.061\ \log T + 0.16\ \log S$
$$(2.868)\ (1.877) \qquad (0.868) \qquad (0.918)$$

$$-0.152\ D(1960) + 0.29\ Mg_3 + 0.053\ Tk_7 + 0.028\ Tk_8$$
$$(1.662) \qquad (2.066) \qquad (0.598) \qquad (0.239)$$
$$R^2(\text{adj}) = 0.974 \qquad SEE = 0.076 \qquad DF = 16$$

*Variables:* H, Herfindahl index; R, Rosenbluth index; M, numbers of passenger cars imported; Tk, takeovers (1, Panhard by Citroën in 1965; 2, Auto-Union by Volkswagen in 1966; 3, NSU by Volkswagen in 1969; 4, Glas by BMW in 1968; 5, Autobianchi by Fiat in 1968; 6, Lancia by Fiat in 1970; 7, Jaguar by BMC in 1966; 8, Rover by Leyland in 1967; Mg, large-scale mergers (1, Peugeot and Citroën in 1976; 2, Peugeot-Citroën and Chrysler-Europe in 1978; 3, Leyland and British Motor Corporation in 1968); Y, income variable; T, weighted tariff variable; S, competitiveness variable; NTB, non-tariff barrier variable; D (1960), dummy variable for Britain, 1960 = 1 and 0 otherwise.

The equations are estimated with the OLS method and for most of them corrected for serial correlation with the Cochrane–Orcutt procedure. The Durbin-Watson statistic is given for non-corrected equations. The critical values of the $t$-statistic (in parentheses) at the 5 and 10 per cent levels with a one-tailed test are $t(17) = 1.740$ and 1.333, and $t(16) = 1.753$ and 1.337.

structure profiles observed in the five countries under study and illustrated in Figures 5.1 and 5.2. Actually, a 10 per cent increase in imports led to a 2.35, 0.84, 2.95, 0.83 and 1.65 per cent decrease in market concentration (as measured by the H index) in France, West Germany, Italy, Sweden and Britain, respectively. A question that arises is, what are the reasons behind such large differences?

The size of the import coefficient depends mainly upon which firms face international competition: the larger the firms that lose portions of their market shares in the presence of foreign entry, the larger the size of the coefficient and vice versa. Behind the large Italian and French coefficients, there is thus a transfer of market shares from the leading firms (or firm) to the importing firms. The low coefficients in West Germany and Sweden suggest that the transfer of market shares took place between medium-sized and importing firms.

The size of the import coefficient and thus the competitive intensity of import inroads also depend upon the volume of captive imports; the larger this volume, the lower the competitive intensity of imports and vice versa. The relatively lower import coefficient in Britain (as compared with Italy and France) is probably the result of the large volume of captive imports in this country.

A third factor influences the size of the import coefficient: the more dominant the position of some importing firms on the domestic market, the more likely that the effects of competitive import inroads will be mitigated (or cancelled) by dominant importing firms' imports. As noted in Chapter 4, of the countries under study only Sweden is concerned by this pattern.[19] The results of Equations 5.9 and 5.10 confirm this by showing an import coefficient that is negative but low and significant only at the 10 per cent level.[20]

These results are roughly confirmed by those obtained from the second specification. The latter indicate that changes in income helped to bring about a more competitive market structure through their effects on foreign entry. The coefficients of the income variable are of the right sign and statistically significant at the 5 per cent level in all countries. They can be interpreted to mean that a 1 per cent increase in income led, other things being equal, to a 0.82, 0.23, 0.66, 0.4 and 1.06 per cent decrease in concentration (as measured by the $H$ index) in France, West Germany, Italy, Sweden and Britain, respectively. A surprising result is the relatively large coefficient in Britain as compared with the cross-country evidence provided by the first specification. A likely explanation is that income increase in Britain also led to the substitution of domestic cars of non-dominant firm(s) for other domestic cars of dominant firm(s).

The competitiveness variable is of the right sign in all countries except Italy, but statistically significant at the 5 per cent level only in France and Sweden. The size of the coefficient in these two countries (0.642 and 0.222 with the $H$ index) suggests that the influence of a change in the domestic industry's competitiveness differs according to the impact of import on market structure. The results for West Germany, Italy and Britain tell us that changes in the domestic industry's competitiveness are not (or to only a limited extent) responsible for changes in market share distribution. A possible explanation is the price policy of firms (price leadership or other forms of collusive practices), which explains why the relative market prices of domestic and foreign firms do not reflect their relative competitiveness. Note also that for West Germany and Britain these results conform to those obtained in Chapter 3, where it was shown that changes in the domestic industry's competitiveness do not explain changes in imports.[21]

The tariff variable is of the right sign and statistically significant only in Sweden and Britain. The absence of significance in France, West Germany and Italy probably originates in the lack of data on market structure at the beginning of the 1960s. The tariff variable for these countries was dropped in the reported regression results. The absence of significance of the British coefficient when the $R$ index is considered is more surprising because of the significant role of the tariff variable in explaining import changes during the period covered by the market structure analysis.[22] A likely explanation is the large volume of captive imports that entered the British market in the wake of tariff abolition between the EEC and Britain and cancelled the competitive effect of non-captive import inroads.

An interesting finding is the statistical significance of the tariff variable in explaining changes in market structure in Sweden (see Equation 1.20). In Chapter 3 no influence of tariff policy on imports could be detected in Sweden.[23] A reason behind these (at first sight, contradictory) findings is that the last two decades' tariff cuts affected the composition of Swedish imports but not their volume. Tariff changes might have resulted in a transfer of market shares from the three oligopolistic importing firms (Opel, Ford and Volkswagen) to the relatively small importing firms.[24] Two complementary factors may explain this result. First there may exist a low cross-elasticity of substitution between Swedish and foreign passenger cars but a high cross-elasticity between different sorts of imported passenger cars. Second, as a result of price leadership practices, the three oligopolistic importing firms did not incorporate the tariff reductions that took place between 1973 and 1977 in their local prices.

Another reason behind the absence of statistical significance of the tariff variable in Italy is the introduction of purchase taxes discriminating against imports during the period of tariff removal within the EEC. It is supported by Equation 1.17. This shows that the coefficient of the non-tariff variable reflecting changes in the Italian tax structure is of the right sign and statistically significant at the 10 per cent level. The other non-tariff variables included in the second specification are not significant except for Sweden. In this country, the results point out the significant effect of the introduction of technical obstacles to trade on foreign entry. The *NTB* variables reflecting the voluntary export restraint in West Germany in 1981 and 1982 and the marketing agreement in Britain between 1975 and 1984 turned out to be insignificant and were dropped. A main reason behind the low and insignificant *NTB* coefficients is probably that most non-tariff restrictions 'leak' and affect the country composition of foreign entry, leaving the volume of total foreign entry rather unchanged.

An important aspect of the results is the small temporal shifts in market share distribution that are unexplained by changes in the international environment and the fact that concentration in a given year is strongly dependent upon concentration the year before. Such a result is illustrated by the high explanatory power of the regressions corrected with the Cochrane–Orcutt procedure. It can depend upon three sets of factors. First, it can be caused by the absence of destabilising factors such as a high rate of growth of demand or rapid changes in technology. Second, it can originate in the existence of product differentiation and brand loyalty that reduce responsiveness to price and product quality changes. Third, it can be brought about by the presence of some form of collusion (tacit or overt) between firms. The reason for this is that stability in market shares is expected to increase as collusion becomes more complete and more effective, and vice versa.[25]

The high rate of growth of demand observed in all countries, with the exception of Sweden, up to the end of the 1970s and the changes in technology that have occurred in the motor industry since the mid-1970s cast some doubt on the influence of the first set of factors.[26] As regards product differentiation, its impact on market share stability is undeniable but should not be exaggerated since, as illustrated in Chapter 2 in relation to imports, consumers are not indifferent to changes in the relative prices of passenger cars or to new car models. Thus, the tentative conclusion that emerges is that market share stability is the result of a combination of several factors such as absence of vigorous price competition or presence of some form of collusion, and some degree of consumer brand loyalty.

As pointed out earlier, the wave of takeovers experienced by the West European industry during the second half of the 1960s was caused by the process of international integration, which forced small inefficient car manufacturers out of business. The regression results of Table 5.1 show that the effects of the 1960s takeovers on market structures were rather small. Actually, the takeover variables are statistically significant only for the takeover of NSU by Volkswagen in West Germany (see for example Equations 5.15 and 5.16). The size of the coefficients of the takeover variable is nevertheless limited. According to Equations 5.15 and 5.16, the takeover of NSU by Volkswagen in 1969 resulted in a 14- and 15-point increase in market concentration in West Germany. In view of the substantial competitive effects of import inroads, we can thus reject the U-shape hypothesis on the relationship between integration and market concentration for all countries except France.

As illustrated in the preceding chapter, large-scale mergers in the British and French passenger car industries were mainly the result of public and large firm policy. The exit of Citroën as an independent firm was also the result of the integration process. Our findings show that large-scale mergers were an important source of variation of market structures over time. According to the results obtained with the second specification and the Herfindahl index, the mergers between Leyland and BMC, Peugeot and Citroën, and Peugeot-Citroën and Chrysler-Europe are responsible for a 58-, 51- and 67-point increase in the level of market concentration in 1968, 1976 and 1978, respectively. The upward effect of the two French mergers on the level of market concentration is in absolute value lower than the downward effect caused by the rise in import penetration. (French imports were multiplied by 10 during the 1963–1984 period.) This finding means that the experience of the French passenger car market also leads to the rejection of the U-shape hypothesis between integration and concentration.

A final interesting result concerns the concentration measures. The regression results produced with the Herfindahl and Rosenbluth indexes are roughly similar in sign, statistical significance and order of magnitude. However, a certain number of differences can be noticed. For example, the tariff variable in Sweden and Britain is statistically significant with only one of the indexes. Another example is the very different level of statistical significance obtained in several cases with the two indexes. These differences support the view that the choice of concentration index is not a negligible matter.[27]

## SUMMARY AND CONCLUSIONS

The main conclusion that emerges from this chapter concerns the great importance of international factors in explaining changes in market structure over time. It should be stressed that the period examined brought considerable changes in the international environment. Hence the determinants of changes in market structures are not just a first-difference version of the determinants of their levels before the start of the integration process.

In the first part of the present chapter, it was shown that concentration has decreased in most markets since the very beginning of the 1960s. In the second part, it was seen that the process of integration in Western Europe was the main factor behind this decrease and the emergence of more competitive market structures. An important aspect of the results concerns the very different impact of a similar change in imports, or its determinants, on market structure and competition in the different countries under study. Such a result means that the effect of foreign competition on domestic firms varies from country to country. This being so, changes in the international environment may be expected to induce various responses from the domestic firms in terms of price policy, lobbying activity and product policy. The analysis of corporate price policy in Chapter 7 will shed some light on this issue.

The rise in foreign competition following from international integration prompted takeovers of small and medium-sized firms by larger firms during the second half of the 1960s. It was shown that these takeover operations affected market concentration only marginally. In Chapter 4 we provided some evidence of the shift of public policy from trade policy to industrial policy in the wake of international integration. Furthermore, we illustrated the interplay between public and firm policies in bringing about large-scale mergers in Britain and France. Our findings in the present chapter show that large-scale mergers significantly altered market structures in Britain, and even more so in France. In both countries their effect on market structure was nevertheless smaller than the opposite competitive effect of rising import penetration.

All this suggests that the U-shape hypothesis between international integration and market concentration can be rejected for all countries. The process of integration has favoured the emergence of more competitive market structures and contributed to make collusion less likely. This constitutes one of the so-called dynamic effects of integration. As mentioned in the preceding chapter, such a result has worthwhile implications for the welfare outcome of integration. It indicates that the welfare gains to consumers of increased imports are unlikely to be cancelled out by the possible welfare losses that may result from an increase in concentration.

In most West European countries there are competition policies that are directed towards market structure. Their purpose is to combat increases in concentration in order to curb its possible effects on economic performances. The empirical findings of the present chapter suggest that a liberal trade policy can be considered an effective competitive policy that does not incur costs (no anti-trust authorities).

A substantive finding of the second part is the small size of year-to-year changes in market structures that are not accounted for by the explanatory variables included in the model. It seems reasonable to argue that the stability of market shares is the result of the absence of vigorous competition combined with the presence of product differentiation and brand loyalty. This combination explains the low range of variation of market structure in Sweden and West Germany during the whole period examined and in Britain and Italy since the mid-1970s. As a result, there have been limited dynamic competitive gains in these countries over the past decade.

Furthermore, the stability in the distribution of market shares between firms of different size indicates that scale advantages or disadvantages do not affect market share distribution. This confirms that economies of scale are not responsible for changes in market structure over time, apart from their influence on small and medium-sized firm exit during the second half of the 1960s.

The stability of market shares also raises the question of the role of market conduct, which is embodied in changes in market structure over time. During the course of the study, several patterns of conduct were found to exert a worthwhile influence on market structure. The merger policy of large firms in cooperation with public policy, product differentiation policy, price policy and all kinds of measures used by firms to relax the scale constraint are the main channels through which firm conduct reshapes market structure. This aspect of the results supports

135

the view that the structure–conduct relation is not a one-way relationship: conduct is not only influenced by the structural elements that surround firms but feeds back substantially into them.

In the present chapter, we have examined the determinants of changes in market stucture in West European car-producing countries. On inspecting these determinants, it was found that today's market structure is dependent upon several, often interacting factors such as yesterday's market structure, today's market conduct (past market conduct is embodied in yesterday's market structure), public industrial and merger policy, trade policy and international integration as well as structural elements such as product differentiation. A central concern of the next two chapters will be to see whether, to what extent and how market structure affects corporate behaviour and price policy in an internationally integrated economy.

## NOTES

1. See for example Caves (1976), p. 4:

I shall argue that there is a strong case for shifting some of the emphasis in research to the determinants of market structure, and that parallel investigation in several countries and the use of cross-country comparative analysis provide particularly attractive strategies for research in this area.

See also Wahlroos (1980), p. 176.
2. On concentration measures, see Stigler (1968), Marfels (1972a, 1972b, 1975) and Phlips (1975).
3. Marfels (1972a, 1972b, 1975) and Phlips (1975).
4. Ibid.
5. For a survey of concentration studies in OECD countries, see OECD (1979).
6. See Table 4.4 (Sources), this volume.
7. See Chapter 4, p. 104.
8. See Chapter 1, p. 6.
9. In 1963 new car registration in West Germany, Italy, France and Britain amounted to 1,271,000, 916,600, 1,047,000 and 979,000, respectively. L'Argus de l'automobile et des locomotions, yearly statistical issue (1964).
10. Adams (1981), p. 204.
11. Caves (1976), p. 11.
12. See Chapter 3, p. 69.
13. See Pindyck and Rubinfeld (1981), p. 322.
14. For an illustration, see Table 4.7.
15. See Chapter 3, p. 69.

16. See Table 4.4.
17. See Chapter 4, pp. 103–9.
18. See Chapter 3, pp. 69–72.
19. See Chapter 4, pp. 93–94.
20. To remove the impact of dominant importing firms' imports in Sweden, we defined a new import variable ($NOM$, non-oligopolistic imports) equal to all imports minus imports by Opel, Ford and Volkswagen. The coefficients of the new import variable are of the right sign and much more significant than in Equations 5.9 and 5.10:

$$\log H = 6.388 - 0.132 \log NOM$$
$$(16.616) \quad (3.822)$$

$$R^2 = 0.989 \qquad SEE = 0.041 \qquad DF = 23 \qquad (5.23)$$

$$\log R = 5.968 - 0.097 \log NOM$$
$$(13.813) \quad (2.501)$$

$$R^2 = 0.991 \qquad SEE = 0.039 \qquad DF = 23 \qquad (5.24)$$

21. See Chapter 3, pp. 74–75.
22. See Chapter 3, p. 75.
23. Ibid.
24. A proof of this is given by the estimation of the model used in Chapter 3 with, as the dependent variable, the number of passenger cars imported by the non-oligopolistic importing firms instead of total imports and the same explanatory variables. The regression covers the same period, 1958–1984. The results (with $t$-statistics in parentheses) are as follows:

$$\log NOM = 5.832 + 1.24 \log Y - 0.311 \log T - 0.479 \log S$$
$$(2.477) \quad (2.748) \qquad (2.236) \qquad (1.751)$$

$$- 0.673 \, NTB \qquad\qquad\qquad (5.25)$$
$$(3.102)$$

$$R^2 \text{(adj)} = 0.845 \qquad DW = 1.87 \qquad SEE = 0.155$$

The equation produces results that are statistically significant and identical in coefficient sign and order of magnitude to the results of equations 3.8 and 3.9 except for the tariff and non-tariff barrier variables. The tariff variable, which is now statistically significant, shows that tariff policy affected non-oligopolistic imports in Sweden. The larger $NTB$ coefficient (0.7 instead of 0.35) and the higher degree of statistical significance in the present specification confirm that technical barriers are more effective against medium- and small-sized firms than against large importing firms.

25. On the relation between market share stability, product differentiation and collusion, see Caves and Porter (1978), pp. 289–313; Gort (1963), pp. 51–63; McGuckin (1972), pp. 363–70; and Jacoby (1964), pp. 83–107.
26. See Figure 3.4 and pp. 91–92.
27. The same conclusion is reached in another study. See Kwoka (1981).

137

# 6

# International Integration, Market Imperfections and Prices

In the previous chapters of the present work, emphasis has been placed on the process of integration and its impact on trade and competition. The present chapter concentrates on economic integration regarded as a state of affairs.[1] Its main purpose is to analyse how the removal of trade barriers between national economies affects the formation of prices in member countries.

According to the well-accepted definition of Augustin Cournot, a market is 'not a certain place where purchases and sales are carried on, but the entire territory of which the parts are so united by the relations of unrestricted commerce that prices there take the same level throughout, with ease and rapidity'.[2] A central concern of the present chapter is to see whether prices are identical throughout the integrated area or, in other words, whether integration results in the creation of an enlarged market out of several national markets.[3] Emphasis is laid on the role of different forms of integration and of two market imperfections, imperfectly competitive market structures and product differentiation. The reason for selecting these two factors is twofold. First, both are main characteristics of the passenger car industry. Second, both are expected to affect the price outcome of integration and stand in the way of the completion of a truly integrated enlarged market.

The chapter is divided into three parts. In the first part we will present the expected price effects of different forms of international integration with the help of a partial equilibrium model. Our main concern will be to show how the establishment of a customs union or a free-trade area affects prices when competitive conditions prevail in the markets. We will focus more particularly on the free-trade area case because of its greater relevance for the analysis of integration since the breakdown of the customs union in the mid-1970s.

The second part is concerned with the interplay between international integration and market structure in affecting prices. We will show how the introduction of imperfectly competitive market structures into the analysis changes the expected effects of integration on prices. Another aspect that will be examined is the institutional condition necessary for price disparities to arise and persist over time.

The third part concentrates on the role of product differentiation. Its purpose is to see how the existence of product differentiation changes what was said above on the price outcome of imperfectly competitive market structures. We will attempt to answer three questions. First, does product differentiation favour the emergence of price disparities among member countries of a tariff-unified area? Second, does the growth of intra-trade in product-differentiated markets create incentives for price leadership practices that lead to price disparities? Third, what is the necessary condition for price disparities in product-differentiated markets to last?

In the next chapter we will illustrate in detail the price policy of passenger car manufacturers and test the relevance of the different hypotheses put forward in the present chapter.

## INTERNATIONAL INTEGRATION AND PRICES

Since the late 1950s and the early 1960s, European trade policy has evolved through a number of stages the purpose of which was to free intra-European trade and to create a large and unified economic area. This process was expected to lead to an intensification of competition among West European firms and, in the long run, to the emergence of competitive product prices throughout the whole integrated area.

As regards the effects of international integration on product prices, economic theory tells us that they can differ according to the form of the economic association, that is whether the countries involved decide to form a customs union or a free-trade area.

In the customs union case, the suppression of trade barriers between the member countries and the fixation of a common external tariff with third countries result in a common price throughout the whole customs union area. In the case of the free-trade area, the price of the same commodity may in some cases differ in the member countries. Two characteristics of free-trade areas explain this result. The first is the likely existence of different tariff rates on trade with third countries. These differences are the result of the power that each member country retains to fix its own tariff rate on trade with third countries. The second is the existence of rules of origin that prevent the deflection of trade, which should have levelled out eventual price disparities among the members of the free-trade area.

The effect of customs union versus free-trade area on prices can be illustrated with the help of a two-country, one-product, partial equilibrium model (see Figures 6.1 and 6.2).[4] Let country $A$ be an efficient producer of the product $X$ and country $B$ be a less efficient producer of the same product $X$. The two countries have different demand schedules and the world's lowest-cost producer remains outside the economic union. Country $B$ is protected by a relatively high tariff $T_b$ while country $A$ is insulated by a lower but prohibitive tariff $T_a$.[5] Before the integration, country $B$ produces $OL$, consumes $OM$ at price $P_{tb}$ and imports $LM$ from the world's lowest-cost producer at price $P_w$. For its part, country $A$ produces and consumes $OR$ at the pre-association equilibrium price $P_{ta}$. Note that $A$ and $B$ together satisfy the small-country assumption and that $P_w$ is exogenously given.

## Customs union

Countries $A$ and $B$ decide to form a customs union. They eliminate their internal tariffs and establish a common external tariff $CET$. Let this tariff be equal to the unweighted average of the pre-union tariffs, as was actually the case when the EEC was formed. The outcome of integration is illustrated in Figure 6.1.

Once the customs union is established, a single equilibrium price prevails over the whole integrated area. Country $A$ produces $OE$, consumes $OF$ and exports $EF$. For its part, country $B$ produces $OG$, consumes $OH$ and imports $GH$. The post-integration equilibrium price depends upon the demand and supply conditions within the customs union. Nevertheless,

**Figure 6.1:** Customs union and price

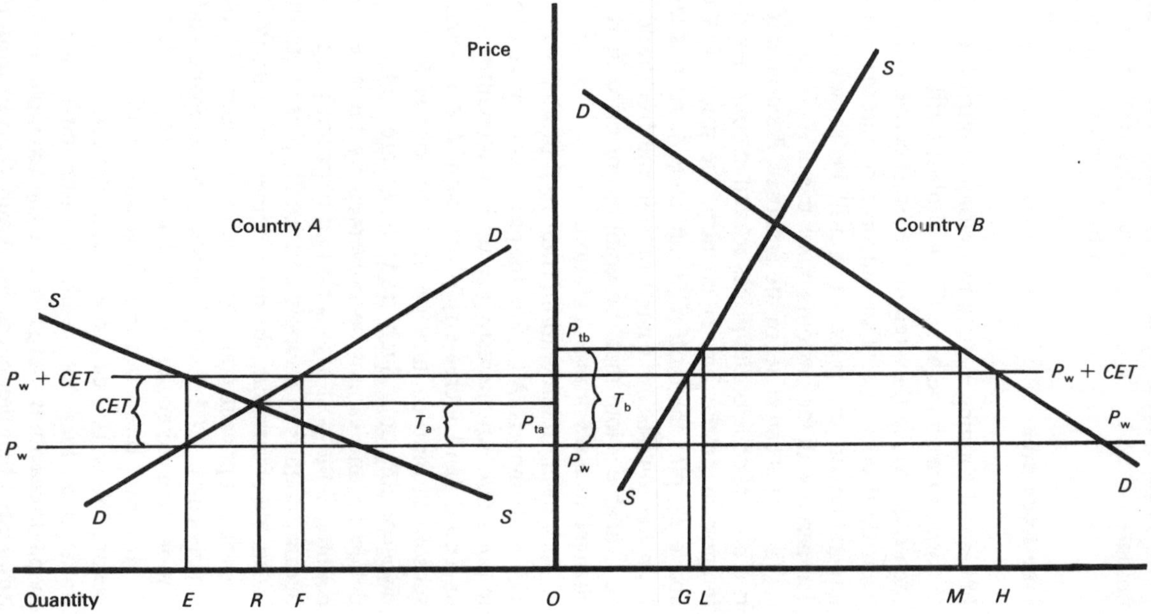

this price will never rise above the world's price $P_w$ plus the common external tariff *CET*, which constitutes the upper limit of the equilibrium price for the product $X$ in the whole customs union.

### Free-trade area

Instead of forming a customs union, countries $A$ and $B$ decide to form a free-trade area. They abolish tariffs on imports from each other while they retain their respective tariffs on imports from third countries. The outcome of international economic integration on the price of $X$ will be somewhat different as compared with the customs union case.

Two cases can arise. In the first case, illustrated in Figure 6.2, two distinct equilibrium prices prevail in countries $A$ and $B$ after integration. In the former country, the price of $X$ cannot rise above $P_w$ plus the tariff $T_a$ (that is, $P_{ta}$). At this level imports from the lowest-cost source outside the free-trade area would be available. Note that the equilibrium price in $A$ will not be changed as a result of integration.

As a result of integration, country $B$ produces $ON$, consumes $OV$ and imports $NV$. For its part, country $A$ consumes and imports $OR$. An interesting result is that country $A$ exports now its entire (and increased) production $OZ$ to country $B$ and substitutes third-country products for domestic products in its own consumption. Such trade flows are called indirect trade deflection and cannot be prevented by the rules of origin. In country $B$ the post-association equilibrium price will be higher because country $A$'s supply at price $P_w$ plus the tariff $T_a$ ($P_{ta}$) is incapable of satisfying the extra demand in country $B$. The post-association price in country $B$ will be $P_b$ where $A$'s and $B$'s joint supply curve, $S(A + B)$, intersects $B$'s demand and where $B$'s import demand equals $A$'s production ($OZ = NV$).

However, this is not the whole story and a second case may occur. The second case means that the establishment of a free-trade area does not result in price differences among the member countries. As stated in the example above, the price differential between countries $A$ and $B$ arises from the incapacity of country $A$'s supply to satisfy country $B$'s extra demand at price $P_w$ plus the tariff $T_a$ ($P_{ta}$). It arises, also, from the existence of a rule of origin that prevents the deflection of trade, that

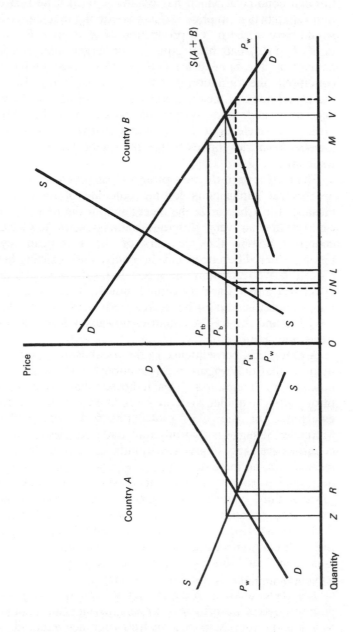

**Figure 6.2:** Free-trade area and price

is imports from the lowest-cost source outside the association through country $A$ which has the lower tariff. The first condition suggests that no price differential among member countries would have arisen if $A$'s production of $X$ at price $P_w$ plus the tariff $T_a$ ($P_{ta}$) had been equal to or larger than $B$'s import demand at the same price ($OR \geqslant JY$). Thus, under certain conditions, the formation of a free-trade area may also lead to the equalisation of member countries' prices and to the emergence of a single-price system throughout the whole economic area. This single price is equivalent to the lower of the two member countries' prices before the establishment of the free-trade area.

The drift toward the new protectionism over the past decade has several implications for the outcome of integration. As illustrated in Chapter 2, the emergence of the new protectionism resulted in very different trade policies towards third countries among the members of the European 'customs union'.[6] Such differences and the equivalence existing between a quantitative restriction and a certain tariff level as far as their effects on imports are concerned indicate that the EEC is no longer a customs union but a free-trade area.[7] By implication, the EEC and the EFTA countries nowadays form an enlarged free-trade area.

A theoretical consequence of the breakdown of the customs union is that only Figure 6.2 is suitable for the analysis of the outcome of integration. This indicates that price disparities throughout the unified area are more likely now than before the emergence of the new protectionism in the mid-1970s. Moreover, it suggests that different trade policies towards third countries are likely to give rise to indirect trade deflection. This means, first, an increase in imports from a partner country for the member country having the most restrictive trade policy towards third countries and, second, an increase in imports from third countries for the least protected member country. Such a result supports the view that a source-specific quantitative restriction introduced by only one member of a free-trade area 'leaks' and mostly affects the composition of imports, leaving the volume of total imports unchanged.

The above analysis of the impact of economic integration on domestic prices nevertheless presents certain limitations which stem largely from the partial analysis approach adopted. Firstly, the method concentrates on the direct effect of an economic association on a single final product's price. It ignores the secondary repercussions that may affect this price through other final products' or inputs' prices. Secondly, the small-country assumption implies that the formation of an economic association does not affect the terms of trade of the member countries. This is hardly a realistic assumption. The increase in imports in the wake of tariff abolition or decrease can only by chance be matched by a corresponding increase in exports that leaves the terms of trade unchanged.

In addition, the partial equilibrium analysis above assumes that competitive market conditions prevail throughout the entire area of the economic association. This, however, need not be the case. It might be specially important to see whether the results on price convergence hold when the analysis takes into account non-competitive market conditions.

## MARKET STRUCTURE AND PRICES

Market structures can influence international trade in different ways. Firstly, non-competitive market forms may have an impact on firms' pricing policies which in turn may affect trade flows. For example, the highly concentrated nature of some markets is likely to make it easier for a few firms to escape the free play of competitive forces. They may dominate the domestic market and affect international trade flows through price discrimination between the domestic and foreign markets. Empirical evidence suggests that price discrimination between various national markets is common in international trade and more widely practised by West European firms than by US or Japanese firms.[8]

### Monopoly

Price elasticities among the members of an economic association may vary according to different income structures, preferences or availability of substitute products. Such differences may prompt large industrial companies to charge different prices for the same product, higher prices in countries with low price elasticities and lower prices in countries with high price elasticities. Price discrimination policy is compatible with profit-maximising behaviour. It is illustrated in Figure 6.3 in the monopoly case.[9]

Let $DD$ be the domestic demand curve, $MR$ be the marginal revenue curve derived from it and $MC$ be the domestic monopolist marginal cost curve. First, we assume that the domestic market is not protected by any barrier to trade and thus that the world price prevails in the domestic market. In this case, the monopolist is a price-taker and maximises his or her profit at the world price $P_w$. $OQ_2$ is the quantity produced, $Q_1Q_2$ is the quantity exported and $OQ_1$ the quantity sold on the domestic market. Note that in such a case no differences exist between a monopolist and a competitive industry as regards production and export.

**Figure 6.3:** Monopoly and price

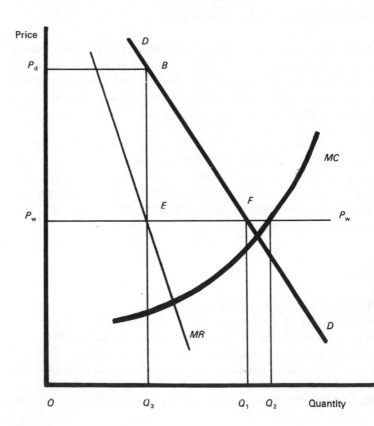

Suppose now that the monopolist can, for some reason, segment his markets and prevent the world price from prevailing in the domestic market. In order to maximise his profit, he will equate marginal revenue with marginal cost in both home and export markets. This will be done by producing $OQ_2$ and by charging two different prices, $P_d$ at home and $P_w$ on the export market. The price difference that arises for the same product will persist as long as a trade barrier permits the monopolist to set a domestic price that is higher than the world price. The quantity produced does not change, but the monopolist now exports $Q_3Q_2$ and only sells $OQ_3$ on the domestic market. An interesting result emerges, namely that a monopolist exports more than a competitive industry if he can discriminate between the domestic and foreign markets.

This result has two important implications. First, assuming that the maximisation of export revenues is one of the government objectives, it increases the opportunity for corporate lobbying activities to succeed in obtaining some form of public protection. Second, it justifies a more passive government policy towards firms that depart in varying degrees from conditions of pure competition on the domestic market. The reason for this is that some form of import protection or higher domestic prices improves the export performance of domestic industries and facilitates the realisation of one of the main objectives of industrial policy in West European countries.[10] Note that this might be particularly true in countries like France, Italy or Britain which, in order to combat chronic balance of payments deficits, are more eager to increase exports.

The example above shows that market structures can generate price differences among members of an 'integrated' economic area provided that there are some non-tariff barriers to trade among members (since tariff barriers are prohibited in customs unions or free-trade areas). The numerous non-tariff barriers that have arisen since the mid-1970s or still exist 25 years after the creation of the Common Market and the European Free-Trade Area suggest that this necessary condition for the emergence and persistence of price differences is still fulfilled in many West European markets. This was illustrated in Chapter 2 in the case of passenger car trade and is confirmed by several studies. For example, the head of the division for 'Safeguard measures and removal of non-tariff barriers' in the European Commission gives a list of 29 measures of neo-protectionist character that impede the free flow of goods within the EEC.[11] This list comprises measures such as frontier control, import formalities, obligation to have a representative established on the territory of the importing member state, and so on. It is neither exhaustive nor definitive since 'the fertile imagination of the public authorities will never cease to amaze us'.[12]

To illustrate the impact of market structure on prices in an 'integrated area', we have used the monopoly case. However, this is only a rough approximation to reality. In fact, most markets exhibit forms of competition in which a few relatively large sellers supply the lion's share of output in the market that they serve. In other words, most markets belong to an intermediate form of competition between the two standard cases of pure competition and monopoly. One might wonder, therefore, whether the presence of only a few sellers affects the results obtained in the monopoly case as regards the possible emergence of price disparities among union members.

## Oligopoly

Although oligopolistic market structures conform more closely to what is observed in most marketplaces, economic theory has mainly concentrated its attention on either monopoly or perfectly competitive market structures.[13] The reason behind this partial neglect is probably the fuzziness surrounding oligopoly theory with regard to prices and output. There are nevertheless a certain number of tentative works that attempt to analyse how interdependence among large firms is likely to affect price and output in a market.[14]

Before making any commitment to collective action, the few firms acting in a market will balance the prospective gains from such action against its costs. If costs are large relative to gains, firms would see competition as more lucrative than collusion and the market would remain competitive. In the opposite case, firms would strive to collude. Thus it might be important to see how market structure affects the likelihood of collusion through its impact on costs and benefits.

The incentive for a few sellers to behave as a monopolist in order to maximise their combined profits may be represented in Figure 6.3 by the rectangle $P_w P_d BE$. This corresponds to an income transfer from domestic consumers to the organised sellers. How much each collusive firm will benefit from this transfer depends upon the size of the market group. The larger the number of firms that will benefit from the income transfer, the smaller the share that will accrue to the individual firms. This implies that the incentives for the firms to act as a monopolist are all the more important when the number of firms in a market is small and vice versa. Collusive action is thus more frequent in markets with few sellers than in markets with numerous sellers.[15]

The number of firms in a market affects the likelihood of collusion in another way: the smaller the number of firms, the lower the cost of reaching and policing a collusive arrangement and the more likely this agreement.

The costs of attaining an agreement are positively related to the number of firms that attempt to organise due to the costly time-consuming process of negotiations in large groups. The role of these coordination costs in affecting the likelihood of collusion is all the more determinant since the collusive firms are forced to renegotiate continuously. This may be the result of frequent and unexpected changes in market conditions such as changes in demand or in production costs. All this suggests that collusive agreements between a few partners are easier to reach and as a consequence more likely, particularly when market conditions are stable over time.

There is an incentive for individual firms to break the collusive agreement.[16] If one of the firms can secretly violate the agreement and increase its output up to the point where the cost of producing another unit exceeds the price of that unit, it will gain larger profits than by conforming to the agreement. This vulnerability of collusive agreements to price violations means that the policing of agreements is a necessary condition of their durable enforcement. We may expect the cost of policing to influence the likelihood of collusion. The higher this cost, the less likely is collusion. It is easier to determine what the different firms are doing and to detect at an early stage any secret price-cutting when the number of firms in the marketplace is small. This suggests that the cost of policing an agreement is a negative function of the number of firms. Hence, the striking point that emerges is that collusive agreements ought to be more frequent and more stable in markets with few sellers.

Other factors such as the price elasticity of market demand, the presence of different production costs among the firms in the market, the fear of government intervention or the fear of new entry may also affect the likelihood of collusion. We have ignored them in order to concentrate on the impact of small numbers on collective behaviour and pricing policy.[17]

Two other aspects of collusion have also been ignored above: the decision variable and the form of collusion. The former tells us whether firms will agree on price or on quantity. The latter tells us whether firms will engage in overt collusion or in tacit collusion such as price leadership. In respect to our main purpose, this neglect is not too worrying. Whatever the decision variable and the form of cooperation, the effect of collusion on price should rather be the same.[18] Nevertheless, it may be worth adding two points. First, in order to be successful, price collusion between oligopolistic firms should also entail an agreement on quantity so that the collusive price can be achieved. Second, the form of collusion can in fact influence the cost of collusion and accordingly its likelihood.

## Barriers to reimport

In open economies such as those forming an economic union, price agreements between firms in order to achieve the joint profit-maximisation goal cannot be successful if the domestic market is not protected against foreign rivals. Actually, no protection means that the foreign competitive price prevails in the domestic market (foreign supply is assumed to be competitive). If there is no natural protection provided by substantial transport costs, collusive firms will also be in need of a collective good, for example a non-tariff barrier. The latter allows firms to raise their prices above their costs in the domestic market and to price-discriminate between the home and foreign markets. It is thus likely that collusive firms will also strive to obtain 'favourable' obstacles to trade and in this way build a form of *cordon sanitaire* around the domestic market. This permits firms to charge a higher price at home, to shift more of their production to the foreign markets and to gain more revenue than before at the expense of domestic consumers.

Regarding the relationship between international market integration, market structures and prices, the above arguments suggest that price disparities may arise in an 'integrated' economic area provided that market structures result in non-competitive behaviour among firms and that there is some kind of barrier to internal trade. This result is obtained when the analysis deals with a homogeneous product, that is when home products are perfect substitutes for foreign products. However, this need not be the case. It might be interesting to see whether the above results hold when the differentiated nature of most products is taken into account.

## PRODUCT DIFFERENTIATION, MARKET STRUCTURE AND PRICES

A striking feature of most markets for consumer durables (cars, consumer electronics, electrical goods, etc.) in industrialised countries is that products are highly differentiated. Product differentiation is the result of either real differences in the inherent characteristics of the products or imaginary differences due to advertisting or selling activities. Differentiated products are imperfect substitutes for one another, although they belong to the same industry. This means that the responsiveness among consumers to changes in the relative prices of such products can be rather limited.

Product differentiation has two main sources. Firstly, it is the result of different consumer preferences which in turn are the product of a combination of historical, sociological and economic factors. Among the latter factors, the level of per capita income and the structure of income distribution (more or less even) play a determinant role. Secondly, it is the result of the product policy of firms whose horizons are often limited to the domestic markets, i.e. to the national tastes. However, for products whose production is subject to large economies of scale, the existence of national preferences is a necessary but not sufficient condition for their production by domestic firms. Another factor is the size of the domestic market, which should be large enough to make home production viable.[19]

The passenger car industry provides an outstanding example of a highly differentiated product whose production is subject to large economies of scale.[20] The design of most passenger cars reflects different consumer preferences in the countries of production; for example, there are preferences for two-door cars in West Germany, for four-door cars in France, for cars

151

able to face cold winters and adapted to countries with wide, straight roads in Sweden or for cars with limited displacement in Italy.[21] Further, the large economies of scale in production explain the location of the industry in relatively large countries where a substantial demand for the product exists.

One of the main consequences of product differentiation is that products originating in different firms and countries can be rather different in the eyes of consumers although they require the same inputs and are close substitutes in use. The passenger car industry provides a good illustration of this point since a low elasticity of substitution exists between the different passenger cars. For example, a decrease in the price of high-quality cars is likely to hardly affect the demand for low-quality cars.

The product policy of the main West European car manufacturers is illustrated in Figure 6.4. The larger proportion of small and light cars in the production mix of British, Italian and French firms confirms that the level of per capita income in the home country is one of the main factors behind firm product policy.

With regard to the interaction between economic integration, market structures and prices, the presence of product differentiation in a market has two important implications: intra-industry trade competition and some degree of price insulation.

### Intra-trade and price insulation

The main effect upon the pattern of international trade of the differentiated nature of many consumer durables whose production entails large economies of scale, is the export by a country of brands that are most popular with its own population and the import of brands that appeal to minority tastes. This phenomenon, which has been called intra-industry trade or two-way trade, implies that countries are both importers and exporters within a specific commodity market.[22]

This form of trade has grown rapidly as a result of the liberalisation of trade and the formation of economic unions in Western Europe. Another explanatory factor is the increased consumer demand for product variety as a result of the rapid rise in income observed in Western Europe since the mid-1950s.[23] Table 6.1 illustrates this development in the case of trade in passenger cars. It shows that intra-trade increased

**Figure 6.4:** Production mix of the main West European car makers

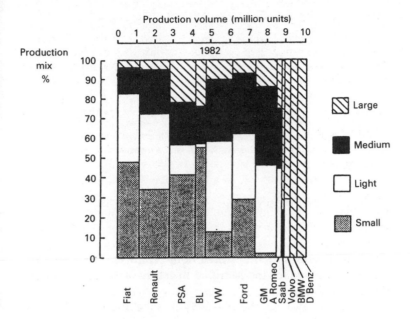

Source: Jones, 'SPRU databank of the Western European auto industry', quoted by Altschuler *et al.* (1984), p. 166.

Notes: Small: up to 1,200 cc (cubic centimetres); Light: 1,200–1,400 cc; Medium: 1,400–1,800 cc; Large: 1,800 cc and up.

rapidly up to the mid-1970s and has stagnated or decreased since then, except for France.[24] The rapid expansion of intra-industry trade has brought about a new form of market competition, 'reciprocal competition', where firms compete in each others' home markets.

The second implication of product differentiation concerns the degree of power over price that it confers on firms. This was called price insulation above. The loyalty of domestic consumers towards home products that mostly reflect their tastes allows domestic firms to charge higher prices than foreign producers without sacrificing the entire sales volume. How large will the sacrifice be? In other words, how many home buyers will, as a result of the higher price, prefer the foreign rivals' products to the domestic products? The answer depends upon the cross-

**Table 6.1:** Changes in intra-industry trade in passenger cars

| Year | W. Germany | France | Italy | Sweden | Britain | Average |
|------|------------|--------|-------|--------|---------|---------|
| 1955 | 9.4 | 13.3 | 8.4 | 6.6 | 5.8 | 8.7 |
| 1960 | 18.7 | 9.4 | 16.9 | 61.8 | 19.3 | 25.2 |
| 1965 | 32.2 | 41.4 | 50.2 | 60.0 | 16.4 | 40.0 |
| 1970 | 50.7 | 35.3 | 84.2 | 78.4 | 37.2 | 57.2 |
| 1975 | 68.5 | 36.8 | 72.8 | 90.3 | 93.0 | 72.3 |
| 1980 | 70.8 | 50.4 | 70.4 | 94.7 | 58.8 | 69.0 |
| 1984 | 66.4 | 74.0 | 77.6 | 86.4 | 35.4 | 68.0 |

The intra-trade measure varies between 0 (no intra-trade) and 100 (all trade is intra-trade, that is exports are exactly matched by imports). The calculations are based on import and export statistics according to a measure proposed by Grubel and Lloyd (1975):

$$\text{Intra-industry trade} = \frac{(X + M) - |X - M|}{(X + M)} \times 100$$

elasticity of substitution between both products. The lower this elasticity the smaller the sacrifice in terms of sales volume for the domestic firms.

The role played by the elasticity of substitution implies that firms in differentiated markets cannot neglect other more or less close substitute products and other firms when they fix their prices. Hence the discretion a differentiated firm enjoys over the price of its product is limited. It is likely that the price charged on the domestic market will be dependent upon the availability of more or less imperfect substitutes and the degree of competition prevailing on this market. The higher this degree, the less likely that the price charged by the differentiated firm(s) will approach its monopoly level.

All this suggests that the impact that product differentiation has on intra-industry trade and price insulation produces somewhat contradictory effects on international market integration and prices. On the one hand, product differentiation is responsible for greater inroads from one country into the domestic markets of another, and for the promotion of a form of competition that seems to further market interpenetration and international economic integration. On the other hand, it tends to insulate domestic markets from foreign competition and to confer on home sellers more power over their prices. In this way, product differentiation creates the conditions for the occurrence of price disparities, which are often regarded as the proof of the absence of a truly integrated economic area.

## Product differentiation and collusion

A question that arises in the present context is whether product differentiation modifies to some extent what has been said in the previous section regarding the relationship between lack of numbers and collusive price behaviour. We may expect two main effects of product differentiation on the likelihood of collusion, one through its impact on coordination costs among oligopolistic firms and another through its influence on intra-industry trade.

As regards the first effect, it is clear that the task of coordinating firms is more difficult in relation to differentiated firms than with firms producing homogeneous products. Differentiated firms have to coordinate their actions not only on price but also on other product dimensions such as product quality and advertising expenditures. The coordination difficulties associated with product differentiation ought to entail a substantial cost and render collusion less likely.[25] Note that the deterrent effect of product differentiation pertains more particularly to explicit forms of collusion that necessitate time-consuming bargaining on prices and other product dimensions.

Moreover, if firms, in order to limit their coordination costs, agree on the price but not on the other dimensions of the product, the collusive arrangement would tend to be rather unstable and short-lived.[26] The reason for this is non-price competition and its destabilising effects on market share distribution. Price-constrained firms can increase their market shares and maximise their gains by varying product design and/or selling expenses. Such incentives are all the stronger since successful changes in product design or advertising campaigns can only be replicated with a lag. For example, three years are required for a new car model to appear on the market.[27]

The second effect of product differentiation is a consequence of the interpenetration of markets resulting from the expansion of intra-industry trade and the subsequent emergence of reciprocal competition. If a firm engages in price or advertising wars abroad, the risk of retaliation in its own market (home base) is all the more important since the degree of interpenetration through intra-trade is high. This is because firms that are already in the marketplace do not bear penetration costs. Thus, one may expect firms that face 'reciprocal competition' to be more willing to enter into some form of collusion (reciprocal agreement) for fear of retaliation against their home base. In this respect, it may be worth stressing that differentiated firms often consider the defence of the home base as a prerequisite for their survival.[28] This is explained by the existence of a home demand — what Staffan Burenstam Linder calls a representative demand[29] — which is in most cases a necessary condition for exports and for the survival of firms in the long run. This argument is especially true if production is subject to large economies of scale.

However, the fact that firms are of different nationalities can be an important limit to the ability of sellers to reach an agreement. Differences in languages and culture make coordination among firms more difficult and thus collusion more costly and less likely.[30] This argument is more applicable to overt forms of collusion that necessitate frequent negotiations and explicit agreements.

The above two effects of product differentiation on collusion are somewhat contradictory. Heterogeneity of the products and the sellers renders collusion less probable, whereas the necessity to preserve a home base should incite firms facing 'reciprocal competition' to enter into some form of arrangement. A likely answer to this situation can be some form of tacit collusion such as price leadership, with domestic firm(s) as the price leader(s) and foreign firms as the followers, combined with some form of non-price competition (in product design, advertising activities, etc.). Such an answer has two advantages. First, price leadership results in lower coordination costs. Second, it confers on domestic firms — which are better informed on the prices that the market can bear — the power to set prices on their home markets.

Price leadership is a widespread collusive practice in the business world.[31] It implies that one firm sets the price with other firms following its price leadership. Each follower would gain by not following but by instead increasing its output up to the point where the cost of producing another unit exceeds the price of that unit. The reason for this apparently non-economic pattern of behaviour on the part of the followers is the uncertainty about the leading firm's reaction to a non-cooperative follower's behaviour.

The tentative conclusion that emerges is that product differentiation increases the probability of price disparities among countries that form some sort of economic union. This may be explained in two ways. Firstly, it confers on firms some discretion over their prices, allowing them to price-discriminate. They can charge a higher price at home where they face a low price elasticity of demand (as a result of home buyer loyalty) and a lower price abroad where the elasticity of demand is likely to be higher. This policy is made possible by the fact that domestic and foreign products are imperfect substitutes. Secondly, oligopolistic interdependence and 'reciprocal competition' may incite firms to adopt a special price for each foreign market. They may follow the price leader(s) in foreign markets and fix their own price on the domestic market according to how much the market can bear. However, such tacit collusive practices are likely to be somewhat unstable. This result is due to the presence of non-price competition, which is a positive function of the number of dimensions of the product. It is worth adding that, in case of price leadership practices, the price on the foreign market can be higher than on the domestic market.

**Barriers to parallel trade flows**

Nevertheless, price leadership and discrimination practices are conditional upon the prevention of arbitrage-induced trade flows. Actually, price disparities create an incentive for arbitrage operations that may endanger firms' price discrimination policy. These arbitrage-induced trade flows can either take the form of re-imports or parallel exports. They take the form of re-imports if prices charged abroad are lower than on the domestic market. They take the form of parallel exports (i.e. exports outside the official distribution network of the firm) if prices are higher abroad as a result of price leadership practices or other forms of collusive arrangements.

Therefore, it is likely that differentiated oligopolists will strive to prevent parallel trade flows in order to maintain a lucrative market fragmentation. To achieve this, they can enter some form of exclusive territorial distribution agreements with foreign dealers and, hence, ban reselling to distributors other than to the appointed retailers. Another measure with equivalent effect is to establish their own distribution networks abroad and impede re-imports of their own products.

Price discrimination has often a positive impact on exports, at least in the short run.[32] This result suggests that measures whose purpose is to maintain divisions between the national markets will probably benefit from government support. It is worth pointing out that this is true only when the price charged abroad is lower than the price charged on the domestic market. If the price set abroad is higher than the home price, government support is more unlikely since price discrimination has negative effects on exports.

Are barriers to parallel trade flows more likely to exist in oligopolistic than in atomistic markets? Barriers to parallel trade flows can, in Mancur Olson's terminology, be regarded as a collective good.[33] They make possible lucrative price discrimination among various national markets, and their benefits accrue to all the firms in the market. The likelihood of such barriers is dependent upon the number of firms that may benefit from them. The smaller the group of firms, the more likely that firms will organise collectively to obtain some form of regulation that prevents parallel trade flows.

The presence of a trade association increases further the chance of obtaining a favourable regulation. It minimises the costs of coordination among the firms and provides a selective incentive for the individuals that act in the interest of the firms, that is the active members of the trade association.[34] The main conclusion to be drawn therefore is that the prevention of parallel trade flows in differentiated markets is all the more probable when firms are effectively organised and their number is fairly small.

## SUMMARY AND CONCLUSIONS

It is a well-accepted proposition that the price for internationally traded commodities must be identical in the different national markets of an integrated area except for transport costs, tax disparities and costs of search. In the first section of this chapter we showed that this is the case when competitive conditions prevail in the unified trade area, with the exception of countries forming a free-trade area under certain special assumptions. This last result suggests that price disparities among West European passenger car markets are more likely now than at the beginning of the 1970s. The reason behind this argument is the transformation of the EEC into a free-trade area over the past decade.

The introduction of a first market imperfection, non-competitive market structures, into the analysis, shows that price differences between members of an economic union may arise. These can be the result of the presence of only one discriminating monopolist in the marketplace or of some form of collusive action between several discriminating firms. Necessary conditions are that firms succeed in erecting barriers that maintain market segmentation and that price elasticities differ among national markets. Further, it is suggested that the smaller the number of firms in a market, the more likely that collective action will be undertaken in order to achieve higher prices and the joint maximisation of profits.

The introduction of a second market imperfection, product differentiation, increases the likelihood of price disparities in a tariff-unified area. A necessary condition is that discriminating firms constrain the arbitrage-resale by low-price buyers to high-price buyers through strict control over the distribution network. Moreover, it is argued that product differentiation and intra-trade foster tacit forms of collusion, such as price leadership. The reason for this is that tacit collusion minimises coordination costs among differentiated oligopolists. It is suggested that price leadership practices may contribute to the emergence of price disparities between members of an economic association.

In the next chapter, this interplay between international economic integration, and oligopolistic and differentiated market structures in affecting prices will be discussed in the context of the West European passenger car markets.

## NOTES

1. See Chapter 1, p. 1.
2. Cournot (1897), pp. 51–52.
3. A central aim of the study is to see whether price differences emerge in an integrated area. It should be stressed that we are not concerned with price differences that may arise from transport costs or tax disparities. An additional source of price dispersion ignored here is the volatile and limited price differences that reflect the cost of search and are 'the measurement of ignorance in the market' (Stigler, 1961,

p. 172). It will be shown in the next chapter that the observed price differences among passenger car markets cannot be ascribed to these three factors.

4. On the use of partial equilibrium models to analyse the outcome of economic integration, see Robson (1980), Chapter 2, and Curzon (1974), Chapter 10.

5. For the sake of diagrammatic simplification, we chose a prohibitive tariff in country A. Note that the use of a non-prohibitive tariff does not affect the results on the price outcome of integration.

6. Chapter 2, pp. 28–52.

7. On the equivalence between tariffs and different forms of quantitive trade restriction, see Bhagwati (1965), pp. 53–67, and Hansson (1983), Chapter 4.

8. See for example Kravis and Lipsey (1978), pp. 193–246.

9. On non-competitive market structures and international trade, see Caves and Jones (1973), Chapter 11, Södersten (1978), Chapter 8, and White (1974), pp. 1013–20.

10. See Chapter 4, pp. 97–98.

11. Mattera (1984), pp. 283–308.

12. Ibid., p. 284.

13. An exception is the path-breaking study of Chamberlin (1935), Chapters 4 and 5. See also Fellner (1949), Chapters 6, 7 and 8, and Bain (1972), pp. 186–210.

14. See for example Stigler (1964), pp. 39–63, and Olson (1982), Chapter 2.

15. See Olson and McFarland (1962) and Olson (1982), Chapter 2.

16. See Stigler (1964), pp. 39–63.

17. On the influence of these factors on collusion, see for example Koutsoyiannis (1975), Chapter 10.

18. On the different forms of collusion, see any textbook on industrial economics. For example, Shepherd (1979), Chapter 15.

19. See Drèze (1960), pp. 5–26.

20. See Chapter 4, pp. 88–95.

21. In an analysis of the factors behind trade in passenger cars in Western Europe, it is shown that manufacturers produce first for the home market — that is to satisfy home market tastes — and then export if the varieties produced are demanded abroad. See Hocking (1980), pp. 504–9. See also Burenstam-Linder (1961), pp. 87–91.

22. On intra-trade see Grubel and Lloyd (1975), Greenaway and Milner (1986) and Caves (1981), pp. 203–23.

23. See Greenaway and Milner (1986), pp. 91–92.

24. See Figure 3.1 for the sources of import and export data. On the intra-trade measure, see Grubel and Lloyd (1975), Chapter 2.

25. On product heterogeneity and collusion, see Scherer (1980), pp. 200–205.

26. See Caves and Porter (1978), pp. 292–93.

27. See Chapter 4, pp. 87–88.

28. On the importance of a home base for firms, see Burenstam-Linder (1961), pp. 87–91, and Wells (1972), pp. 6–10.

29. Burenstam-Linder (1961), p. 87.

30. See Caves (1974), pp. 11–12.
31. See for example Mitchell (1978), pp. 28–31, and Scherer (1980), pp. 176–84.
32. In the longer run, however, price discrimination may loosen the pressure on the firm to reduce costs, entail a higher degree of X-inefficiency and, thus, negatively affect exports. On the relation between price discrimination and X-inefficiency, see Leibenstein (1976), pp. 172–73.
33. See Olson (1982), p. 19.
34. See Olson (1965), pp. 51, 144–48.

# 7

# International Integration, Market Conduct and Price Dispersion

Two and a half decades after the formation of the European Economic Community and the European Free-Trade Area and some eight years after the creation of an enlarged free-trade area including the EEC and EFTA countries, substantial price differences still exist for identical car models within the tariff-unified economic area. These differences cannot be explained by transport costs or tax disparities. Their large and growing extent over the past decade suggests that they cannot be ascribed to the cost of search and the ignorance of the market, either. Such a price outcome questions the reality of international economic integration in Western Europe. In a truly integrated market, consumers purchase the product where it is cheapest and, hence, equalise its price over the whole economic area. The analysis of the emergence and permanence of these price disparities provides an outstanding illustration of the interplay between international integration and market structure in affecting prices in a differentiated market. In other words, it allows for a powerful test of the different hypotheses put forward in the preceding chapter.

The present chapter is arranged in three parts. Firstly, we will provide ample evidence of the substantial price disparities among West European passenger car markets and of their changes over the past decade. Several sources will be used to illustrate these disparities.

In the second section we will analyse the logic of price disparities. A central concern will be to see whether the factors that give rise to price disparities conform to the hypotheses developed in the preceding chapter. We will see whether price disparities throughout the tariff-unified economic area can be related to tax disparities, different non-tariff barriers towards third countries or different degrees of competition in the five countries under study. Thereafter, several aspects of the pricing policies of the passenger car manufacturers, such as price discrimination and price leadership, will be the subject of particular scrutiny. Another possible explanatory factor, government price control policy, will be investigated as well.

In the third part we will concentrate on the factors that contribute to price disparities. Several examples will be used to illustrate the interacting factors behind the existence of a certain number of integration-retarding rigidities. These examples will highlight the interplay between, on the one hand, manufacturers and their trade associations and, on the other hand, national authorities and the European Commission. The main result of this interplay is the prevention of parallel trade flows which, if present, will iron out price disparities and create a truly unified economic area in Western Europe.

In the third section trade associations in the passenger car industry will be shown to be partly responsible for the emergence and permanence of a certain number of integration-impeding barriers. In the appendix we will discuss the institutional organisation of the passenger car industry, at the national as well as international levels, and analyse its role as an obstacle to integration.

## PRICE DISPARITIES IN THE TARIFF-UNIFIED ECONOMIC AREA

It was at the beginning of the 1970s, a few years after the complete removal of tariff barriers within the EEC, that several studies evidenced persistent price disparities for a certain number of similar goods among the six initial members. For example, in its First Report on Competition Policy in April 1972, the Commission of the European Community presented a study concerned with prices for identical products among the Six. A striking conclusion was that 'price differences *still* exist within the Common Market'.[1] One of the products examined in the EEC study was passenger cars, and we will now focus our attention on them.

International comparisons of passenger car prices in Western Europe have been made by several organisations and authors.

163

Most of these studies pertain to dealer prices, that is, to prices paid by consumers (transaction prices). A question that arises is therefore whether such prices reflect passenger car manufacturers' pricing policies or distributors' pricing policies. As far as passenger cars are concerned, price competition, if any, does not come from the bargaining of distributors but from manufacturers. Distributors are much weaker than passenger car manufacturers, and dealer prices for passenger cars can be regarded as highly representative of manufacturer pricing policies. This point will be illustrated in depth in the third section. Dealer prices depart only moderately from manufacturer list prices, especially at the beginning of the model year, when discounting is generally at a minimum. This observation further supports the above view on the predominant role of manufacturers in price determination.

International comparisons of passenger car prices (dealer prices net of taxes) for a certain number of models of different makes were made by the European Community for the EEC countries.[2] Table 7.1 presents the main results of these studies and the year on which they are based. To facilitate the cross-country comparison, the average prices (net of taxes) are expressed as a percentage of the French prices (base 100 for France).

**Table 7.1:** Comparison of prices (net of taxes) of similar passenger car models

| Year | W. Germany | France | Italy | Britain | Sweden | Benelux* | Denmark |
|---|---|---|---|---|---|---|---|
| 1970 | 106 | 100 | 107 | n.a. | 148 | 104.3 | n.a. |
| 1974 | n.a. | 100 | n.a. | n.a. | 139.3 | n.a. | n.a. |
| 1975 | 96.5 | 100 | 102.1 | 98.7 | 123 | 90.4 | 85.3 |
| 1978 | n.a. | 100 | n.a. | n.a. | 126.8 | n.a. | n.a. |
| 1980 | 100.5 | 100 | 108.3 | 124.5 | 118 | 90.9 | 80.6 |
| 1981 | 100.4 | 100 | n.a. | 139.5 | 124 | 90.8 | 74.3 |
| 1982 | 103.7 | 100 | 106.6 | 138.1 | 129.5 | 90.3 | 76 |
| 1984 | n.a. | 100 | n.a. | n.a. | 114.5 | n.a. | n.a. |

*Sources:* Commission of the European Communities (1972), p. 193; studies made by the European Community (1983), available in Ferrier (1984), p. 70; *Jan Ulléns Bilfakta* (1970, 1974, 1975, 1976, 1978, 1980, 1981, 1982, 1984); *L'Argus de l'automobile et des locomotions* (1970, 1974, 1975, 1978, 1980, 1981a, 1981b, 1982, 1984).

*Average for the Netherlands, Belgium and Luxembourg.

To include the Swedish passenger car market in the cross-country comparison, we collected the Swedish dealer prices (net of value-added taxes, excise taxes and, since 1975, car-scrapping charges) of a certain number of models.[3] We selected the models according to two criteria. Firstly, we chose the models that sold most on the Swedish market. Secondly, the models selected had also to be sold on the French market for the sake of comparison.[4] The Swedish prices were first converted into French francs at the exchange rate prevailing on the date (month) of the comparison. Then they were compared with the dealer prices (net of VAT) of the same models in Paris during the same period.[5]

The figures of Table 7.1 should be interpreted with some care. The models considered in the various countries may not be totally identical and may present certain small differences in accessories (seat belts, head rests, etc.) or in the services included in the price (delivery charges, etc.). However, such small product differences are unlikely to explain large and, moreover, changing ranges of price variation among West European countries. Another shortcoming of the results stems from the role of exchange rates in cross-country comparisons. Volatile exchange rates — such as those experienced since the breakdown of the Bretton Woods system — can actually create momentary price disparities.

With these limitations in mind, the following interesting conclusions emerge from the above studies. First, passenger car prices (net of taxes) vary greatly from country to country in the West European 'integrated' economic area. The large size of price differences suggests that they cannot be attributed to small product differences. Second, and rather surprisingly, since the last tariffs on intra-European trade were removed in 1977, the price differences have increased substantially since the mid-1970s. Third, the British prices are much higher than the continental prices since the early 1980s or, possibly, the latter half of the 1970s. Fourth, prices were much higher in Sweden than in other countries at the beginning of the 1970s, but the differences were getting narrower over time. Fifth, prices in non-producer countries like Benelux countries or Denmark are much lower than in car-producing countries.

Other cross-country comparative studies of passenger car prices were made by the BEUC (Bureau Européen des Unions des Consommateurs), which is a consortium of consumer organisations in the member states of the EEC. Their studies were based on a sample of 25 passenger car models from 18 different makes in 1981 and 1982 but on a sample of only ten models from ten different makes in 1983. The main results of the BEUC studies are presented in Table 7.2.

As above, the average prices (net of taxes) are expressed as a percentage of the French prices in order to facilitate the cross-country comparison. The BEUC studies give the list of the passenger car models taken into account. Thus it was possible to gather the Swedish prices for the same models on, approximately, the same date and to include the Swedish market in the comparison. The exchange rate prevailing between the Swedish krona and the European Unit of Account at the time (month) of the study was used to convert the Swedish prices. Some of the passenger car models considered in the BEUC studies were not sold on the Swedish market. The Swedish sample was consequently reduced and covered 20 models from 16 makes in 1981, 17 models from 15 makes in 1982 and 7 models from 7 makes in 1983.

The BEUC studies support the results of the EEC studies as regards the price differences that exist between the Common Market countries. They also confirm that prices in Britain and, to some extent, Italy are higher than in other EEC countries and that prices in non-producer countries are lower than in producer countries. Moreover, the 1983 study suggests that price disparities among EEC countries have become somewhat smaller since the beginning of the 1980s. However, the small size of the sample in 1983 — ten observations for EEC countries and seven observations for Sweden — means that only

**Table 7.2:** BEUC comparison of prices (net of taxes) of similar passenger car models

| Year | W. Germany | France | Italy | Britain | Sweden | Benelux[a] | Denmark |
|------|-----------|--------|-------|---------|--------|-----------|---------|
| 1981 | 97  | 100 | n.a. | 139 | 114 | 91   | 76   |
| 1982 | 104 | 100 | 109  | 135 | 108 | 92   | 80   |
| 1983 | 103 | 100 | n.a. | 123 | 103 | 89[b] | n.a. |

Sources: BEUC (1981, 1982a, 1983a); Jan Ulléns Bilfakta (1981, 1982, 1983).
[a]Average price for the Netherlands, Belgium and Luxembourg.
[b]Only Belgium.

tentative conclusions can be derived from the 1983 results. The results indicate that the large price disparities in Sweden observed during the first half of the 1970s (see Table 7.1) decreased at the beginning of the 1980s. The Swedish results differ widely from those obtained with a larger sample (compare Tables 7.1 and 7.2). Two reasons explain this difference. First, there is a much larger proportion of medium and large models in the BEUC sample than in our own sample in Table 7.1. Second, the price disparities between Stockholm and Paris for medium and large models are much less pronounced than for small and light models.

## THE LOGIC OF PRICE DISPARITIES

What are the factors behind such price disparities? The answer to this question is arranged in five parts. Part one will concentrate on the role of tax disparities among West European countries. Part two concerns the role of trade policy. Its main purpose will be to see whether it is the breakdown of the customs union in the mid-1970s and the creation instead of an enlarged free-trade area which are responsible for price disparities between West European passenger car markets. The role of other trade policy-related factors, such as the extent of non-tariff barriers, will also be investigated in this second part. There follows in part three an analysis of the influence of competition on prices: Are price disparities in the 'integrated' area the result of different degrees of competition and different market structures in the countries under study? Part four will discuss the role of firm behaviour that may not be mechanically determined by market structure. Its purpose will be to see whether the observed price differences can be related to market conduct. There still exist national and to some extent independent economic policies in Western Europe. One example is that of government price control policies. Part five will scrutinise the role of this factor, which might have played a non-negligible role in the creation and permanence of price disparities.

### Tax disparities

In Chapter 2 it was shown that indirect taxes differ widely from country to country and that divergent tax changes have

167

occurred over the past decade.[6] Taxes imposed on the purchase of a new car have increased in Britain, West Germany, Italy and Sweden while they have remained constant in France. A first question that arises is whether the different rates of tax imposition and their changes over time explain the growing price disparities observed over the past decade. Note that this factor is often put forward by the passenger car manufacturers and their trade association in Brussels to explain price disparities among West European markets.[7]

The effect of indirect taxes on prices net of taxes can be illustrated with the help of a two-country, one-product, partial equilibrium model (see Figure 7.1). Country $A$ imposes a high purchase tax $t_1$. The price paid by consumers is $P_e$ and the price net of tax $P_a$. This latter price is the price received by producers. Country $B$ imposes a lower tax $t_2$. In this country, the price paid by consumers is $P_b$ and the price net of tax $P_a$. The same producer prices in both countries correspond to the situation prevailing in 1975 (Sweden excepted) among the countries under study (see Table 7.1).

Let country $B$ increase its rate of tax imposition, as was actually the case in Britain, West Germany and Italy during the past decade. What will be the effects of this increase (from $t_2$ to $t_3$ in Figure 7.1) on the relative prices net of taxes?

Two cases can arise. The first is more relevant to our discussion because we deal with an integrated area where trade obstacles have been removed and transport costs are likely to be limited. In such a case, an increase in the rate of tax imposition in only one country does not result in a price disparity. If no trade takes place, the tax increase from $t_2$ to $t_3$ will result in a decrease in the producer price in $B$ (from $P_a$ to $P_d$). As there are no trade barriers between $A$ and $B$, a producer price disparity cannot exist. This is because the emergence of a disparity will lead $B$ producers to export a part of their production to $A$, where it can be sold at a higher price. This will result in turn in a lowering of the producer price in $A$, an increase of the corresponding price in $B$ and an equalisation of both prices at a level between $P_d$ and $P_a$.

The existence of a trade obstacle or substantial transport costs can prevent $B$ producers from exporting to country $A$, where they can sell their products at a higher price. In such a case, a change in the rate of tax imposition from $t_2$ to $t_3$ will bring about a decrease from $P_a$ to $P_d$ in the net of tax price in

**Figure 7.1:** Price and tax disparities

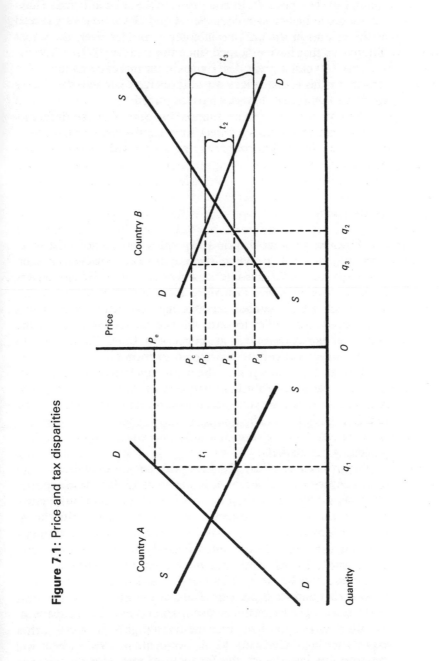

169

country *B*. The price $P_a$ in country *A* will not be affected. Thus a price disparity between countries *A* and *B* will arise as a result of the change in the tax rate in country *B*. However, the price differences that have emerged since the mid-1970s (see Tables 7.1 and 7.2) cast a great deal of doubt on this explanation. The reason for this is that prices net of taxes have *increased* in those countries where tax increases have occurred.

The results of both cases support the view that the different tax rates and their changes over time cannot explain the price disparities observed throughout the integrated area over the past decade.

## Trade policy

As shown in Chapter 6, price disparities should not exist in a customs union under competitive conditions. However, as was also suggested with regard to passenger cars, the EEC no longer forms a customs union but, since the mid-1970s, a free-trade area. Each EEC member country has its own specific non-tariff-based trade policy towards third countries. By implication, and as far as passenger cars are concerned, the EEC and EFTA countries together can be considered to form an enlarged free-trade area. As regards prices, the main conclusion that emerged from the partial equilibrium analysis was that price disparities might occur under certain special assumptions among members of a free-trade area.[8] The question is now whether this development can explain the observed differences in prices among the passenger car markets.

Since the mid-1970s, the European countries under study have adopted very different attitudes towards Japanese exports of passenger cars.[9] In addition to a 10–11 per cent tariff rate, EEC countries are protected by quantitative restrictions towards Japanese exports. Italy is the most protected country, since import licences are granted for only 1,700 passenger cars every year. France and Britain, which are somewhat less protected, benefit from 'voluntary' restrictions on Japanese exports that allow a 3 per cent share of the French market and an 11 per cent share of the British market. Since 1981 Japanese exporters have agreed to limit the annual growth rate of their exports to West Germany to 10 per cent. In 1981, when the measure was introduced, the Japanese exports already enjoyed a 10 per cent share of the German market. Tariff barriers facing Japanese — as well as other third countries' — exports are lower in Sweden than in the EEC countries. They have amounted to between 8 and 10 per cent during the past decade.[10] Moreover, no quantitative restrictions are imposed by Sweden on Japanese exports.

What are the likely effects on prices of these various trade policies towards Japanese exports? In addition to their effects on import volumes, quantitative restrictions give rise to a discrepancy between foreign and domestic prices. At first sight we may expect different levels of quantitative restrictions and of tariff rates — as between Sweden and the EEC — to result in different discrepancies between foreign and domestic prices. The tighter the import control, the larger this discrepancy would be. Thus Italy ought to exhibit the highest discrepancy between foreign and domestic prices followed in descending order by France, Britain, Germany and Sweden. By implication, a price differential is likely to arise within the enlarged free-trade area.

However, this is not the whole story. A different outcome is possible if we take into account the fact that we are concerned with a free-trade area. As illustrated in Chapter 6, the introduction of a quantitative restriction by only one of the member countries of a free-trade area may not result, under certain conditions, in a price differential between member countries.[11] A price differential is avoided if the member country that does not impose any import control can increase its exports to the member country protected by a restriction and satisfy the extra demand in the latter country at a price corresponding to the world price plus their own tariff.

When applied to the passenger car markets, this indicates that the introduction of more or less severe quantitative restrictions by Italy, France and Britain during the second half of the 1970s did not lead to price differentials. A necessary condition for this result is that the two remaining car-producing countries, West Germany and Sweden, could increase their exports to these three markets and satisfy the extra demand at a price amounting to the world price plus their own tariffs. Two factors, however, suggest that such an outcome was unlikely. The first is the size of the two latter countries relative to the three former in terms of production capacities. This means that the German and Swedish production could hardly satisfy the extra demand from the three other members of the free-trade area. The second is the fact that we are concerned with a differentiated market with limited substitution possibilities. West Germany and Sweden produce mostly high-quality passenger cars that are imperfect substitutes for Japanese and other European vehicles. These two factors argue in favour of a trade policy-induced price differential within the unified economic area.

The observed price differences provide, nevertheless, very little support for the trade policy explanation (see Tables 7.1 and 7.2). This cannot explain the high level of British prices compared, for example, with the French. The reason is that, since the mid-1970s the French market is protected from Japanese export of passenger cars by a much more severe 'voluntary' export restraint than the British market (3 per cent instead of 11 per cent of the domestic market). Neither can the trade policy explanation tell us why French prices are lower than the West German. However, the price differential between, on the one hand, the West German and the French markets and, on the other hand, the Italian market can to some extent be related to the effects of different trade policies towards Japanese exports.

Table 7.1 shows that passenger car prices were higher on the Swedish market than on other markets. This is all the more surprising since Sweden does not benefit from any quantitative restriction towards Japanese exports.[12] Moreover, this country is protected by the lowest tariff towards third-country exports. Two other trade policy-related factors may explain the huge and changing difference between the Swedish and continental passenger car prices. The first is the enforcement of the free-trade area between Sweden and the EEC, which resulted in the removal of the 10 per cent tariff imposed on continental cars in Sweden up to 1973.[13] This probably caused the decreasing price differential observed between the beginning of the 1970s and the mid-1970s (see Table 7.1). The second factor is the extra costs brought about by the existence of much more stringent technical and administrative barriers to trade in Sweden.[14] As pointed out in Chapter 2, such barriers negatively affect firms that capture a small share of the market.[15] In Sweden they negatively affect small and light cars which only capture around 30 per cent of the limited Swedish market. The differences noticed between Tables 7.1 and 7.2 in Swedish prices confirm the role of technical and administrative barriers. This is accounted for by the fact that these differences arose from the

172

much larger proportion of small and light cars in the sample of Table 7.1.

Do the changes in the real price of passenger cars over the last decade give more support to the trade policy explanation? Table 7.3 shows that the behaviour of the consumer price index for new cars has been very different in the five countries under study since 1975. Passenger car prices have risen in Italy and Britain while they have decreased to various extents in France, West Germany and Sweden. If one excludes the behaviour of the British prices, such results are more in accordance with the trade policy explanation. Prices have decreased most in the two countries that are the least protected against Japanese car exports, namely Sweden and West Germany, and increased most in Italy, the country that is the most protected against Japanese exports.[16]

Before turning to the next possible explanation, it should be noted that neither cross-country comparisons nor new-car consumer price indexes capture the impact that quantitative restrictions have on prices through their impact on quality upgrading. Quantitative restrictions apply to the number of products imported, as the Italian quota, or to a share of the domestic market, as the French and British VER. As far as differentiated products are concerned, one of the main effects of such restrictions is to shift exports towards higher-price and quality products, that is, to lead to an upgrading of product quality.[17] The resulting change in the mix of passenger cars is

**Table 7.3:** Average annual change in the ratio of new passenger-car consumer price index to total consumer price index

| Period | W. Germany | France | Italy | Sweden | Britain* |
|--------|-----------|--------|-------|--------|----------|
| 1961–1975 | −0.7% | −0.6% | −1.1% | −0.04% | n.a. |
| 1975–1984 | −0.4% | −0.2% | +0.8% | −1% | +1.5% |

*Sources:* Statistiches Bundesamt (West Germany); INSEE (France); Department of Trade and Industry (Britain); SCB (Sweden); and ISTAT (Italy) for the new-car consumer price indexes and OECD for the total consumer price indexes.
  *The figures for Britain should be interpreted with some care because they represent producer prices and cover British manufacturers with no allowance for imports.

173

reflected neither in cross-country comparisons, since the same models are taken into account in various countries, nor in the new-car consumer price index, because this index corrects for quality changes. This failure of new-car consumer price indexes to fully reflect price changes induced by quantitative restrictions is likely to be more serious in Britain than in France and Italy. This is because quantitative restrictions are concerned with a much larger share of the market in the former country than in the latter two.

## Market competition

In Chapter 6 it was suggested that the existence of imperfectly competitive market structures could *per se* be conducive to oligopolistic conduct and the raising of prices above costs. Such market structures could lead to the emergence of price dispari-ties throughout the tariff-unified area, assuming that discriminat-ing firms could prevent arbitrage-induced trade flows. Price disparities can actually be the result of different degrees of competition prevailing in the various national markets and of barriers to parallel trade flows. The higher the degree of compe-tition the more unlikely that the price charged by the firms will approach its monopoly level.[18]

Simple correlation coefficients between cross-country price differences and degrees of competition were calculated to give a rough idea of their relationship. The reason for selecting this procedure instead of regression analysis is the low number of observations available for each year. We made use of the price differences estimated by the EEC and our own studies in 1970, 1975, 1980, 1981 and 1982. In order to express the level of competition prevailing in the five countries examined, use was made of the concentration measures introduced and utilised in Chapter 5, namely the Herfindahl and Rosenbluth indexes.[19] The statistical results are given in Table 7.4.

The results of Table 7.4 should be interpreted with some care because of the small number of observations and the method used. They show that a negative correlation exists between market concentration and price. This finding suggests that the higher the level of concentration, the lower the prices. Such an unexpected result gives some support to the view that the degree of concentration prevailing in the different countries is

**Table 7.4:** Simple correlation coefficients between cross-country differences in price and competition

| $P_d(t)$ | H | R | $H_{t-1}$ | $R_{t-1}$ | $\|\Delta H(\%)\|$ | $\|\Delta R(\%)\|$ |
|---|---|---|---|---|---|---|
| P(1970) | −0.40 | −0.69 | −0.35 | −0.55 | −0.83 | −0.85 |
| P(1975) | −0.31 | −0.43 | −0.33 | −0.50 | −0.61 | −0.44 |
| P(1980) | −0.53 | −0.54 | −0.61 | −0.63 | −0.42 | −0.66 |
| P(1981) | −0.54 | −0.60 | −0.54 | −0.56 | −0.48 | −0.40 |
| P(1982) | −0.62 | −0.68 | −0.64 | −0.69 | −0.33 | −0.15 |

*Sources:* Table 7.1 and Chapter 5, pp. 117–18.

*Notes:* $P_d(t)$, price differences in year $t$; $H$ and $R$, concentration as measured by the Herfindahl and Rosenbluth indexes in year $t$; $H_{t-1}$ and $R_{t-1}$, concentration as measured by the Herfindahl and Rosenbluth indexes in year $t - 1$; $\|\Delta H(\%)\|$ and $\|\Delta R(\%)\|$, changes in concentration between years $t$ and $t - 1$.

not responsible for the price disparities observed among these countries. Passenger car prices do not tend to be higher when markets are highly concentrated and lower when markets are less concentrated.

A limitation of the present approach may be the omission of the demand side in the reasoning. Prices may be the result of an interaction between market concentration and some demand characteristics: the higher the level of concentration and the lower the price elasticity of demand, the higher the level of prices and vice versa. The level of price elasticity varies inversely with the level of per capita income. This will be illustrated in the next section. The observed price differences tend to refute the concentration–price elasticity interaction hypothesis. For example, the high British prices cannot be explained by the relatively low level of concentration in Britain combined with an expected relatively high price elasticity. Another factor that suggests that the omission of the demand side is not too worrying is the identical prices prevailing in the four largest countries in the mid-1970s. No drastic and explanatory changes on the demand side could have occurred over the past decade.

Do market structures affect prices with a lag? One reason can be put forward to support this hypothesis. Passenger car prices are set at the beginning of the year and are only adjusted — to a moderate extent — to the state of the market in the course of the year. This being so, we may expect the degree of competition prevailing a year before to be more important as far as price-determining factors are concerned. The simple correlation

175

coefficients between prices and concentration a year before turn out to be identical in sign to those obtained when prices and concentration are taken for the same year. This result is not surprising in view of the narrow range of variation of market structures in all countries except France over the past decade. They confirm that passenger car price disparities cannot be ascribed to different levels of market concentration.

Do the preceding results mean that competition has no influence on prices or that the level of concentration is a poor indicator of the intensity of competition in the marketplace? One of the most likely results of a highly competitive market is market share instability. Competitive markets should generate substantial changes in market share distribution and in market structure over time.[20] Thus, one may expect large (small) shifts in market structures to be correlated with low (high) prices. In order to provide a rough test of this hypothesis, simple correlation coefficients between changes in market structures between years $t - 1$ and $t$ and the price level in year $t$ were calculated. Note that only the size of the changes in market structures but not their direction were considered. As above, the Herfindahl and Rosenbluth indexes are used in the statistical test. The results are given in the fifth and sixth columns of Table 7.4.

The results are of the right sign. They tend to indicate that larger changes in market structure lead to lower prices in the national market and vice versa. This finding tends to support the view that market share instability, as measured by year-to-year changes in market structure, is a good proxy for the degree of competition prevailing in the marketplace. It seems to be a more accurate indicator of the degree of competition than the level of concentration, probably because it embodies the role of market conduct and consumer brand loyalty.[21]

A striking finding of Chapter 5 was the low range of variation in market structure in Sweden and West Gemany during the whole period examined and in Britain and Italy since the mid-1970s.[22] It was shown that only France has experienced a high degree of market share instability over the past decade. An interesting result is that the lower prices noticed in France can probably be ascribed in part to this higher degree of instability.

In sum, market structure as defined by the market share distribution of domestic and foreign firms does not seem to be responsible for the price disparities within the 'integrated' area.

On the contrary, changes in market structure seem to partly explain price disparities. A likely reason behind this result is that such changes embody the role of consumer brand loyalty and market conduct. In the next section we will concentrate more particularly on firm behaviour and see whether it can shed more light on the logic of price differences.

## Firm conduct and price leadership

Do the substantial price disparities for identical models of passenger cars arise from the discriminatory pricing policy of car producers and their success in erecting barriers to parallel trade flows?

As far as discriminatory pricing policies in differentiated markets are concerned, two plausible hypotheses were put forward in Chapter 6.[23] The first one suggests that firms charge a higher price in the domestic market than abroad because they face a lower price elasticity at home than abroad. The lower price elasticity in the home market follows from home buyer loyalty and the fact that the design of passenger cars reflects mainly national tastes.[24] According to the second hypothesis, firms facing reciprocal competition are likely to enter into some form of tacit agreement and, as a consequence, charge different prices in different markets. They should follow the price leader in each foreign market and they should set their own prices at home. In this section, we will try to see whether these explanations fit the pricing policies of passenger car manufacturers.

### High home price–low export price hypothesis

The main reason behind the first kind of discriminatory pricing policies is the existence in each national market of different price elasticities of demand: a high one for foreign products and a low one for domestic products. Whether this assertion conforms to reality is, however, difficult to prove. No separate price indexes for domestic and foreign cars exist in most West European countries. An exception is France, where price indexes for domestic and foreign passenger cars have been calculated by the central statistical office (INSEE) since 1962. From these indexes, it was also possible to estimate the short-run price elasticities for domestic and foreign passenger cars in the French market.[25] Different specifications were tried. The

177

regression results (with $t$-statistics in parentheses) are given in Table 7.5.

Equations 7.1 and 7.2 assume that the markets for foreign and French passenger cars are two different markets. They show that the two markets are characterised by very different price and income elasticities of demand. The results indicate that the short-run price elasticity for foreign cars is statistically significant and rather large (around $-1.6$), while the price elasticity for domestic cars is not statistically significant and, furthermore, very low ($-0.25$). Equations 7.1 and 7.2 indicate that the

**Table 7.5:** Price and income elasticities for domestic and foreign passenger cars on the French market, 1962–1984

| | |
|---|---|
| (7.1) | log $RegF(nb)$ = 0.056 + 2.025 log $Y$ − 1.566 log $P_f$ − 0.31 $D74$–$75$ |
| | (0.063) (13.967) (2.467) (3.521) |
| | $R^2$(adj) = 0.982  SEE = 0.103  DF = 19 |
| (7.2) | log $RefD(nb)$ = 10.073 + 0.63 log $Y$ − 0.256 log $P_d$ − 0.126 $D74$–$75$ |
| | (9.258) (3.527) (0.475) (2.108) |
| | $R^2$(adj) = 0.996  SEE = 0.073  DF = 19 |
| (7.3) | log $RegF(sh)$ = − 8.555 + 1.112 log $Y$ − 4.436 log $P_f$ + 3.322 log $P_d$ |
| | (7.175) (5.683) (4.005) (3.098) |
| | −0.142 $D74$–$75$ |
| | (1.989) |
| | $R^2$(adj) = 0.896  SEE = 0.085  DF = 18 |
| (7.4) | log $RegF(sh)$ = − 8.859 + 1.177 log $Y$ − 3.754 log $P_f/P_d$ − 0.102 $D74$–$75$ |
| | (6.681) (5.442) (3.507) (1.457) |
| | $R^2$(adj) = 0.880  SEE = 0.089  DF = 19 |

*Sources:* New car registration: *L'Argus de l'automobile et des locomotions,* yearly statistical issues, 1962–1985; price indexes for passenger cars: *Annuaire statistique de la France,* 1962–1985 (Paris: INSEE, Institut National de la Statistique et des Études Économiques); consumer price index: OECD; GNP: see Chapter 3.

The equations are estimated with the OLS method and corrected for serial correlation with the Cochrane–Orcutt procedure. The critical values of the $t$-statistic (in parentheses) at the 5 and 10 per cent levels with a one-tailed test are $t(19)$ = 1.729 and 1.328 and $t(18)$ = 1.734 and 1.330.

*Variables: RegF(nb),* number of foreign passenger cars registered in the French market; $Y$, GNP at constant prices; $P_f$, price index for foreign cars divided by the total consumer price index; *RegD,* number of French passenger cars registered in the French market; $P_d$, price index for French cars divided by the total consumer price index; *D74–75,* dummy variable 1974 and 1975 = 1, and 0 otherwise; *RegF(sh),* foreign share of new registration in France; $P_f/P_d$, relative price ratio of foreign-to-domestic passenger cars.

income elasticity for foreign cars is three times larger than the corresponding elasticity for domestic cars (+2 instead of +0.6).

Another interesting result concerns the dummy variable that captures the effect of the oil embargo and the subsequent increase in the price of petrol. It turns out to be of the right sign and statistically significant in both equations. The rather different size of the dummy variable coefficients (−0.31 and −0.126) suggests that the sharp increase in the oil price had a much greater effect on the demand for foreign cars than for domestic cars.

Equation 7.3 produces results that are of the right sign and statistically significant. They confirm that price elasticities for foreign and domestic passenger cars differ widely. They indicate that a 1 per cent increase in foreign car price results in a 4.4 per cent decrease in the foreign share in new registration, while the same increase in domestic car price leads to a 3.3 per cent increase in the foreign share. Equation 7.4 confirms that the foreign share in new registration is greatly influenced by foreign prices relative to domestic prices.

The sign and statistical significance of the income variable in Equations 7.3 and 7.4 provide evidence of a continuous change in the composition of passenger car purchases, in favour of foreign cars and at the expense of domestic cars. This change is not explained by a change in relative prices. It is probably the result of two kinds of factors. An increase in per capita income leads to a shift in the consumer demand towards higher-quality cars. The specialisation of the French industry in the production of relatively small and light passenger cars implies that this shift means a substitution of imported for domestic cars.[26] The non-price-related causes of international integration represent another kind of factor. The opening up to trade results in an internationalisation of tastes or a reduction of cultural heterogeneity, regularly improved information on foreign passenger cars and a reduction of uncertainty. The positive influence of these factors on imports is captured by the income variable because of parallel changes in these factors and income over time.[27]

What will be firm price policy if a similar difference exists in all European countries between the price elasticities of demand for foreign and domestic passenger cars? It is likely that discriminating firms will charge a higher price at home, where the demand is less price-elastic, and a lower price abroad, where the demand is more responsive to the price charged. Does this theory explain the price disparities illustrated in the previous section?

In order to test this theory, we used the BEUC studies for 1981 and 1982. We compared the passenger car prices on the foreign markets with the prices of the same models on the domestic markets. An analysis of the net prices for cars based on a sample of 124 observations including German, Italian, British and French passenger cars and their prices on various foreign markets (Belgium, Netherlands, Denmark, France, Germany, Italy and Britain) suggests that export net prices were on average about 5 per cent lower than home market net prices. This finding shows unambiguously that transport costs are not responsible for the observed price differences. The average difference between home and foreign markets is larger (about 20 per cent) if only Belgium, Denmark and Netherlands are taken into account among the foreign countries (44 observations). If, on the other hand, the markets considered are those of countries that have a passenger car industry (Germany, Italy, France and Britain), the calculation based on 80 observations shows that the export prices were on average 3 per cent higher than the home market prices. This low figure conceals, however, large differences between foreign prices in Britain (more than 20 per cent higher than home market prices) and foreign prices on other markets whose difference with home prices is less pronounced. The main conclusion that emerges is that the high home price–low abroad price hypothesis pertains only to exports to non-producer countries. In these countries passenger car manufacturers are putting out their products at lower net car prices than in their own home markets. This explanation has very little merit for foreign car prices in producer countries.

*Price leadership hypothesis*

Does the second firm-conduct hypothesis have more merit as far as price determination in producer countries is concerned? The second hypothesis suggests that the growth of intra-industry trade and the resulting interpenetration of European markets has encouraged collusive cooperation among firms. Further, it pointed out that collusion was more likely to take the form of price leadership.[28] The main reason for this is that coordination costs among differentiated firms are much lower with this form of collusive action. According to this explanation, firms are expected to fix the prices in their own home market and to follow the price leader(s) in foreign markets. The reciprocal competition hypothesis does not apply to Japanese producers because of the very limited extent of intra-industry trade between Western Europe and Japan. This means that Japanese producers have no interest in adopting price follower practices and that trade policy-related factors should be taken into account to explain their possible collusive behaviour in Western Europe.

This aspect of passenger car manufacturer pricing policy is illustrated in Figure 7.2, which shows price movements for domestic and foreign passenger cars in the French market between 1962 and 1984.

Although prices in the producer countries (see Table 7.3)

**Figure 7.2**: Price indexes for foreign and domestic passenger cars on the French market (base 100 = 1962)

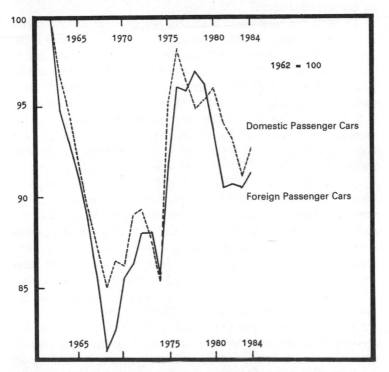

*Sources:* Price indexes for passenger cars: *Annuaire statistique de la France, 1962–1985* (Paris, INSEE); consumer price index: OECD.

181

exhibit divergent changes after 1975, foreign prices in the French market follow approximately the prices of French passenger cars (about 50 per cent of foreign passenger cars are German). Furthermore, it is likely that the small differences between the two indexes can be ascribed, to some extent, to different and changing mixes of passenger cars in the foreign and French samples (proportionally more high-quality cars in the foreign sample). It is worth adding, however, that this illustration should be accepted with some reservations since causality may run the other way, that is from foreign to French prices.

The question that now arises is, of course, which factors are behind the prices charged by the passenger car manufacturers over the past decade? Does a lower price elasticity in Britain and Sweden explain the higher prices charged by passenger car manufacturers in these two markets? Are the lower German and French passenger car prices due to the fact that French and German consumers are more responsive to the prices charged by car manufacturers?

To illustrate this issue, price elasticities were estimated for the countries under study. Equations 7.5–7.9 regress new registration in West Germany, France, Italy, Sweden and Britain on income, passenger car prices deflated by dividing by consumer price indexes and a dummy variable. This dummy variable takes on the value of 1 in 1974 and 1975 and 0 otherwise. Its purpose is to capture the effect of the oil embargo and the subsequent increase in the price of petrol on passenger car demand. The regression results, with $t$-statistics in parentheses, are given in Table 7.6.

A striking feature of the results of Table 7.6, when compared with those of Table 3.2, is that income elasticities for new cars (imported and domestic) are much lower than for only new imported cars.[29] Income elasticities for new cars range from +0.5 in Sweden to about +1 in France and West Germany, while the corresponding elasticities for imports range from around +1 in Sweden to +3.5 in France. The results for Britain were not considered because the periods covered by the two studies are too different, 1958–1984 in Chapter 3 and 1970–1984 in the present chapter. This result means that income elasticities for imports are much larger than income elasticities for domestic products. It has important implications for the trade effects of international integration and the empirical results of Chapter 3.

**Table 7.6**: Estimation of price and income elasticities for passenger cars

France

(7.5)  $\log R =$  1.478 + 1.04  $\log Y -$ 0.647 $\log P -$ 0.142 $D74-75$
         (0.690) (12.451)        (1.633)        (2.305)

$R^2$(adj) = 0.958    $SEE$ = 0.073    $DF$ = 21    $OBS$: 1960–1984

West Germany

(7.6)  $\log R =$  −3.845 + 1.127 $\log Y +$ 0.334 $\log P -$ 0.13 $D74-75$
         (0.818)  (7.753)        (0.424)        (2.122)

$R^2$(adj) = 0.964    $SEE$ = 0.072    $DF$ = 21    $OBS$: 1960–1984

Italy

(7.7)  $\log R =$  5.819 + 0.932 $\log Y -$ 1.298 $\log P -$ 0.202 $D74-75$
         (4.452) (10.708)        (4.934)        (2.5)

$R^2$(adj) = 0.867    $SEE$ = 0.097    $DF$ = 20    $OBS$: 1961–1984

Sweden

(7.8)  $\log R =$  −1.542 + 0.464 $\log Y +$ 0.777 $\log P +$ 0.031 $D74-75$
         (0.345) (1.973)        (0.996)        (0.309)

$R^2$(adj) = 0.911    $SEE$ = 0.118    $DF$ = 21    $OBS$: 1960–1984

Britain

(7.9)  $\log R =$  −6.872 + 2.272 $\log Y -$ 0.993 $\log P -$ 0.112 $D74-75$
         (1.963) (3.804)        (1.982)        (1.535)

$R^2$(adj) = 0.968    $SEE$ = 0.084    $DF$ = 11    $OBS$: 1970–1984

*Sources:* Price indexes for passenger cars: see Table 7.3; GNP: see Chapter 3; new registration: see Figure 3.4.

The equations are estimated with the OLS method and corrected for serial correlation with the Cochrane–Orcutt procedure. The critical values of the $t$-statistic at the 5 and 10 per cent levels with a one-tailed test are $t(21) = 1.721$ and 1.323, and $t(11) = 1.796$ and 1.363.

*Variables:* R, new registration of passenger cars; P, price index for passenger cars divided by the total consumer price index; Y, income variable (GNP at constant prices); $D74-75$: dummy variable 1974 and 1975 = 1, and 0 otherwise.

First, it confirms the results of Table 7.5 on the existence of trade effects that are not explained by changes in relative prices. International integration affected trade not only through the price mechanism, as in the case of tariff changes, but also through changes in trade obstacles of more qualitative character such as consumer loyalty towards home products and inform-ation about foreign makes.

Second, concerning the empirical results of Chapter 3, it suggests that the trade effects of international integration are much larger than those derived from Table 3.2. The reason for this is that some of these effects are captured by the income variable. This is true particularly for France and, to a lesser extent, Italy. These two countries present the largest discrepancy between the income elasticities for imported cars and for all new cars (3.5:1 and 2:0.9).[30] The relatively low tariff elasticities in these two countries (−0.313 and −0.315), as compared with West Germany (−0.465), indicate that income elasticities for imports may also capture delayed tariff effects not captured by the tariff variable.

The regressions produce very different results for price elasticity in the various West European countries. The coefficient of the price variable is of the right sign and statistically significant in France, Italy and Britain. The price coefficient is of the wrong sign and not statistically significant in West Germany and Sweden. The results for these two countries and the fact that the price elasticity is lower in France than in Britain and Italy suggest that such differences are partly the result of different per capita income levels. The higher the per capita income the lower and less significant the price elasticity of demand. It is likely that other factors of economic, historical and sociological nature are also responsible for the different price elasticities.[31]

The level of the price elasticity of demand for passenger cars has important implications for car manufacturer pricing policy. The fact that the price elasticity varies with income implies that consumers are becoming less responsive over time to changes in prices. It implies also that consumers in high per capita income countries are less responsive to higher prices than consumers in lower per capita income countries. This means in turn that the ability of car manufacturers to charge higher prices — and thus their market power — is larger now than during the 1960s and larger in high per capita income countries than in low per capita income countries. Assuming that arbitrage-induced trade flows can be impeded, it is therefore likely that collusive firms will try to charge high prices in high per capita income countries and low prices in lower per capita income countries. Empirical evidence on price disparities among European passenger car markets indicates, however, that the validity of this theory, too, can be questioned.

The high per capita income in Sweden, according to this theory, can explain why manufacturers charged higher passenger car prices on the Swedish market. Nevertheless, this theory cannot explain why manufacturers charge higher prices in Britain and Italy than in Germany and France. The reason for this is that the per capita income is lower in the two former countries and the price elasticity of demand is likely to be higher.

A final interesting result of Table 7.6 is that the oil crisis affected negatively and significantly the demand for new passenger cars in all countries except Sweden. The absence of effects in this last country must be due to the highly expansive fiscal policy adopted by the government in 1974–1976 to tide the economy over the slack period of foreign demand.

Does the introduction of exchange rate movements into the analysis, in combination with price leader–follower practices, shed more light on the logic of price disparities and on the abnormally high passenger car prices in the British market? If exchange rate changes are not passed on in import prices, we may expect large and changing price disparities to occur throughout the enlarged free-trade area on condition that arbitrage-induced trade flows can be prevented. The reason behind this is that foreign firms follow the price decisions of domestic firms, and change prices for similar amounts and around the same time as domestic firms regardless of exchange-rate movements. It is likely that the break-down of the Bretton Woods system at the beginning of the 1970s and the more volatile exchange rates observed in Western Europe since the first oil crisis have both contributed to the development of these exchange-rate-induced price disparities. This argument pertains more particularly to Britain, whose exchange rate has been subject to erratic day-to-day fluctuations over the last 12 years, mainly because it chose to remain outside the different systems of monetary cooperation in Western Europe. The pound left the European snake in June 1972, four months after its creation, and did not join the European Monetary System (EMS) in 1979.

To illustrate this issue, Figure 7.3 shows the developments of effective exchange rates for the countries under study over the past 18 years. For the sake of comparison with Table 7.1, which shows that price disparity was at its minimum in 1975, the year 1975 was chosen as the base year.

Figure 7.3 shows an appreciation of the British currency after 1977 with a peak in 1981. The higher British prices are probably due to the fact that this appreciation was not passed

185

**Figure 7.3:** Effective exchange rates, 1967–1984

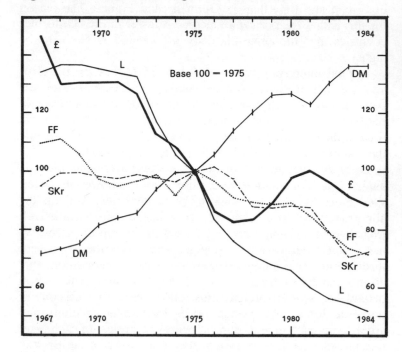

Source: OECD, Economic Outlook, 38, July 1981 and December 1985.
Notes: £, British pound; SKr, Swedish krona; L, Italian lira; DM, German mark;
FF, French franc.

on to British consumers and did not result in lower prices for imported passenger cars. Importers fixed their prices according to the prices charged by the highly inefficient and loss-making domestic industry, which acted as the price leader on the British market.[32] The reason put forward above on the logic of collusive behaviour and price leadership pertains to the behaviour of West European car manufacturers in other European manufacturers' home markets. Beside this reason, two factors highlight the behaviour of importers on the British market.

Around 40 per cent of British imports are so-called captive imports, that is imports by firms like Ford and Vauxhall (Opel), which are also established as manufacturers in Britain.[33] Such firms have an interest in avoiding price warfare and adopt a price leadership strategy to maintain the viability of the British subsidiaries. In this respect, it is interesting to note that what was put forward in Chapter 6 on the relationship between the growth of intra-trade, home market defence and collusion is still more valid when intra-firm intra-trade is concerned.[34]

The second factor that has played a likely role is the existence of a 'voluntary' export restraint (VER) that limits to 11 per cent the rate of penetration of Japanese car producers in the British market. Already in 1977–1978, Japanese exporters captured 10–11 per cent of the British market. Since that time, they have not been allowed to increase their market share. Thus they had no interest in violating the tacit collusive agreement and passing on the appreciation of the British pound in passenger car prices. Another consequence of the VER is a *modus vivendi* for competition between Japanese and continental producers on the British market.[35] In sum, the rise of the British currency against the other currencies combined with a VER towards Japanese exporters and the large extent of reciprocal competition resulted in higher prices and larger profits for Japanese and continental car manufacturers.

Changes in exchange rates do not seem to have produced the same harmful effects on prices and consumer welfare in other countries. For example, the appreciation of the German currency did not have the same upward effect on passenger car prices in West Germany. The depreciation of other currencies against the DM was passed on in the prices of imported vehicles. Two factors helped to keep low passenger car prices in West Germany. The first is the absence of a quantitative restriction towards Japanese exports in this country. The second is the higher degree of efficiency of the German motor vehicle industry, which is price leader on its home market.[36]

The Italian passenger car market provides evidence that increasing prices can be combined with a steady decrease in the exchange rates (see Figure 7.3). Here, too, price leader–follower practices from West European car manufacturers and a nearly prohibitive quantitative restriction against Japanese exports explain the divergent movements of Italian car prices after 1975. The economic difficulties of the main Italian producer, Fiat, during the second half of the 1970s and the necessity of charging higher prices in order to survive explain the higher level of Italian prices during this period.

The introduction of exchange rates into the analysis partly explains the divergent movements of passenger car prices within the enlarged free-trade area since the mid-1970s. It is worth emphasising that it is not exchange rate movements *per se* that explain price dispersion but their combination with price following practices.

## Price control policies

The lower level of car prices in some countries might be the result of price control policies that prevented domestic as well as foreign car manufacturers from passing on the increase of their production costs in their prices. If valid, this argument is only appropriate for those passenger car markets that were not characterised by increasing relative prices during the second half of the 1970s, that is for West Germany, France and Sweden.

This explanation has little merit. In West Germany, price control is permitted only in so far as it serves anti-monopolistic purposes and was never exercised against car prices.[37] In France the widespread price controls exercised in most industrial sectors since 1945 were abolished for all industrial products, including passenger cars, in 1978.[38] However, it was reintroduced in conjunction with the devaluation of the French franc in October 1981.[39] Four years later, in 1985, the price controls on passenger cars and on several other industrial products were removed in France. In Sweden, besides short periods of price freeze in relation with exchange-rate readjustments, control of car prices was exercised between July and December 1976 and between May 1979 and December 1980.[40]

It should be added that price control policy in France and Sweden does not imply that firms cannot increase their prices. It only consists of an apparatus of surveillance and means that firms must obtain the authorisation of a Price Commission in order to increase their prices. An exception is the freeze of car prices decreed in Sweden for a duration of five months in 1976. The fact that price control policies in France and Sweden were exercised during short periods and the absence of price control policy in West Germany suggest that the growing price disparities observed during the second half of the 1970s cannot be ascribed to this factor.

Price control policies are thus of no help in explaining price disparities. Yet the behaviour of foreign car manufacturers during periods of price control is worth analysing because it is illustrative of some leader–follower practices.

For example, the price control introduced in France in October 1981 did not apply to foreign car manufacturers. These were free to pass on exchange-rate changes in the prices of imported cars. Between 1981 and 1984 the French currency was devalued three times and lost around 25 per cent of its value in relation to the German mark. As suggested by Figure 7.4, the appreciation of foreign currencies was passed on only to a very limited extent in the prices of imported cars (50 per cent of imported cars in France are German). Foreign producers continued to follow the prices charged by the French manufacturers subject to the price control.[41] Such results tend to support the price–leadership hypothesis. However, they should be interpreted with some care. The similarity of price changes over time in the presence of exchange-rate movements can follow from divergent cost developments.

In Sweden the interplay between importer pricing policy, government control policy and exchange-rate changes is less conclusive for price-following practices. As noted above, prices for domestic and foreign passenger cars were frozen in Sweden between July and December 1976. In October the same year, the DM was revalued by 3 per cent in relation to the Swedish krona. Importers of West German passenger cars demanded and obtained the permission to increase their prices in the Swedish market.[42] A likely reason behind this departure from price-following might be the lower degree of price-responsiveness of demand on the Swedish market.

However, another picture emerges from an analysis of corporate pricing policy in the Swedish market in the absence of exchange-rate changes. This points out that importers and foreign car manufacturers do take into account the timing and extent of price adjustments by the leading domestic companies, Volvo and Saab, when they fix their local prices.[43]

## Concluding remarks

Pricing is like a tripod. It has three legs. In addition to cost, there are the two other legs of market demand and competition. It is no more possible to say that one or another of these factors determines price than it is to assert that one leg rather than either of the other two supports a tripod.[44]

189

190

**Figure 7.4:** Price changes for foreign and domestic passenger cars on the French market, 1981–1984 (base 100 = March 1981)

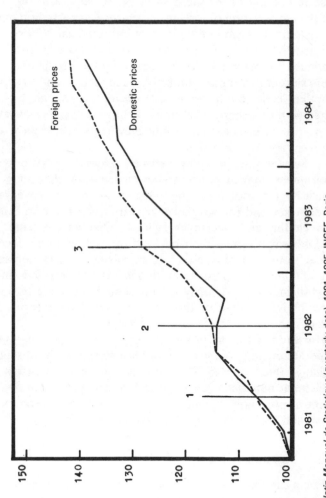

*Sources: Bulletin Mensuel de Statistique* (quarterly data), 1981–1985, INSEE, Paris.

*Notes:* 1, FF devalued by 3 per cent and DM revalued by 5.5 per cent; 2, FF devalued by 5.75 per cent and DM revalued by 4.25 per cent; 3, FF devalued by 2.5 per cent and DM revalued by 5.5 per cent.

This definition expresses the complex nature of business pricing and explains why our analysis does not provide a monocausal and precise explanation of the factors governing price disparities among passenger car markets within the enlarged free-trade area.

The merit of our analysis is to focus on a certain number of probable factors and to show how they interact to create price differences. A main conclusion is that price dispersion is the manifestation and indeed represents the measurement of price leading–following in the West European market combined with more or less severe trade restrictions towards foreign producers, exchange-rate volatility and different characteristics of consumer demand.

As for the factors behind the prices charged by the car manufacturers in their national markets — which are the prices that will prevail in the different markets — we suggested that the level of price elasticity, combined with the presence of high non-tariff barriers, plays a non-negligible role in Sweden. In other countries like Britain and Italy, the level of price elasticities does not seem to be taken into account when domestic firms set their prices. In these countries it is mostly the cost situation, trade restrictions towards Japanese exports and price following that motivate the level of car prices. The low car prices that prevailed in West Germany seem mainly the result of a more competitive domestic industry combined with the absence of trade restrictions towards Japanese car exporters. Note that the first factor is probably in part a consequence of the second.

Our findings on the relatively low French prices are somewhat disappointing. We could expect higher car prices in France (above all after 1980–1981) for two main reasons. Firstly, the French market is protected by a severe VER towards Japanese car producers. Secondly, serious economic difficulties have characterised the French passenger car industry since the beginning of the 1980s.[45] A combination of several factors probably explains the French results. An erroneous estimation of the price elasticity for French cars by French producers can be a possible explanation. This may be the result of an inaccurate interpretation of the income coefficient in Table 7.5 or a misunderstanding of the non-price-related causes of integration. A second factor is the greater intensity of import competition against leading domestic firms and the higher degree of competition noticed in this country over the past decade. A third

191

factor can be the price control (introduced in 1981 and removed in 1985), which has postponed the intended upward adjustments of prices on the French market.[46] A fourth factor can be the presence among the domestic price leaders of a state-owned firm, Renault, that is less sensitive to losses because these are spread over taxpayers.[47]

## BARRIERS TO PARALLEL TRADE FLOWS

Parallel trade flows refer to arbitrage-induced imports or exports that take place outside the official distribution network. In Chapter 6 it was shown that barriers to parallel trade flows are a necessary condition for the maintenance of a lucrative market fragmentation.[48] As far as passenger cars are concerned, such barriers can take two forms. The first is exclusive dealing agreements. These imply that manufacturers do not supply foreign dealers who refuse to prohibit passenger car re-exports and that the appointed dealers have no right to sell in another dealer's territorial market. This last restriction is of course not necessary if manufacturers distribute their own products through their subsidiaries abroad. The second form of barriers is corporate or collective action in the domestic market so as to obtain a regulation that impedes passenger car parallel imports. In the car markets under study, there are several examples of barriers to parallel trade flows. They provide a good illustration of the way car manufacturers and dealers split up markets and of the attitude of authorities. We will concentrate our attention on four of them.

The first example concerns Opel, the German subsidiary of General Motors. During a short period in 1973, Opel prevented parallel imports of new Opel cars not marketed through its own distribution network in Belgium and which could be purchased at a lower price in other EEC countries. According to Belgian law, passenger car manufacturers had exclusive power to issue certificates of conformity establishing that their new passenger cars conformed to the general approved type.[49] This legislation was used to impede parallel imports. General Motors charged a much higher inspection fee on parallel imports than on imports sold by Opel subsidiaries. The parallel trade barriers were nevertheless rapidly removed by General Motors. This was the main reason invoked by the Court of Justice of the European

Communities for annulling the fine imposed on General Motors by the Commission.[50]

The second example concerns the German company BMW and the trade association for BMW importers in Belgium (BMW Belgian Dealers' Advisory Committee). In 1977, to curb parallel trade flows, this trade association addressed a circular to all BMW Belgian dealers in which they asked them not to re-export new BMW passenger cars to other EEC countries where prices were higher than in Belgium.[51] However, this attempt was not successful. It was reported to the Commission of the European Community which, on 23 December 1977, fined BMW-Belgium and most of the BMW Belgian 'independent' importers for being involved in a ban of re-exports of new BMW vehicles from Belgium to other EEC countries. It is worth noting that the fine imposed on BMW-Belgium was much higher than the fines paid by the 'independent' dealers but that the Commission insisted on fining the latter. The Commission pointed out that they could have refused to enter into the agreement in spite of their dependence upon BMW-Belgium.[52]

The third example dates from some years later in Britain. In 1980 and 1981 the growing price differentials observed between the British passenger car market and other EEC markets gave rise to a violent press campaign in Britain: 'Anybody who buys a new car in Britain today is a mug.'[53] Several newspapers pointed out these differences and encouraged British consumers not to purchase British or foreign cars in Britain but on the continent, where they could be bought at a saving of up to 30 per cent. The press campaign gave rise to a large flow of private parallel imports. According to some estimations, these amounted to not less than 50,000 units per year, around 3 per cent of new passenger car sales in Britain.[54]

In order to curb this growing intra-EEC parallel import flow and consumer exit from the British market, car manufacturers adopted two measures. First, they strove to stop the distribution of right-hand-drive motor vehicles in Western Europe (Britain and Ireland excluded) and more particularly in West Germany and Belgium. Second, they intervened directly in Britain so as to block entry of parallel imports and of re-imports.

Ford-Germany for example decided to end the distribution of right-hand-drive motor vehicles by the continental Ford companies from 1 May 1982.[55] Note that the same Ford vehicles were 30 per cent cheaper in the German market than in the British market, where Ford enjoyed a dominant position. Ford's decision can be regarded as a barrier to exit for dissatisfied consumers. It led to vigorous protests by the British press, the BEUC and several German dealers who were more particularly affected. This in turn drew the attention of the Commission. In August 1982 it issued an interim order to Ford to resume supplies of right-hand-drive passenger cars to German dealers but, and as a temporary measure, to an aggregate number limited to the level attained before Ford's measure in question was introduced.[56] The Commission decision was confirmed by the Court of Justice but contested by Ford.[57]

Two other companies, Fiat and Alfa-Romeo, tried to hamper parallel imports of right-hand-drive vehicles into Britain mainly by delaying their delivery in Belgium.[58] Their action was, however, short-lived as a result of the intervention of the Commission. It is likely that this only marginally affected parallel exports to Britain.[59]

The second measure that contributed to impede parallel imports was the use of the British type-approval legislation. This provides car manufacturers exclusive authority to issue the certificates of conformity — concerning safety and technical standards — required to register new passenger cars in Britain. The large extent of parallel imports threatened established firms' dominant positions in Britain. To curb such imports, manufacturers made use of the above regulation. The certificates of conformity were difficult and costly to obtain for private persons or commercial importers outside the official dealer network.[60] A good illustration is given by British Leyland in 1984. In a first stage, the state-owned firm refused to provide independent importers with type-approval numbers for some BL cars necessary to licence vehicles in Britain. In a second stage and once it changed its mind, it charged a high fee aimed at deterring parallel importers. This was reported to the Commission, which ordered British Leyland to put an end to such practices and imposed a fine of 350,000 ECU (BL has appealed to the European Court of Justice against this decision).[61]

A loophole in the British legislation, however, enabled the individual import of passenger cars provided that they had been 'used' abroad. The liberal interpretation of this requirement by British authorities was questioned by the car manufacturers and their trade association, the Society of Motor Manufacturers and

Traders. The latter approached the British government during 1981 in order to extend to six months the required period of use abroad.[62] The British government resisted these pressures and decided not to tighten up the regulation on personal parallel imports. Furthermore, in February 1982 it proposed that commercial importers outside the official dealer network should obtain automatically the necessary conformity certificates from the official distributors. This liberalisation announcement was, however, not followed by any systematic action from the British government. The probable reason behind this attitude is that free parallel imports and price equalisation between Britain and the continental countries would have meant more difficulties for the state-owned and already loss-making British Leyland and, consequently, more public subsidies.

The fourth example concerns the French passenger car market. In 1983 an independent dealer, E. Leclerc, reimported French passenger cars from Belgium and marketed them at a price that was around 15 per cent lower than the price charged by the official distributors for the same makes of cars in France. His attempt was not successful. Rumours originating in the car manufacturers' and official sellers' lobbying groups were circulated that the warranty services would not be available for the Leclerc vehicles. Furthermore, it was suggested that the official authority responsible for the type-approval certificate (Service des Mines) would extend the delay of attribution of the conformity certificates for the Leclerc vehicles. This prevention of reimports benefited from the goodwill of the French government, which was afraid of the consequences of falling prices on the already loss-making domestic car producers.[63]

Official French importers have the sole power to issue certificates of conformity establishing that individual parallel imports conform to the general approved type. Individual parallel imports threaten the monopoly position of official importers. Thus it is not surprising that the latter took advantage of this regulation so as to hamper free import. According to a survey, official importers in France either keep individual importers waiting for several weeks or make them travel several hundred kilometres to have their cars examined or charge high inspection fees (in one case up to the price differential between France and Belgium).[64] It may be worth adding by way of concluding the French example, that neither the practices of official importers nor the Leclerc case drew the attention of the Commission on the French passenger car market.

Of course, these four examples do not constitute an exhaustive review of the actions by the car manufacturers, their trade associations and the official dealers to prevent free-trade flows. Nevertheless, they provide evidence of a certain number of interesting aspects concerning the extent of barriers to parallel trade flows — and their changes over time — in the West European 'unified' economic area.

A first striking conclusion that emerges from these examples is that large firms do strive to segment the West European economic area and prevent a complete interpenetration and integration of national products markets. The behaviour of firms is thus responsible for the permanence of price dispersion. This is not a manifestation of ignorance in the market. Such a result has important implications for the role of market conduct and the outcome of the integration process. It suggests that integration-retarding market distortions of private origin are common and recurrent.

A second conclusion concerns the role of national governments. The four examples show that national governments either adopt a passive attitude or support, in one way or another, the attempts of firms to fragment the European economic area. Three reasons can be put forward to explain public policy. The first is that free parallel trade flows are expected to worsen the financial difficulties of several car manufacturers and lead to more public subsidies. The second is that market fragmentation and price discrimination policies may help to accomplish — at least in the short run — one of the main goals of industrial policy which is to promote exports. The third is that public policy reflects the success of the efforts of the car producers and their trade associations to obtain a regulation (that is a public good) that hampers free parallel imports. (The structure and role of trade associations will be examined in detail in an appendix to the present chapter.) Further, the passive government policy in Britain and France indicates that the presence of state-owned firms facilitates the achievement of a free-trade-impeding regulation.

A third conclusion concerns the growing number of cases of intra-EEC trade impediments reported to the Commission during the last decade. This development reflects the greater room for profitable parallel trade flows operations over the past ten years. The small number of cases before the mid-1970s must be due in large part to the absence of arbitrage-inducing price disparities. This confirms indirectly the results of Table 7.1 on the small price differentials among the EEC countries prior to 1975. A complementary factor may be the vigorous press campaigns (above all in Britain) which, by spreading information about price differences, have decreased the cost of search for the cheapest products for most consumers and encourage exit.

Fourth, the above four examples illustrate the dependence of official dealers upon car manufacturers. This is a consequence of the exclusive dealing arrangements. Such arrangements imply a fear of losing one's concession if one refuses to accept the recommendations of the manufacturers on prohibition of re-exports and sales to non-residents. The dependence between manufacturers and official dealers reduces the chances of detecting measures of a protectionist nature. The reason for this is that these measures are often taken by individual dealers at the grass-roots level in form of, for example, reservations about reparations under the guarantee or excessive delivery delays.

Fifth, with regard to cases referred to the European Commission and the distribution among EEC countries, the above review shows that Belgium has been involved in most cases. This result reflects the fact that passenger car prices are lower in this country but also, probably, the fact that the European Community has its headquarters in this country and is therefore more able to investigate notified cases. A somewhat surprising result concerns the absence of France and to some extent Italy in the cases considered by the Commission, although there is some room for lucrative re-imports in these countries. Such evidence confirms previous studies dealing with EEC competition policy towards restrictive practices that ascertained the surprisingly small number of French and Italian cases considered by the Commission.[65]

Finally, it is interesting to note that the policy of the Commission towards parallel imports has been twofold. On the one hand, it has furthered competition and the free flow of intra-EEC trade by defending the right of each consumer to buy a car wherever he or she wants within the Common Market (the so-called individual parallel imports). On the other hand, it has contributed to limiting free trade by exempting exclusive dealer arrangements in the motor vehicle sector from the general ban stipulated in Article 85 of the Rome Treaty and, consequently, by hampering free parallel trade flows by dealers outside the official distribution network.

The enactment of EEC-type approval for automobiles from 1 July 1985 is an illustration of the first aspect of the Commission policy. It gives each consumer the right to purchase anywhere in the Common Market a passenger car with the specifications appropriate in the country where the vehicle is to be used. It also gives each buyer the conformity certificate necessary to register the vehicle in this country.[66] This measure facilitates individual parallel trade flows and undeniably constitutes a step towards a higher degree of integration of passenger car markets.

The exemption for selective distribution agreements of motor cars from Article 85 of the Rome Treaty has the opposite effect on free parallel trade flows and integration. Article 85 prohibits 'agreements which may affect trade between Member States and which have as their object or effect the prevention, restriction or distortion of competition within the Common Market'.[67] The exemption will be valid up to 1993. It implies a certain number of restrictions imposed on all motor vehicle dealers by manufacturers. Dealers have no right to sell new vehicles (or replacement parts) obtained from the manufacturer to commercial dealers outside the official distribution network. They have no right either to actively seek customers outside their allotted territorial market or to sell other manufacturers' vehicles or parts. These restrictions necessarily impede arbitrage-induced intra-EEC trade flows and help to maintain substantial price disparities.

It is interesting to note that trade policy considerations (mostly the desire to limit Japanese penetration in the EEC) influenced the Commission in coming to the decision. The Commission considered that a strenghtening of the ties between dealers and manufacturers and the density of motor vehicle distribution networks in EEC countries were 'powerful weapons in the fight against competition from abroad'.[68]

In a first stage, the Commission proposed a regulation with an automatic suspension of selective distribution agreements when prices net of tax differ by more than 12 per cent for a period of more than six months between any two EEC markets.[69] This clause was supported by the European consumer organisation BEUC.[70] The vigorous opposition of West European car manufacturers and their trade association in

Brussels probably explains its rejection by the Commission in a second stage.[71] A complementary reason was the firm opposition of certain national governments, which considered that the Commission was going beyond its prerogatives by adopting a price control measure.[72]

## SUMMARY AND CONCLUSIONS

Viewed as a state of affairs, integration can be defined by the creation of a new and larger market out of several originally different national markets.[73] The main purpose of international integration is thus to favour the emergence of a new economic area 'of which the parts are so united by the relations of unrestricted commerce that prices there take the same level throughout'.[74]

The main conclusion that can be drawn from the analysis of the present chapter is that there are still different national markets in Western Europe and that the present state of integration is far from the one described above. As pointed out in Chapter 6, several factors may prevent the creation of an enlarged market and a unique price from prevailing throughout the entire integrated area, namely a free-trade area under certain special assumptions or the presence of some market imperfections.

In the first section, we provided ample evidence of the substantial price differences that exist among West European passenger car markets. Furthermore, we showed that such price differences have increased over the past decade.

In Chapter 6 it was shown that the break-down of the customs union in the mid-1970s and its transformation into a free-trade area could favour the emergence of price disparities within the tariff-unified area. In this chapter, we have suggested that it is not this transformation *per se* that is responsible for the observed price disparities among the members of the enlarged West European free-trade area (EEC plus EFTA countries). Further, we have indicated that it is not purchase tax disparities or different levels of market concentration, either. The main conclusion of the second section is that different characteristics of consumer demand, different trade policies towards third countries, different leading firms' pricing policies and price leading-following practices, and the presence in some countries

199

of substantial non-tariff barriers interact to create these substantial price disparities. Such an explanation gives some support to the hypothesis introduced in Chapter 6 on the relationship between the growth of intra-trade and the subsequent emergence of reciprocal competition and price leadership. A consequence of this result is that dynamic competitive gains are substantial during the first years of formation of an economic association but small once intra-trade has become sizeable and oligopolistic firms have become aware of their interdependence. This latter result is all the more likely since firms of member countries organise at the multinational level.

Another conclusion that arises from the second section is the non-significance of market concentration but the non-negligible role of changes in market structures in explaining price dispersion. Such a result suggests that the analysis of conduct embodied in changes in market structures over time offers a much better indication of the degree of competition prevailing in a market. Firms are not passive agents through which the market structure works its influence on industrial performance, but active agents that mould their environment and partly determine the degree of competition. A tentative conclusion emerges concerning the stability in the distribution of market shares over time and the small changes in market structures noticed in most countries over the past decade.[75] Our analysis of corporate pricing policies confirms that they ensue mostly from the absence of vigorous competition (price leading–following practices).

The interplay between market conduct and the political sphere at national as well as European Community levels explains the permanence of price dispersions over time. This interplay resulted in a legislation and a public policy favourable to market fragmentation and to the prevention of arbitrage-induced trade flows. Several factors explain the success of lobbying activities at the national and EEC levels. It was suggested that the high degree of organisation of the West European motor vehicle industry, at the national and international levels, is one of the main factors behind this success. Other factors are some characteristics of the passenger car industry (large in terms of employment, high concentration, presence in some countries of state-owned firms, etc.). As pointed out in Chapter 2 when non-tariff barriers were analysed, such characteristics increase the chances of receiving assistance from national governments and the Commission of the EEC.[76]

## NOTES

1. See Commission of the European Communities (1972), p. 189.

2. The results of the EEC studies are given in Ferrier (1984).

3. We selected 40 models from 11 different makes in 1970, 48 models from 11 different makes in 1974, 44 models from 11 different makes in 1975, 48 models from 15 different makes in 1978, 58 models from 16 different makes in 1980, 83 models from 19 different makes in 1981, 91 models from 17 makes in 1982 and 100 models from 18 makes in 1984.

4. Only Swedish, West German, French and Italian makes were taken into account in 1970, 1974 and 1975. In 1978, 1980, 1981, 1982 and 1984, Japanese, British and East European makes were also included in the sample.

5. Because of the absence of information on the Swedish passenger car prices during October 1975, we compared for the year 1975 the average of the Swedish prices of the same 44 models in May 1975 and January 1976 with the October prices in Paris.

6. See Table 2.4, pp. 35–36.

7. See CLCA (1985a, 1985b).

8. See Chapter 6, pp. 142–45.

9. See Chapter 2, pp. 28–33.

10. See Chapter 2, pp. 26–27.

11. See Chapter 6, pp. 142–44.

12. By creating an artificial scarcity of Japanese imports, the voluntary export restraints are expected to increase the prices charged for these cars. This probable effect implies that prices for the same models of Japanese cars should be lower in Sweden than in France, which benefits from a quantitative restriction. However, empirical evidence — which relates to the second half of the 1970s and the beginning of the 1980s — invalidates this argument. It shows that the prices (net of taxes) of the same models of Japanese passenger cars were significantly higher in Stockholm than in Paris (see Table 7.1).

13. See Chapter 2, pp. 26–27.

14. Ibid., pp. 37–46.

15. Ibid., pp. 37–38.

16. The inclusion of taxes into the consumer price index for new cars means that a move in the price index may not actually ensue from a change in the net price of cars but from a change in the rate of tax imposition on new car purchases. For example, it is likely that the peculiar behaviour of the Swedish prices up to the mid-1970s (see Table 7.3) is the result of the increases in the excise tax (see Table 2.4). Note that if the change in tax imposition concerns all products, no effect will of course be observed on the ratio of new-car to total price indexes.

17. For an illustration of the impact of quantitative restrictions on

passenger car quality upgrading in the United States, see Feenstra (1985), pp. 49–68; and Gomez-Ibanez, Leone and O'Connell (1983), pp. 196–219.

18. Potential competition is ignored here. The main reason behind this is the high barriers to entry that characterise the passenger car industry and which explain the absence of fresh West European entry over the past two and a half decades. Another reason is the trade barriers facing non-European new entry. A third reason is the difficulties of measurement of this form of competition.

19. See Chapter 5, pp. 119 and 122.

20. See Gort (1963), pp. 51–63; Jacoby (1964), pp. 83–107; McGuckin (1972), pp. 363–70; and Caves and Porter (1978), pp. 289–313.

21. See Chapter 5, pp. 132, 135–36.

22. Ibid., pp. 120–21, 132, 135–36.

23. See Chapter 6, pp. 151–58.

24. Ibid., pp. 151–55.

25. It should be noted that the price index for domestic cars refers to home made cars and to captive imports.

26. The specialisation of French firms is illustrated in Figure 6.4, p. 153.

27. These non-price effects cannot be captured by the introduction of a trend variable in Equations 7.3 and 7.4 because of a high degree of collinearity between such a variable and the income variable.

28. See Chapter 6, pp. 155–57.

29. See Chapter 3, pp. 74–75.

30. Ibid.

31. The large and growing part of company purchases in new car registration in West European countries is one of the factors behind lower price responsiveness. In Sweden, for example, this part amounted to not less than 40 per cent of new car purchase in 1983. See Bilindustriföreningen (1985), p. 11.

32. On the productivity and financial performance of the British motor vehicle industry in an international perspective, see Bhaskar (1979), pp. 58–63.

33. See Chapter 3, pp. 62–63.

34. See Chapter 6, pp. 155–56.

35. On the relation between quantitative restriction and collective action among importing firms, see Adams and Dirlam (1977).

36. On the competitiveness of West German manufacturers and other Western Europe manufacturers, see Altschuler et al. (1984), pp. 155–71.

37. See Schmidt (1981), pp. 492–503.

38. See Jenny (1981), pp. 477–90.

39. See L'Expansion (1985).

40. See Jonung (1984), pp. 23–41; and SOU (1981) (Bilagor 7–12), pp. 557–88.

41. Empirical evidence indicates that the causality runs from domestic to foreign firms, since importer price changes take place after domestic firm price changes. See L'Expansion (1985).

42. See SOU (1981), pp. 578–79.

43. Ibid., p. 566.

44. President of General Motors, quoted by Alfred (1972), p. 3.

45. The two French firms, Renault and Peugeot, began to make losses in 1981 and 1980. In 1981, 1982, 1983 and 1984, the state-owned Renault lost FF 875, 2,563, 1,875 and 11,234 millions, respectively. In 1980, 1981, 1982, 1983 and 1984, Peugeot lost FF 1,473, 2,034, 2,148, 2,590 and 340 millions, respectively (the figures are after-tax profits; sources are annual company reports).

46. This is partly confirmed by a recent episode. The French car manufacturers raised their prices by 4.5 per cent a few days after the freeing of their prices in July 1985. See L'Expansion (1985).

47. See Table 2.6 on public subsidies to Renault, p. 50.

48. See Chapter 5, pp. 150–51, 157–58.

49. See Commission of the European Communities (1975), pp. 65–66.

50. See Commission of the European Communities (1976), p. 29.

51. On the BMW case, see Commission of the European Communities (1975), pp. 57–60, and (1980), pp. 25–27.

52. The Commission fined BMW-Belgium BFR 7,500,000, each of the eight members of the BMW Belgian Dealers' Advisory Committee between BFR 75,000 and 100,000, and 39 other BMW dealers BFR 50,000. See Commission of the European Communities (1975), p. 25.

53. See The Economist (1980), p. 75, (1981a), pp. 68–72, and (1981b), p. 63.

54. See Commission of the European Communities (1983c), p. 12.

55. See BEUC (1982b), and Burnside (1985), pp. 34–53.

56. See Commission of the European Communities (1983a), pp. 55–56, and (1984a), pp. 75–76.

57. Ford dealers were involved in another anti-competition case when at the very beginning of 1983 they placed an advertisement in West German newspapers: 'We do not carry out guarantee work on new Ford cars reimported after being purchased elsewhere in the European Community.' Complaints by individuals and the BEUC led the Commission to intervene and to oblige the same dealers to place further advertisements stating that Ford cars reimported will no longer be handicapped in this way. See Commission of the European Communities (1984a), pp. 78–79.

58. See Commission of the European Communities (1985), pp. 64–66.

59. Several other car manufacturers (Toyota, Honda, Mazda, Volkswagen, BMW and Mercedes) tried to deter buyers of right-hand-drive passenger cars in Belgium. However, these car manufacturers were not prosecuted by the Commission although their anti-competitive practices were reported to it. See The Economist (1982a), p. 47.

60. See Swann (1983), pp. 28–30.

61. See Commission of the European Communities (1985), pp. 79–80.

62. See Swann (1983), p. 29.

63. See Le Monde (1984a).

64. BEUC (1982a).
65. See George and Joll (1975), p. 210.
66. See *Official Journal of the European Communities* (1985a).
67. The exemption was first granted in 1974 in the BMW case. A new regulation, which came into force in July 1985, confirms the main principles of the BMW decision. On the EEC exemption for selective distribution of motor vehicles, see Commission of the European Communities (1975), pp. 57–60, (1983c), pp. 15–18; Van Houtte (1984), pp. 349–57; *Official Journal of the European Communities* (1985a).
68. See Commission of the European Communities (1981b), pp. 43–44.
69. See Van Houtte (1984), pp. 353–54.
70. See BEUC (1983b).
71. *The Economist* (1983b) and *Financial Times* (1984).
72. See *Le Figaro* (1985).
73. See Chapter 1, p. 1.
74. Cournot (1897), pp. 51–52.
75. See Chapter 5, pp. 85–92.
76. See Chapter 2, pp. 15, 53.

## APPENDIX: TRADE ASSOCIATIONS

The main objective of business associations is to provide a service to all the members of the association.[1] This service can be considered as a public or collective good since it goes to every member of the association. It is assumed that, as is actually the case in the passenger car industry, all the firms of the industry belong to the trade association. A higher price, a trade-impeding measure — such as a VER or a quota — or any regulation that benefits the members of the industry are examples of public goods provided by trade associations. As seen above, one of the main services provided by the trade associations in the passenger car industry has been to prevent parallel trade flows, the effects of which, if present, would have levelled out price disparities and fully integrated the West European passenger car market.[2] Another example is the role of the British and Italian trade associations in the introduction of non-tariff barriers.[3] These services can of course be regarded as public goods. They permit all the firms to remain inefficient, to enjoy a quieter competitive life or, eventually, to benefit from monopoly profits and economic rents.

The high degree of organisation of the passenger car industry is the likely result of the small number of firms that comprise the industry.[4] This high degree is indubitably one of the major factors behind its influence on political decisions at the national as well as at the international level. The interests of the motor vehicle industry are crystallised and defended by trade associations that have existed in most producer countries since the beginning of the century (see Table 7.7). A noteworthy aspect of the institutional organisation of the industry is the existence of a separate trade association for passenger car importers in Italy, Germany and France while domestic and foreign producers belong to the same trade association in Sweden and Britain. This is all the more interesting since the two latter countries were characterised by relatively high prices and had little price competition to contend with from imports.

The establishment of the European Common Market resulted in the organisation of the industry at the international level and in the formation of a new trade association in Brussels in 1958. The BPICA, created in Paris in 1919, performs a primarily informative role with no lobbying activities. The European trade association (CLCA) consists of national trade associations of motor manufacturers established in the EEC, that is of French, German, Italian and, since 1973, British car manufacturers. Although a non-EEC producer, Volvo belongs

**Table 7.7**: Trade associations in the European passenger car industry

| Country | Trade associations | Date of foundation |
|---|---|---|
| | National Trade Associations | |
| France | Chambre Syndicale des Constructeurs d'Automobiles | 1909 |
| West Germany | Verband der Automobilindustrie | 1901 |
| Italy | Associazione Nazionale fra Industrie Automobilistiche | 1912 |
| Sweden | Bilindustriföreningen | 1941 |
| Britain | Society of Motor Manufacturers and Traders | 1902 |
| | Multinational Trade Associations | |
| All producer countries | Bureau Permanent International des Constructeurs d'Automobiles, Paris | 1919 |
| EEC producer countries | Comité de Liaison de la Construction Automobile, Brussels | 1958 |

*Sources:* Publications of the trade associations.

to it through its subsidiaries in Belgium and the Netherlands. An interesting finding is that the CLCA was reinforced, first in 1974, by the establishment of a permanent Secretariat on a part-time basis, and, then in 1979, by the establishment of a permanent Secretariat with a full-time Secretary General and staff.[5] It is likely that this high degree of organisation contributed to the success of the CLCA in persuading the European Commission to grant a long-standing block exemption on selective distribution of motor vehicles and to remove those aspects of the proposal that were considered to be damaging by the European car manufacturers.

Nevertheless, the trade association does not constitute the only way through which an industry exerts its influence on political decisions. The more dominating a firm is in a business branch, the more likely that the firm will bypass the branch trade association and be in direct and permanent contact with government officials. Further, and what is not always the same, the larger the size of a business firm, the more intense the direct contacts with government officials.[6] Of course, the presence of state-owned firms in an industry increases the likelihood of such direct contacts.

The passenger car industry confirms these points. Besides the political influence of the industry through its trade associations, there exists in each country direct contacts between motor vehicle manufacturers and government officials. Chapters 2 and 4 gave several examples of such direct relations between car manufacturers and the national governments.[7] The huge public subsidies received by state-owned firms in France and Britain provide another example.[8] These examples do not, however, form an exhaustive list. The fixing (up to 1978) of French prices by discussion between the administration and the business firms constitutes another example of direct relations between the industrial firms and the government. It did not involve trade associations and lead to a measure (a higher price, the formation of a cartel or the condemnation of price warfare) benefiting all the firms in an industry.[9] The direct relation existing in Sweden between Volvo and government officials is another illustration of a relation that bypasses the trade association level.[10]

The way the passenger car industry attempts to influence the Common Market Commission constitutes an exception. It does not take place directly but through the EEC car manufacturers' trade association in Brussels and through national governments.

An example of the latter case is when national governments interceded with the Commission to withdraw its proposal on the automatic suspension of selective distribution agreements if prices net of taxes differ by more than 12 per cent for a period of more than six months between any two EEC markets.[11]

Four main conclusions emerge from an analysis of the associations working on the behalf of the passenger car industry. First, it indicates that the industry is highly organised and that this is the likely result of the oligopolistic structure of the industry. Second, it shows that the opening up to trade led to the organisation of the industry at the international level. Third, it suggests that this high degree of organisation has helped to maintain (and in some way create) market segmentation in the enlarged European free-trade area. Finally, it gives some support to the view that trade associations are not the only channel through which the business community — above all if it is composed of very large, industry dominating and state-owned firms — influences the public choices.

## NOTES TO APPENDIX

1. The aim of trade associations emerges clearly from the annual report of the British motor vehicle association: The motor industry trade association 'needs the highest standards of professionalism, the most effective levels of parliamentary and media lobbying and it must provide a vital range of services to you, our members'. See Society of Motor Manufacturers and Traders (1984), p. 3.

2. See p. 198.

3. See for example Chapter 2, pp. 29–31, 34–36.

4. According to Mancur Olson, 'The high degree of organization of business interests, and the power of these business interests, must be due in large part to the fact that the business community is divided into a series of (generally oligopolistic) "industries", each of which contains only a fairly small number of firms' (Olson, 1965, p. 143).

5. See CLCA (1984).

6. For an illustration for Sweden, see Henning (1977), pp. 18–19.

7. See for example Chapter 2, pp. 29–31, and Chapter 4, pp. 103–10.

8. See Chapter 2, pp. 47–51.

9. On the French Plan as the scene of ententes and coalitions, see Cotta (1984), pp. 110–11, and Dirlam (1975), pp. 103–36.

10. On the relations between Volvo and government officials in Sweden, see Henning (1977), pp. 111–13.

11. See pp. 198–99.

# 8

## Summary and Conclusions

The main purpose of the present book has been to examine the interplay between international economic integration, market structure, firm behaviour and public policy with reference to the West European passenger car industry and markets. During the course of the analysis, it was shown that the removal of traditional trade barriers in the 1960s and the first half of the 1970s contributed a great deal to bringing national markets closer to each other. On the other hand, it was suggested that imperfectly competitive firm behaviour and its interplay with the public sphere, at the national and multinational levels, have played a central role as an obstacle to a higher degree of integration over the past decade. This was illustrated with the help of an analysis of the corporate and institutional factors behind the large price differences noticed throughout the 'integrated' area. A second illustration of this interplay is the emergence of a certain number of non-tariff barriers over the past decade. A third is the creation of institutional impediments to resource mobility that take the form of barriers to exit for large firms.

The main conclusion that emerges is that the rapid move towards an integration of national markets initiated at the end of the 1950s was stopped in the mid-1970s and that the present state of integration is imperfect. The existence of a certain number of non-tariff barriers and market imperfections of industrial and political origin explains this latter result. It confirms that empirical works on integration should not be confined to only the trade effects and that industrial and institutional factors should be incorporated to understand the scope of integration and its welfare effects.

Our final comments upon this conclusion are arranged in

three parts. Part one concerns the nature of international integration in Western Europe and its likely future. There follows in the second part some considerations on the nature of market power, some general issues about its social costs and some public policy implications. Finally, the third section discusses the roles of market conduct and public policy in international integration. It touches upon their growth-retarding effects and discusses some general issues regarding the limits of the process of international integration.

## THE NATURE AND FUTURE OF INTERNATIONAL INTEGRATION

A manifestation of the interplay between the public sphere at the national level and car manufacturers' behaviour is the erection of quantitative restrictions towards third-country exports. The form and extent of these restrictions vary widely from country to country. The conclusion derived from the experience of the car industry is thus that, contrary to the official EEC opinion, the EEC is no longer a customs union but a free-trade area. The reason for this is that member countries have different trade policies towards third countries. Another conclusion is that member countries of the two West European trading blocks, the EEC and EFTA, together form an enlarged free-trade area dating from the mid-1970s.

As shown in Chapter 6 with the help of a two-country, one-product, partial equilibrium model, the form of integration, whether customs union or free-trade area, has important implications for the outcome of international integration. For example, price dispersion is more likely in a free-trade area than in a customs union and, thus, more likely within the EEC now than prior to the mid-1970s. Another consequence of the transformation of the EEC into a free-trade area lacking formal rules of origin is a waste of resources due to the necessary time-consuming decisions taken by the EEC Commission in order to prevent trade deflection.

Tariff removal is a necessary but not sufficient condition for the creation of a truly integrated market out of several national markets. The formation of such a market also requires the suppression of a certain number of trade distortions and market imperfections, the origin of which often is firm behaviour.

Chapter 2 pointed out that there are several non-tariff barriers, such as public subsidies, technical and administrative rules and trade-distorting tax structures, which hamper the free flow of passenger cars within an economic area that is integrated with regard to tariffs. Moreover, it was argued that the extent of non-tariff trade barriers has increased significantly over the last decade. For example, public subsidies are more sizeable, particularly in France and Britain now than before the mid-1970s. Technical obstacles are more stringent in Sweden, and the Italian tax structure discriminates more against imports.

There is another factor of private origin that prevents the integration of national markets into a larger multinational one. In product-differentiated markets such as the passenger car market, exclusive distribution agreements permit firms to ban trade flows outside the official network system (so-called parallel trade flows), to price-discriminate and to fragment economic areas that are integrated with regard to tariffs. Chapter 7 showed that this factor has been the main source of fragmentation of the passenger car economic area embracing both the EEC and EFTA countries.

The question that now arises is whether the present nature of economic integration will change in the foreseeable future. Two main reasons suggest that the EEC will remain a free-trade area. The first follows from the observed shift over the last decade in the centre of decision-making of trade policy from the EEC to the national organs. The passive attitude adopted by the EEC Commission towards the different quantitative restrictions introduced by individual countries against third-country passenger car exports illustrates this change. The second reason follows from the enlargement of the EEC, which makes more problematic an agreement on trade policy towards third countries now than at the end of the 1950s because of the increasing effect of the enlargement on coordination costs. A complementary factor may be the different degrees of competitiveness of the national passenger car industries in EEC countries and the different protective measures to which this is likely to give rise.[1]

An important conclusion is that the internal market should remain fragmented in the foreseeable future. There are two primary explanations for this likely outcome. The first is the policy of the EEC Commission and the resulting EEC legislation. This legislation grants a block exemption for selective distribution agreements between car manufacturers and their dealers from Article 85 of the Rome Treaty.[2] It bans parallel trade flows by non-official dealers but permits parallel imports by individual consumers. The exemption was first granted in 1974. It was renewed under a slightly different form in July 1985 and will be valid up to 1993. At least up to this latter date, it is likely that car manufacturers will continue to price-discriminate, to prevent arbitrage-induced trade flows and to segment the West European economic area.

The limited exit that the EEC legislation affords to consumers dissatisfied with the level of domestic prices is insufficient to equalise prices and fully integrate the West European passenger car markets. This was illustrated in Chapter 7. It is further supported by the large price disparities that continue to exist one and a half years after the renewal of the EEC legislation in 1985.[3]

A second reason explains why the EEC enlarged market will remain fragmented. This is a consequence of the de facto transformation of the EEC into a free-trade area. The removal of border controls within an economic area and the creation of an enlarged market is only possible if this economic area forms a customs union. If countries form a free-trade area, internal border controls are necessary in order to prevent trade deflection. This was illustrated in Chapter 2 in the case of Italy. Thus, as long as the EEC remains a free-trade area, the creation of an enlarged market free from internal border controls is unlikely.

A main point to be stressed in this context is that this finding runs counter to the official EEC statements about the removal of 'physical, technical and tax frontiers' and the creation of a really unified internal market by 1992.[4]


## THE NATURE, COSTS AND POLICY IMPLICATIONS OF MARKET POWER

In Chapter 5 it was shown that the process of integration has brought about a decrease in market concentration and more competitive market structures. However, our examination of the interplay between market structure, firm behaviour, public policy and international integration in Chapter 7 shows that the role of the structural variables is strongly limited but that the role of market conduct is decisive. A likely reason behind the absence of significance of structural conditions may be the inability of market structure variables and of the traditional structure–conduct–performance paradigm to capture several important features of West European industrial markets. The most striking examples of such features are state-owned companies, widespread collusive practices between firms, different degrees and forms of organisation of business interests and peculiar trade-off relationships between government and industry.

An illustrative example is the nationalisation of British Leyland in 1975, which did not affect our market structure measures although it obviously altered competitive conditions in the British market. Three factors can be put forward to support this argument. The first is the huge public subsidies received by the newly state-owned firm after 1975. The second is the unobtrusive policy of the British government towards the presence of a collusive agreement between British and foreign firms (see Chapters 2 and 7). The third is the passive attitude of the same government towards barriers to parallel imports during the last decade. Another example is provided by the French state-owned Renault and the peculiar relations existing in France between large firms and the government. It is obvious that the non-competitive impact of these two factors is underestimated by market structure measures that consider only market share distribution.

In view of the determining role of market conduct, analyses of non-competitive markets should more particularly scrutinise firm behaviour, especially pricing policy and lobbying activities. The last aspect suggests that the public sphere, at the national and international levels, should be included in empirical studies because 'one of the obvious ways in which a special-interest group can increase the income of its member while reducing efficiency and output of the society is by lobbying for legislation to raise some price'.[5] For example, the existence and permanence over time of price leader–follower practices in the car industry cannot be understood without the study of EEC policy and the behaviour of national authorities. The conclusion that emerges is thus that the exercise of market power is based on the interplay between firm behaviour and the public sphere and that market power cannot last without the help of public policy.

Like other non-competitive practices, price following implies social costs to society, adding further to the social costs of tariff and non-tariff barriers. These welfare-decreasing costs should be particularly sizeable in countries like Britain, where it is obvious that the selling prices of passenger cars depart significantly from their costs.[6]

Other costs arise from the lobbying activity engaged in by motor vehicle manufacturers and their trade associations in order to obtain protection against foreign competition and favourable legislation and public policies. Lobbying expenditures should be important because of the large size of the income transfer from consumers to producers arising from successful collective action and non-competitive practices.[7] The lobbying costs of the consumer organisations (such as the BEUC), which try to prevent the income transfer and influence public choice in the opposite direction, further add to the lobbying costs. Whether total lobbying costs are welfare-improving or welfare-decreasing is, however, difficult to say since we are dealing with a second-best situation. For example, lobbying can decrease the production of the lobbying sector and increase it in other sectors and, thus, be welfare-improving.[8]

The absence of causal relationships between market structure and firm behaviour, as for example between a high level of market concentration and non-competitive practices or between a low level of concentration and competitive firm behaviour, has important policy implications. It indicates that a genuine competition policy cannot bypass the analysis of firm behaviour and be based on the sole consideration of structural market conditions.

In order to combat price practices harmful to consumer welfare and fully integrate passenger car markets, competition policy can act upon the factors that facilitate the exercise of market power. As shown in Chapter 7, this exercise depends primarily upon the existence of exclusive distribution agreements between producers and dealers and, also, upon different forms of quantitative restrictions towards Japanese exports. The removal of both institutional distortions seems to be an appropriate competition policy. It may imply welfare gains for consumers who will be able to buy passenger cars at lower prices.

The suppression of exclusive distribution agreements also suggests the possibility of a welfare loss. This may arise from the deterioration of after-sales services which, according to car makers, may follow from the removal of the selective distribution system.[9] Whether this is true is a moot question. Fewer after-sales services are actually required by modern cars.[10] Furthermore, the removal of exclusive distribution agreements may result in the separation of sales and after-sales service activities and, in a second stage, in the creation of independent servicing networks. Such a development is not necessarily prejudicial to the quality of after-sales services. Note that changes in that direction have already taken place in the United States.[11]

The exclusive distribution system has advantages for car producers. First, it makes price discrimination possible. Second, as suggested in Chapter 7, the density of exclusive distribution networks in Western Europe permits the limitation of Japanese penetration.[12] As illustrated during the course of the present work, the car industry has considerable political influence because of a certain number of characteristics the industry possesses (large in terms of employment, highly organised, presence of state-owned firms, etc.). Both the advantages derived from the exclusive distribution system and the strong political power of the industry suggest that it is doubtful that the above policy recommendation will be achieved in the near future in Western Europe.

## MARKET CONDUCT, PUBLIC POLICY AND THE LIMITS OF ECONOMIC INTEGRATION

One of the main objectives of international integration is to favour the emergence of trade patterns reflecting the patterns of comparative advantages and to reallocate resources among different producers so as to obtain a more rapid economic growth. A necessary condition for the realisation of this objective is the absence of corporate or institutional barriers to resource mobility.

As shown in Chapter 7, in the case of car manufacturer market conduct, price leader–follower practices are common within the tariff-unified economic area in Western Europe. Such practices prevent patterns of comparative advantages from being reflected in trade patterns and changing patterns of comparative advantages from giving rise to new trade patterns. The reason for this is that car manufacturers fix their export prices not according to their costs, which reflect, *inter alia*, comparative advantages, but according to the domestic price leaders. Another consequence of price leadership practices is

214

that they prevent the exit of inefficient firms that should have disappeared if efficient firms had adopted competitive pricing policies.

In Chapter 7 we provided evidence of the price leader–follower practices among passenger car markets in Western Europe. In Chapter 6 we suggested that such corporate practices are the likely result of the large extent of reciprocal competition and intra-industry trade. This finding has huge implications for the growth of trade and welfare following integration. It indicates that trade creation should be substantial during the first years of formation of an economic association when internal tariffs are removed. This was illustrated in Chapter 3. On the other hand, trade creation should be limited once intra-industry trade has become sizeable and oligopolistic firms in member countries have become aware of their interdependence and have organised at the multinational level. In this second stage, changing patterns of comparative advantages are unlikely to be accurately reflected in trade patterns.

Such a result explains the exclusive focus of former studies on the trade effects of integration. On the other hand, it justifies the inclusion of industrial and political aspects in contemporary integration studies. It supports the view that the neglect of these factors leads to inadequate predictions about the growth of trade and welfare following integration.

A strength of the present analysis is that it shows how competitive conditions and market conduct interact with international trade during the process of integration. In other words, its strength is to bring forth the interplay between the so-called dynamic and static effects of integration and to suggest that these two effects can hardly be separated in integration studies.

In passing it should be added that price leading–following practices have important implications for a wide range of other economic issues of international character. Examples of such issues are the impact on trade flows of exchange-rate adjustments and policies and the growth of West European trade and more particularly intra-industry trade.

The same integration-impeding effects result from public policy at the national and EEC levels. As illustrated in Chapter 4 in the case of the West European passenger car industry, most less-than-efficient firms of small and medium size left the market during the second half of the 1960s, whereas some loss-making and apparently inefficient firms of large size remained.

215

It was shown that this last result ensues from a shift in public policy from trade to industrial policy in the wake of integration and its interplay with firm behaviour. The main reasons behind the institutional barriers to exit set up by public policy were the desire to prevent the exit of firms that are large in terms of employment (and votes) and to keep alive a national motor vehicle industry.

The EEC policy concerning exclusive distribution agreements permits individual parallel trade flows, that is import or export by individual consumers, but bans large-scale arbitrage-induced trade flows that take place outside the official distribution network. Such a policy also constitutes a form of institutional barrier to resource mobility because it affords limited exit to consumers dissatisfied with the level of domestic prices and firm behaviour. The Commission policy has thus the same integration-limiting and growth-retarding effects as national public policies and firm pricing policy. The fact that the Commission is not directly responsible — unlike national governments — to voters and consumers does not seem to make it more devoted to the interest of consumers and less devoted to industrial lobbies and national governments.

A final important conclusion that emerges from the analysis is thus that public policy, at the national and international levels, and market conduct interact to prevent — or at least delay — specialisation and the efficient use of resources within the 'integrated' area. Both contribute to the erection of rigidities and distortions that limit significantly the scope and growth effects of international integration in Western Europe.

Recent economic discussion has concentrated on those rigidities that stand in the way of a large and rapid reallocation of resources and, thus, impede West European economies from growing at a faster pace. This phenomenon has been called Eurosclerosis. The present work, which focuses on corporate and institutional barriers to resource mobility, can be regarded as an illustrative analysis of Eurosclerosis at the industry level.

## NOTES

1. For a rough illustration of the competitiveness of national passenger car industries, see Figure 3.2 on changes over time in their export involvement.

2. See Chapter 7, pp. 197–99.

3. The last BEUC study, which covers the years 1985 and 1986, confirms that there are still substantial price disparities among member countries. See BEUC (1986), p. 5.

4. See Commission of the European Communities (1986), pp. 89–98.

5. Olson (1982), p. 44.

6. In terms of Figure 6.3, the costs to society of non-competitive practices amount to the so-called Harberger triangle $BEF$.

7. In terms of Figure 6.3, the income transfer corresponds to the rectangle $P_wP_dBE$.

8. For a formal proof, see Bhagwati (1980), pp. 355–63.

9. See Commission of the European Communities (1975), pp. 57–59.

10. See *The Economist* (1985b), pp. 75–76.

11. Ibid., p. 75.

12. See Chapter 7, p. 198.

# Bibliography

Adams, W. (1976) 'International comparisons in the study of industrial organization', in A. Jacquemin and H. de Jong (eds), *Markets, corporate behaviour and the state*, Nijhoff, The Hague
——— (1981) 'The automobile industry', in H. de Jong (ed.), *The structure of European industry*, Nijhoff, The Hague
——— and Dirlam, J. (1977) 'Import quotas and industrial performance', in A. Jacquemin and H. de Jong (eds), *Welfare aspects of industrial markets*, Nijhoff, The Hague
*Affärsvärlden* (1986) 19 February, 'Industripolitik i nya farliga banor', Stockholm
Alfred, A. (1972) 'Company pricing policy', *Journal of Industrial Economics*, vol. 21
Altschuler, A., Andersson, M., Jones, D., Roos, D. and Womalk, J. (1984) *The future of the automobile*. The report of MIT's International Automobile Program, Allen & Unwin, London
Anderson, K. and Baldwin, R. (1981) 'The political market for protection in industrial countries: new empirical evidence', *World Bank Staff Working Paper*, no. 492, mimeo
*L'Argus de l'automobile et des locomotions*, Paris.
——— (1960–1985) Yearly issues on motor vehicle statistics
——— (1962) 4 April 1962
——— (1970) 8 October 1970
——— (1974) 3 October 1974
——— (1975) 2 October 1975
——— (1978) 5 October 1978
——— (1980) 2 October 1980
——— (1981a) 8 January 1981
——— (1981b) 5 February 1981
——— (1983) 30 September 1982
Associazione Nazionale fra Industrie Automobilistiche, Torino (1985) *Automobile in cifre 1985*
Auquier, A. (1980) 'Sizes of firms, exporting behaviour and the structure of the French industry', *Journal of Industrial Economics*, vol. 24
*L'Avenir de l'automobile* (1976) Rapport du groupe interministériel de réflexion sur l'avenir de l'automobile, La Documentation Française, Paris
Bain, J. (1954) 'Economies of scale, concentration and the condition of entry', *American Economic Review*, vol. 44
——— (1956) *Barriers to new competition*, Harvard University Press, Cambridge, MA
——— (1966) *International differences in industrial structure*, Yale University Press, New Haven, CT and London
——— (1968) *Industrial organization*, John Wiley, New York
——— (1969) 'Survival-ability as test of efficiency', *American*

*Economic Review*, vol. 59
—— (1972) *Essays on price theory and industrial organization*, Little, Brown, Boston, MA
Balassa, B. (1961) *The theory of economic integration*, Allen & Unwin, London
—— (1967) *Trade liberalization among industrial countries*, McGraw-Hill, New York
—— (1975) 'Trade creation and diversion in the European Common Market: an appraisal of the evidence', in B. Balassa (ed.), *European economic integration*, North-Holland, Amsterdam
—— (1978) 'The "New Protectionism" and the international economy', *Journal of World Trade Law*, vol. 12
Baldwin, R. (1971) *Non-tariff distortions of international trade*, Allen & Unwin, London
—— (1982) 'The political economy of protectionism', in J. Bhagwati and T.N. Srinivasan (eds), *Import competition and response*, University of Chicago Press, Chicago, IL
Batchelor, R., Major, R. and Morgan, A. (1980) *Industrialisation and the basis for trade*, Cambridge University Press, Cambridge
Beenstock, M. and Warburton, P. (1983) 'Long-term trends in economic openness in the UK and USA', *Oxford Economic Papers*, vol. 35
BEUC (Bureau Européen des Unions de Consommateurs)
—— (1981) Report on car prices, BEUC 71.81, Brussels
—— (1982a) Report on car prices, BEUC 105.82, Brussels
—— (1982b) 'The "Ford" case', BEUC 136.82, Brussels
—— (1983a) Report on car prices, BEUC 154.83, Brussels
—— (1983b) 'Distribution automobile', *BEUC Actualités*, no. 25, June
—— (1986) 'Car price differences in the EEC', BEUC 121.86, Brussels
Bhagwati, J. (1965) 'On the equivalence of tariffs and quotas', in R. Baldwin *et al.* (eds), *Trade, growth and the balance of payments*, Rand McNally, Chicago, IL
—— (1980) 'Lobbying and welfare', *Journal of Public Economics*, vol. 14
—— (1982) 'Lobbying, DUP activities and welfare', *Journal of Public Economics*, vol. 19
Bhaskar, K. (1979) *The future of the UK motor industry*, Kogan Page, London
—— (1984) *State aid to the European motor industry*, Motor Industry Research Unit, University of East Anglia, mimeo
Bilindustriföreningen (1968) *Internationella bilnormer*, Stockholm
—— (1983) *Sweden out of step*, Stockholm
—— (1960–1985) *Motor traffic in Sweden*, yearly issues, Stockholm
Bilindustrin (1978), Svensk Industri inför 80-talet, Svenska Metallindustriarbetareförbundet, Stockholm
Blackaby, F. (ed.) (1978) *British economic policy 1960–1974*, National Institute of Economic and Social Research, Cambridge University Press, Cambridge

Bloch, H. (1974) 'Prices, costs and profits in Canadian manufacturing: the influence of tariffs and concentration', *Canadian Journal of Economics*, vol. 7

Bloomfield, G. (1978) *The world automotive industry*, David & Charles, Newton Abbot

Bresnahan, T. (1981) 'Departures from marginal-cost pricing in the American automobile industry', *Journal of Econometrics*, vol. 17

Bronckers, M. (1983) 'A legal analysis of protectionist measures affecting Japanese imports into the European Community', in E. Völker (ed.), *Protectionism and the European Community*, Kluwer, Antwerp

Buchanan, J., Tollison, R. and Tullock, G. (1980) *Toward a theory of the rent-seeking society*, Texas A&M University Press

Burenstam Linder, S. (1961) *An essay on trade and transformation*, Almqvist & Wiksell, Stockholm

Burn, D. and Epstein, B. (eds) (1972) *Realities of free trade: two industry studies*, University of Toronto Press, Toronto

Burnside, A. (1985) 'Enforcement of EEC competition law by interim measures, the Ford case', *Journal of World Trade Law*, vol. 19

Busch, K.W. (1966) *Strukturwandlungen der westdeutschen Automobil-industrie*, Duncker & Humbolt, Berlin

*Business Week* (1965) 14 August, 'Fiat toots new horn at its rivals'

Cable, J., Palfrey, J. and Runge, J. (1980) 'Federal Republic of Germany, 1964–1974', in D. Mueller (ed.), *The determinants and effects of mergers*, Oelgeschlager, Gunn & Hain, Cambridge

Cable, V. (1983) *Protectionism and industrial decline*, Hodder and Stoughton, London

Carlsson, B. (1972) 'The measurement of efficiency in production', *Swedish Journal of Economics*, vol. 74

Carlsson, B. (1983) 'Industrial subsidies in Sweden: macro-economic effects and international comparison', *Journal of industrial economics*, vol. 32

Caves, R. (1974) 'International trade, international investment and imperfect markets', *Special Papers in International Economics*, no. 10, Princeton University Press, Princeton, NJ

—— (1976) 'The determinants of market structure: design for research', in A. Jacquemin and H. de Jong (eds), *Markets, corporate behaviour and the state*, Nijhoff, The Hague

—— (1981) 'Intra-industry trade and market structure in the industrial countries, *Oxford Economic Papers*, vol. 33

—— and Jones, R. (1973) *World trade and payments*, Little, Brown, Boston, MA

—— and Khalilzadeh-Shirazi, J. (1977) 'International trade and industrial organization: some statistical evidence', in A. Jacquemin and H. de Jong (eds), *Welfare aspects of industrial organization*, Nijhoff, Leiden

—— and Porter, M. (1978) 'Market structure, oligopoly and stability of market shares, *Journal of Industrial Economics*, vol. 26

—— (ed.) (1980a) 'Symposium on international trade and industrial organization', *Journal of Industrial Economics*, vol. 24

——, Porter, M. and Spence, M. (1980b) *Competition in the open economy, a model applied to Canada,* Harvard University Press, Cambridge, MA

Central Policy Review Staff, London (1975) 'Future of the British car industry'

Chamberlin, E. (1935) *The theory of monopolistic competition,* Harvard University Press, Cambridge, MA

Clark, K. (1983) 'Competition, technical diversity and radical innovation in the U.S. auto industry', in R. Rosembloom (ed.), *Research on technological innovation, management and policy,* JAI Press, Greenwich, CT

CLCA (Comité de Liaison de la Construction Automobile), Brussels

—— (1984) History, Tasks and Functioning of the CLCA

—— (1985a) Réf. 408/85

—— (1985b) Réf. 463/85

Commission of the European Communities, Luxembourg

—— (1972) First Report on Competition Policy

—— (1974) Third Report on Competition Policy

—— (1975) Fourth Report on Competition Policy

—— (1976) Fifth Report on Competition Policy

—— (1977) Sixth Report on Competition Policy

—— (1978) Seventh Report on Competition Policy

—— (1979) Eighth Report on Competition Policy

—— (1980) Ninth Report on Competition Policy

—— (1981a) Tenth Report on Competition Policy

—— (1981b) The European Automobile Industry, Commission statement, COM(81) 317

—— (1982) Eleventh Report on Competition Policy

—— (1983a) Twelfth Report on Competition Policy

—— (1983b) 'Commission activities and EC rules for the automobile industry (1981 to 1983)', COM(83) 633, series: Documents

—— (1983c) 'Progress report on the implementation of the Commission's statement, "The European Automobile Industry", of June 1981'

—— (1984a) Thirteenth Report on Competition Policy

—— (1984b) *Catalogue of community legal acts and other texts relating to the elimination of technical barriers to trade for industrial products*

—— (1985) Fourteenth Report on Competition Policy

—— (1986) Nineteenth General Report on the activities of the European Communities 1985

Coombs, C. (1976) *The arena of international finance,* John Wiley, New York

Corden, W. (1974) *Trade policy and economic welfare,* Oxford University Press, Oxford

Cotta, A. (1984) *Le corporatisme,* Presses Universitaires de France, Paris

Cournot, A. (1897) *Researches into the mathematical principles of the theory of wealth,* Macmillan, London

Cowling, K., Stoneman, P., Cubbin, J., Cable, J., Hall, G., Domberger,

S. and Dutton, P. (1980) *Mergers and economic performance*, Cambridge University Press, Cambridge

Crandall, R. (1984) 'Import quotas and the automobile industry: the costs of protectionism', *The Brookings Review*, Summer 1984

Curzon, G. (1965) *Multilateral commercial diplomacy*, Michael Joseph, London

Curzon, V. (1974) *The essential of economic integration*, Macmillan, London

Curzon Price, V. (1981) *Industrial policy in the European Community*, Macmillan, London

Dahlström, G. and Söderbäck, B.M. (1972) *Sveriges avtal med EEC*, Rabén & Sjögren, Stockholm

Dashwood, A. (1981) 'The harmonisation process', in C. Twitchett (ed.), *Harmonisation in the EEC*, Macmillan, London

Deardorff, A. and Stern, R. (1983) 'Economic effects of the Tokyo Rounds', *Southern Economic Journal*, vol. 49

De Carmoy, G. (1978) 'Subsidies policies in Britain, France and West Germany: an overview', in S. Warnecke (ed.), *International trade and industrial policies*, Macmillan, London

De Jong, H. (1975) 'Industrial structure and price problem', in G. Means, J. Blair, P. Sargant Florence, J. Dirlam, H. Arndt, H. de Jong, N. Dodge and A. Kahn (eds), *The roots of inflation*, Wilton House Publications, London

——— (1976) 'Theory and evidence concerning mergers: an international comparison', in A. Jacquemin and H. de Jong (eds), *Markets, corporate behaviour and the state*, Nijhoff, The Hague

Denton, G., O'Cleireacain, S. and Ash, S. (1975) *Trade effects of public subsidies to private enterprise*, Trade Policy Research Centre, Macmillan, London

Diekmann, A. (1985) *Die Automobilindustrie in Deutschland*, Deutscher Instituts-Verlag GmbH, Cologne

Dirlam, J. (1975) 'The process of inflation in France', in G. Means *et al.* (eds), *The roots of inflation*, Wilton House Publications, London

Drèze, J. (1960) 'Quelques réflexions sereines sur l'adaptation de l'industrie Belge au Marché Commun', *Comptes Rendus des Travaux de la Société Royale d'Economie Politique de Belgique*, no. 275

Dunnet, P. (1980) *The decline of the British motor industry*, Croom Helm, London

Eastman, H. and Stykolt, S. (1967) *The tariff and competition in Canada*, Macmillan, Toronto

*The Economist*

——— (1975) 29 November, 'The Innocenti suffer with the guilty as the foreigners leave'

——— (1980) 3 May, 'What Common Market?'

——— (1981a) 19 September, 'The common scandal of the uncommon market'

——— (1981b) 3 October, 'Consumers join the Eurocar price row'

——— (1982a) 6 February, 'Right-hand-drive protectionists'

——— (1982b) 1 May, 'Japanese investment, made in Europe'

—— (1982c) 25 December, 'Protectionist overdrive'
—— (1983a) 23 July, 'Peugeot, job cuts, not bails-out'
—— (1983b) 29 October, 'Cars, autosuggestion'
—— (1985a) 23 March, 'British Leyland, greater co-prosperity'
—— (1985b) 26 October, 'Trading-in the old way'
EFTA, Geneva
—— (1968) 'EFTA trade in passenger cars', *EFTA Bulletin*, vol. 9.
—— (1969) *The effects of EFTA on the economies of member states*
—— (1980) *EFTA — past and future*
Ensor, J. (1971) *The motor industry*, Longmans, London
*L'Expansion* (1985) December, 'Quand revient la liberté des prix?'
Feenstra, R. (1984) 'Voluntary export restraint in U.S. autos, 1980–81: quality, employment, and welfare effects', in R. Baldwin and A. Krueger (eds), *The structure and evolution of recent U.S. trade policy*, University of Chicago Press, Chicago, IL
—— (1985) 'Automobile prices and protection: the U.S.–Japan trade restraint, *Journal of Policy Modeling*, vol. 7
Fellner, W. (1949) *Competition among the few*, Alfred A. Knopf, New York
Ferrier, J. (1984) *L'industrie automobile dans la Communauté européene*, CEREC, Paris
*Le Figaro* (1985) 25 January, Druesne G. 'Voitures sans frontières: oui mais ...'
*Financial Times*
—— (1981) 19 March, 'Italian motor industry'
—— (1982a) 29 April, 'Italy holds up BL car imports'
—— (1982b) 28 May, 'Japan car sales in UK agree with forecast'
—— (1982c) 4 June, 'Britain protests to Italy over obstruction of Acclaim imports'
—— (1984) 2 October, 'EEC "threat" to Ford in Britain'
Fontaine, P. (1980) *L'industrie automobile en France*, La Documentation Française, Paris
*Fortune* (1979) 7 May, 'What's good for the world should be good for GM'
Fraas, A. and Greer, D. (1977) 'Market structure and price collusion: an empirical analysis', *Journal of Industrial Economics*, vol. 26.
Frank, I. (1961) *The European Common Market*, Stevens & Sons, London
Franko, L. (1979) 'Industrial policies in Western Europe: solution or problem?' *World Economy*, vol. 2
Frenger, P., Jansen, E. and Reymert, M. (1979) *Modell for norsk eksport av bearbeidde varer*, Statistik Sentralbyrå, Oslo
Frey, B. (1984) *International political economics*, Basil Blackwell, London
George, K. and Joll, C. (eds) (1975) *Competition policy in the UK and the EEC*, Cambridge University Press, Cambridge
—— and Silbertson, A. (1976) 'The causes and effects of mergers,' in A. Jacquemin and H. de Jong (eds), *Markets, corporate behaviour and the state*, Nijhoff, The Hague
Gomez-Ibancz, J., Leone, R. and O'Connell, S. (1983) 'Restraining

223

auto imports: does anyone win?' *Journal of Policy Analysis and Management,* vol. 2

Gort, M. (1963) 'Analysis of stability and change in market shares', *Journal of Political Economy,* vol. 71

Greenaway, D. and Milner, C. (1986) *The economics of intra-industry trade,* Basil Blackwell, London

Grubel, L. and Lloyd, P. (1975) *Intra-industry trade: the theory and measurement of international trade in differentiated products,* Macmillan, London

Hansson, G. (1983) *Social clauses and international trade,* Croom Helm, London

Helpman, E. and Krugman, P. (1985) *Market structure and foreign trade,* MIT Press, Cambridge, MA

Henning, R. (1977) *Företagen i politiken,* SNS, Stockholm

Hirschman, A. (1981) *Essays in trespassing, economics to politics and beyond,* Cambridge University Press, Cambridge

Hocking, R. (1980) 'Trade in motor cars between the major European producers', *Economic Journal,* vol. 90

Husbands, H. (1981) 'The impact of harmonisation on the British motor industry', in C. Twitchett (ed.), *Harmonisation in the EEC,* Macmillan, London

Jacoby, N. (1964) 'The relative stability of market shares. A theory and evidence from several industries', *Journal of Industrial Economics,* vol. 12

Jacquemin, A. (1982) 'Imperfect market structure and international trade, some recent research', *Kyklos,* vol. 35

—— (ed.) (1984) *Industry: public policy and corporate strategy,* Oxford University Press, Oxford

—— and de Jong, H. (eds) (1976) *Markets, corporate behaviour and the state,* Nijhoff, The Hague

—— and de Jong, H. (eds) (1977) *European industrial organisation,* Macmillan, London

Jenny, F. (1981) 'From price control to competition policy in France', *Annals of Public and Co-operative Economy,* vol. 52

—— and Weber, A. (1975) 'French antitrust legislation: an exercise in futility', *Antitrust Bulletin,* vol. 20

*Jans Ulléns Bilfakta* (1970–1984), Stockholm

Johnson, H. (1972), Introduction in D. Burn and B. Epstein (eds), *Realities of free trade: two industry studies,* University of Toronto Press, Toronto

Jonung, L. (1984) *Prisregleringen, företagen och förhandlingsekonomin,* SNS, Stockholm

Junz, H. and Rhomberg, R. (1973) 'Price competitiveness in export trade among industrial countries', *American Economic Review,* vol. 63

Jürgensen, H. and Berg, H. (1968) *Konzentration und Wettbewerb im Gemeisam Markt,* Vandenhoek & Ruprecht, Göttingen

Katrak, H. (1980) 'Foreign competition, tariffs and concentration in Britain, 1963 and 1968', in J. Black and B. Hindley (eds), *Current issues in commercial policy and diplomacy,* St. Martin's Press, New York

Kock, K. (1969) *International policy and the GATT 1947–1967*, Almqvist & Wiksell, Stockholm

Koutsoyiannis, A. (1975) *Modern microeconomics*, Macmillan, London

—— (1977) *Theory of econometrics*, Macmillan, London

Kravis, I. and Lipsey, R. (1971) *Price competitiveness in world trade*, Columbia University Press, New York

—— (1978) 'Price theories in the light of balance of payments theories', *Journal of International Economics*, vol. 8

Kreinin, M. (1973) 'The static effects of EEC enlargement on trade flows', *Southern Economic Journal*, vol. 39

—— and Officer, L. (1979) 'Tariff reductions under the Tokyo Round: a review of their effects on trade flows, employment and welfare', *Weltwirtschaftliches Archiv*, vol. 115

Kwoka, J. (1981) 'Does the choice of concentration measure really matter?' *Journal of Industrial Economics*, vol. 29

Lassudrie-Duchêne, B. (1971) 'La demande de différence et l'échange international', *Economie et Sociétés*, cahiers de l'ISEA, no. 6

Leibenstein, H. (1976) *Beyond economic man*, Harvard University Press, Cambridge, MA

Le Pors, A. and Prunet, J. (1975) 'Les "transferts" entre l'Etat et l'industrie', *Economie et Statistique*, no. 66

Lundgren, N. (1969) 'Customs union of industrialized West European countries', in G. Denton (ed.), *Economic integration in Europe*, Weidenfeld and Nicolson, London

—— and Ståhl, I. (1981) Industripolitikens spelregler, Industriförbundets Förlag, Stockholm

Lustgarten, S. (1984) *Productivity and prices, the consequences of industrial concentration*, American Enterprise Institute, Washington D.C.

Maddala, G. (1979) *Econometrics*, McGraw-Hill, Tokyo

Malmgren, H. (1977) *International order for public subsidies*, Trade Policy Research Centre, London

Marfels, C. (1972a) 'Absolute and relative measures of concentration reconsidered', *Kyklos*, vol. 25

—— (1972b) 'On testing concentration measures', *Zeitschrift für Nationalökonomie*, vol. 32

—— (1975) 'A bird's-eye view to measures of concentration', *Antitrust Bulletin*, vol. 20

Markert, K. (1975) 'EEC competition policy towards mergers', in K. George and C. Joll (eds), *Competition policy in the UK and EEC*, Cambridge University Press, Cambridge

Mattera, A. (1984) 'Protectionism inside the European Community', *Journal of World Trade Law*, vol. 18

Maunder, P. (ed.) (1979) *Government intervention in the developed economy*, Croom Helm, London

Maxcy, G. (1981) *The multinational motor industry*, Croom Helm, London

—— and Silberston, A. (1959) *The motor industry*, Allen & Unwin, London

Mayes, D. (1978) 'The effects of economic integration on trade',

225

*Journal of Common Market Studies*, vol. 17
—— (1981) *Applications of econometrics*, Prentice-Hall International, London
Mazzolini, R. (1974) *European transnational concentration*, McGraw-Hill, London
McGuckin, R. (1972) 'Entry, concentration changes and stability of market shares', *Southern Economic Journal*, vol. 38
Middleton, R. (1975) *Negotiating on non-tariff distortions of trade, the EFTA precedents*, Macmillan, London
Mitchell, J. (1978) *Price determination and prices policy*, George Allen & Unwin, London
*Le Monde*
—— (1979) 21 August, 'Comment le lion Peugeot digérera-t-il l'oursin Chrysler?'
—— (1982) 23 November, 'La montée du protectionnisme, Italie: pas de politique systématique'
—— (1984a) 4 January, 'Les frères Leclerc ou l'embryon d'une dérégulation "à la française"'
—— (1984b) 3 February, 'La stratégie de l'escargot'
—— (1985) 13 March, 'Concours de l'Etat aux groupes nationalisés'
Moneta, E. (1962) *Die Europäische Automobilindustrie*, Verlag Lutzeyer, Baden-Baden
Moreaux, M. (1979) 'Bilan et perspectives de l'industrie automobile française, *Problèmes Economiques*, La Documentation Française, Paris, no. 1611
*Motor Business* (1960–1966), Economist Intelligence Unit, London
Motor Vehicle Manufacturers' Association of the United States (1983 and 1985) *World Motor Vehicle Data*, 1982 and 1984–1985 editions, Detroit
Mueller, D. (ed.) (1980) *The determinants and effects of mergers*, Oelgeschlager, Gunn & Hain, Cambridge
—— (ed.) (1983) *The political economy of growth*, Yale University Press, New Haven, CT
Müller, J. (1976) 'The impact of mergers on concentration: a study of eleven West German industries', *Journal of Industrial Economics*, vol. 25
—— and Hochreiter, R. (1975) *Stand und Entwicklungstendenzen der Konzentrationen in der Bundesrepublik Deutschland*, Verlag Otto Schwartz, Göttingen
*Multinational Business* (1978) 'Peugeot Citroën Chrysler: winners and losers', Economist Intelligence Unit, London, vol. 3
Nême, J. and Nême, C. (1970) *Economie Européenne*, Presses Universitaires de France, Paris
*Newsweek* (1981) 23 March, 'Japan v. Europe: the battle over imports'
OECD, Paris
—— (1956–1985) *Foreign trade statistical bulletins*
—— (1979) *Concentration and competition policy*
—— (1984a) *Competition and trade policies, their interaction*
—— (1984b) *Merger policies and recent trends in mergers*
OEEC (1957) *Liberalization of Europe's dollar trade*, Paris

Official Journal of the European Communities (OJ)
—— (1982a) 4 January, C 287
—— (1982b) 20 January, C 14
—— (1982c) 17 May, C 126
—— (1982d) 17 September, C 243
—— (1982e) 31 December, L 385
—— (1983) 18 January, C 14
—— (1984) 6 September, L 238
—— (1985a) 18 January, L 15
—— (1985b) 18 April, C 98
—— (1985c) 10 July, L 178
—— (1985d) 31 July, C 191
—— (1985e) 18 September, C 267
—— (1986) 12 February, C 32
Ohlin, G. (1978) 'Subsidies and other industrial aids', in S. Warnecke
  (ed.), *International trade and industrial policies*, Macmillan, London
Olson, M. (1965) *The logic of collective action*, Harvard University
  Press, Cambridge, MA
—— (1982) *The rise and decline of nations*, Yale University Press,
  New Haven, CT
—— and McFarland, D. (1962) 'The restoration of pure monopoly
  and the concept of the industry', *Quarterly Journal of Economics*,
  vol. 66
Orcutt, G. (1950) 'Measurement of price elasticities in international
  trade', *Review of Economics and Statistics*, vol. 32
Ouin, M. (1964) 'L'industrie automobile et l'intégration européenne',
  *Cahiers de Bruges*, n.s. 11
Owen, N. (1973) 'Competition and industrial structure: implications of
  entry to the EEC', *Trade and Industry*, vol. 10
Page, S. (1981) 'The revival of protectionism and its consequences for
  Europe', *Journal of Common Market Studies*, vol. 20
Pagoulatos, E. and Sorensen, R. (1976a) 'Domestic market structure
  and international trade', *Quarterly Review of Economics and Business*, vol. 16
—— (1976b) 'Foreign trade, concentration and profitability', *European Economic Review*, vol. 8
—— (1980) 'Industrial policy and firm behaviour in an international
  context', in I. Leveson and J. Wheeler, *Western economies in transition*, Hudson Institute Studies on the Prospects for Mankind,
  Westview Press, Boulder, CO
Phlips, L. (1971) *Effects of industrial concentration, a cross-section
  analysis for the Common Market*, North-Holland, Amsterdam
—— (1975) *The measurement of industrial concentration: a reassess-
  ment based on European data*, Statistical Office of the European
  Communities, Brussels
Pincus, J. (1975) 'Pressure groups and the pattern of tariffs', *Journal of
  Political Economy*, vol. 83
Pindyck, R. and Rubinfeld, D. (1981) *Econometric models and
  economic forecasts*, McGraw-Hill International, Tokyo
Porter, M. (1983) 'The technology dimension of competitive strategy',

227

in R. Rosenbloom (ed.), *Research on technological innovation, management and policy*, JAI Press, Greenwich, CT

Pratten, C. (1971) *Economies of scale in manufacturing industry*, Cambridge University Press, Cambridge

Prewo, W. (1980) 'Trade, interdependence and European integration', in L. Hurwitz (ed.), *Contemporary perspectives on European integration*, Aldwych Press, London

Prodi, R. (1974) 'Italy', in R. Vernon (ed.), *Big business and the state*, Harvard University Press, Cambridge, MA

Raisch, M. (1973) *Die Konzentration in der Deutschen Automobilindustrie*, Duncker & Humbolt, Berlin

Reuss, F. (1963) *Fiscal policy for growth without inflation, the German Experiment*, Johns Hopkins University Press, Baltimore, MD

Rhys, D. (1972a) 'Economies of scale in the motor industry', *Bulletin of Economic Research*, vol. 24

—— (1972b) *The motor industry: an economic survey*, Butterworths, London

—— (1977) 'European mass-producing car makers and minimum efficient scale: a note', *Journal of Industrial Economics*, vol. 25

Rydén, B. (1972) *Mergers in Swedish industry*, Almqvist & Wiksell, Stockholm

—— and Edberg, J. (1980) 'Large mergers in Sweden 1962–1976', in D. Mueller (ed.), *The determinants and effects of mergers*, Oelgeschlager, Gunn & Hain, Cambridge

Robson, P. (1980) *The economics of international integration*, Allen & Unwin, London

Salvatore, D. (1985) 'The new protectionism and the threat to world welfare', *Journal of Policy Modeling*, vol. 7

Scherer, F. (1974) 'Secrecy, the rule of reason and European merger control policy', *Antitrust Bulletin*, vol. 19

—— (1980) *Industrial market structure and economic performance*, Houghton Mifflin, Boston, MA

——, Beckenstein, A., Kaufer, E. and Murphy, R. (1975) *The economics of multi-plant operation*, Harvard University Press, Cambridge, MA

Schmidt, I. (1981) 'Price control in Germany', *Annals of Public and Co-operative Economy*, vol. 52

Scitovsky, T. (1958) *Economic theory and Western European integration*, George Allen and Unwin, London

Shepherd, W. (1979) *The economics of industrial organization*, Prentice-Hall, Englewood Cliffs, NJ

Slot, P. (1975) *Technical and administrative obstacles to trade in the EEC*, Sijthoff, Leyden

Society of Motor Manufacturers and Traders

—— (1967–1983) 'Statistics on new registration'

—— (1984) 'The eighty-third annual report and accounts for the year end, 31st December 1984'

Södersten, B. (1978) *International economics*, Macmillan, London

SOU (Statens offentliga utredningar), Stockholm

—— (1981) *Prisreglering mot inflation?*, SOU 1981:4

228

—— (1983) *Bilar och renare luft,* SOU 1983:27
Stigelin, P. (ed.) (1973) *The European Community and the outsiders,* Longman Canada Limited, Toronto
Stigler, G. (1961) 'The economics of information', *Journal of Political Economy,* vol. 64
—— (1964) 'A theory of oligopoly', in G. Stigler, *The organization of industry,* University of Chicago Press, Chicago, IL
—— (1966) 'The economic effects of the antitrust laws', *Journal of Law and Economics,* vol. 9
—— (1968) 'The measurement of concentration', in G. Stigler, *The organization of industry,* University of Chicago Press, Chicago, IL
Stoléru, L. (1969) *L'impératif industriel,* Seuil, Paris
Swann, D. (1983) *Competition and industrial policy in the European community,* Methuen, London
—— (1984) *The economics of the Common Market,* Penguin Books, London
Taber, G. (1974) *Patterns and prospects of Common Market trade,* Peter Owen, London
Toder, E. (1978) *Trade policy and the US automobile industry,* Praeger, New York
Turner, H., Clark, G. and Roberts, G. (1967) *Labour relations in the motor industry,* Allen & Unwin, London
United Nations
—— (1957) *Economic survey of Europe in 1956,* Geneva
—— (1968) *The Kennedy Round estimated effects on trade barriers,* UNCTAD, Geneva
—— (1983) *Transnational corporations in the international auto industry,* New York
Utton, M. (1975) 'British merger policy', in K. George and C. Joll (eds), *Competition policy in the UK and EEC,* Cambridge University Press, Cambridge
—— and Morgan, A. (1983) *Concentration and foreign trade,* Cambridge University Press, Cambridge
Van Dartel, R. (1983) 'The conduct of the EEC's textile trade policy and the application of Article 115 EEC', in E. Völker (ed.), *Protectionism and the European Community,* Kluwer, Antwerp
van Duijn, J. (1983) *The long wave in economic life,* Allen & Unwin, London
Van Houtte, H. (1984) 'The EEC draft regulation on selective distribution of automobiles', *Journal of World Trade Law,* vol. 18
Verband der Automobilindustrie E.V. (1985) *Tatsachen und Zahlen aus der Kraftverkehrswirtschaft 1975–1984,* Frankfurt am Main
Vernon, R. (ed.) (1974) *The technology factor in international trade,* Columbia University Press, New York
—— (ed.) (1974) *Big business and the state, changing relations in Western Europe,* Macmillan, London
Verreydt, E. and Waelbroeck, J. (1982) 'Europcan Community protection against manufactured imports from developing countries: a case study in the political economy of protection', in J. Bhagwati (ed.), *Import competition and response,* University of Chicago Press,

Chicago and London

Vogelenzang, P. (1981) 'Two aspects of Article 115 EEC: its use to buttress Community-set sub-quotas and the Commission's monitoring system', *Common Market Law Review*, vol. 18

Völker, E. (ed.) (1983) *Protectionism and the European Community*, Kluwer, Antwerp

*Volvo Company Report 1979* (1980)

Wahlroos, B. (1980) *The economics of the Finnish industrial structure, an empirical analysis of industrial concentration, conduct and performance in Finland in the seventies*, Swedish School of Economics and Business Administration, Helsingfors

Walsh, A. and Paxton, J. (1975) *Competition policy, European and international trends and practices*, Macmillan, London

Warnecke, S. and Suleiman, E. (eds) (1975) *Industrial policies in Western Europe*, Praeger, New York

—— (1978) 'The European Community and national subsidy policies', in S. Warnecke (ed.), *International trade and industrial policies*, Macmillan, London

Weiss, L. (1964) 'The survival technique and the extent of suboptimal capacity', *Journal of Political Economy*, vol. 72

Wells, L. (ed.) (1972) *The product life cycle and international trade*, Harvard Business School, Boston, MA

—— (1974) 'Automobiles', in R. Vernon (ed.), *Big business and the state*, Harvard University Press, Cambridge, MA

Wemelsfelder, J. (1960) 'The short-term effect of the lowering of import duties in Germany', *Economic Journal*, vol. 70

White, L. (1971) *The automobile industry since 1945*, Harvard University Press, Cambridge, MA

—— (1974) 'Industrial organization and international trade: some theoretical considerations', *American Economic Review*, vol. 64

Winters, L. (1984) 'British imports of manufactures and the Common Market', *Oxford Economic Papers*, vol. 36

# Index

233